EXPLORER'S GUIDE

CHARLESTON, SAVANNAH & COASTAL ISLANDS

EXPLORER'S GUIDE

CHARLESTON, SAVANNAH & COASTAL ISLANDS

NINTH EDITION

CECILY McMILLAN

THE COUNTRYMAN PRESS
A Division of W. W. Norton & Company
Independent Publishers Since 1923

Interior photographs by the author unless otherwise specified
Maps by Erin Greb Cartography, © The Countryman Press

Book series design by Chris Welch Design
Manufacturing by Versa Press

For information about permission to reproduce selections from this book, write to
Permissions, The Countryman Press, 500 Fifth Avenue, New York, NY 10110

For information about special discounts for bulk purchases, please contact
W. W. Norton Special Sales at specialsales@wwnorton.com or 800-233-4830

Library of Congress Cataloging-in-Publication Data

Names: McMillan, Cecily, 1956– author, photographer.
Title: Explorer's guide Charleston, Savannah & coastal islands / Cecily McMillan.
Other titles: Charleston, Savannah and coastal islands
Description: Ninth Edition. | New York : The Countryman Press, [2021] |
Series: Explorer's guides | Includes index.
Identifiers: LCCN 2020046081 | ISBN 9781682685082 (Paperback) | ISBN 9781682685099 (ePub)
Subjects: LCSH: Charleston (S.C.)—Guidebooks. | Savannah (Ga.)—Guidebooks. | Hilton Head (S.C.)—
Guidebooks. | Sea Islands—Guidebooks. | South Carolina—Guidebooks. | Georgia—Guidebooks.
Classification: LCC F279.C43 M37 2021 | DDC 917.57/9904—dc23
LC record available at https://lccn.loc.gov/2020046081

The Countryman Press
www.countrymanpress.com

A division of W. W. Norton & Company, Inc.
500 Fifth Avenue, New York, NY 10110
www.wwnorton.com

978-1-68268-508-2 (pbk.)

10 9 8 7 6 5 4 3 2 1

To the late George McMillan, who introduced me to the beauty and social complexity of the Lowcountry, and to our son, Tom, with whom I continue to love it; and to Priscilla Johnson McMillan, whose wisdom and support has allowed me to understand it.

EXPLORE WITH US!

This is the ninth edition of *Explorer's Guide Charleston, Savannah & Coastal Islands*. Over the years we've discovered how to make it easier to use before, during, and after your visit. Brief historical summaries introduce each chapter, and recommendations and reviews follow. They cover a range of options according to activity and price, and will help you make decisions, whether you are staying in one area or intend to travel the region. An extensive bibliography closes the book.

All basic information has been checked for accuracy as close to the time of publication in 2021 as possible, but things change, deals appear, and places close, so it's a good idea to check in advance. Wherever possible I've included websites and up-to-date telephone numbers.

Due to the COVID-19 pandemic, travel in the Lowcountry, as with everywhere else, requires more planning for every activity to ensure appropriate social distancing. This means that you should call or check a venue's website to confirm, among other things, if reservations are required where walk-in activity was once the norm. It also means that providers of services from hotels to restaurants or boat rides to carriage tours are likely to be running their businesses differently from in the past, with fewer visitors engaged at any one time. If you are a family group, be sure to mention that, because it may make a difference in the business owner's risk calculations. Ask if there is outdoor seating available at restaurants—many venues have changed their layouts to include more outside dining while they reduce the numbers of tables inside. Meals to go, food service delivery, and curbside pick-up options have expanded dramatically in the spring and summer of 2020; check to see if those options are still available. Annual events, including professional golf and tennis tournaments and house and garden tours, have shifted their dates and ticketing procedures. You'll have a more rewarding travel experience if you arrive prepared and flexible.

WHAT'S WHERE The book starts out with an overview of handy visitor information arranged alphabetically and dives deeply into specifics in subsequent chapters.

LODGING All selections were judged on their own merits and did not pay to be included, nor did we accept compensation or discounts. The rates are for two-person occupancy. Smoking, even on porches or in outdoor spaces on the property, is generally forbidden, as it is in restaurants and bars. Whether accommodations welcome children (and of what age) and pets is highly variable in hotels, fancy bed-and-breakfasts, and boutique inns, so you should ask. Resorts are very family oriented, whether you stay in the main hotel or a house on the property. Costs are calculated based on the number of bedrooms and proximity to the beach or use of a dock. Airbnb rentals, which are becoming more numerous throughout the region, allow visitors and property owners to align their expectations in advance. Please note that this type of short-term stay requires being especially mindful of your neighbors and the neighborhood, as many units are not in commercial areas.

RATES You can expect to pay more in the summer (on the beaches), spring, and fall if a visit coincides with an arts or music festival, or a historic house and garden tour. But, and there are probably more exceptions than rules, the fall has become a prime time for golf groups, and there are packages galore for resort stay and play. If an off-season rate exists, it would likely be from mid-November to early February and reflect up to a 20 percent discount. Minimum stays and the costs generally apply to high-season stays in boutique inns and bed-and-breakfasts. In summer months, if you're renting a house on or near the beach, it usually leases from Saturday to Saturday. Additional accommodations taxes apply in the region, which add to the listed cost.

RESTAURANTS As mentioned, the regional dining scene has exploded and with it the range of options and prices. We've tried to be careful to give you a general idea of cost, but this is where an establishment's social media pages, or other sites where you can see a menu or read reviews, would be instructive if you're on a budget. Casual places, breakfast, pizza dinners, and the like tend to cost under $15 and are noted as $. Prices indicate the cost of a meal, including appetizer, entrée, and dessert, but not bar beverages, tax, or tip. All of the more expensive restaurants provide online reservations, which is probably a good idea, given that Charleston has become a city with trophy restaurants that visitors have heard raves about and want to try.

PRICE CODES
Lodging
$ Up to $90
$$ $90 to $150
$$$ $150 to $250
$$$$ Over $250

Dining
$ Up to $15
$$ $15 to $35
$$$ $35 to $50
$$$$ Over $50

Please send any comments or corrections to:

Explorer's Guide Editor
The Countryman Press
500 Fifth Avenue
New York, NY 10110

The Lowcountry

⭐ Point of Interest

Orangeburg

SOUTH CAROLINA

Francis Marion National Forest

Colleton State Park

Givhans Ferry State Park

Cypress Gardens

Awendaw

Cape Island

Cape Romain National Wildlife Refuge

Hampton

Walterboro

Audubon Swamp Garden

Charleston

Bull Island

Isle of Palms

Ft. Sumter

Johns Island

Sullivan's Island

James Island

Folly Island

ACE Basin National Wildlife Refuge

Kiawah Island

Seabrook Island

Ridgeton

Edisto Island

Beaufort

St. Helena Sound

St. Helena Island

Hunting Island

Hunting Island State Park

Fripp Island

Pritchards Island

Bluffton

Savannah National Wildlife Refuge

Hilton Head Island

Daufuskie Island

Savannah

GEORGIA

Ft. Pulaski

Ft. McAllister

Tybee Island

Richmond Hill

Skidaway Island State Park

ATLANTIC OCEAN

Port Royal Sound

N

0   12.5   25
Miles

© The Countryman Press

CONTENTS

INTRODUCTION | 11
HISTORY: "NO FAYRER OR FYTTER PLACE" | 13
WHAT'S WHERE IN CHARLESTON, SAVANNAH & COASTAL ISLANDS | 21

CHARLESTON | 29

SAVANNAH | 71

BEAUFORT, EDISTO & BLUFFTON | 101

BEAUFORT | 102
EDISTO | 133
BLUFFTON | 137

HILTON HEAD | 141

BIBLIOGRAPHY | 164
INDEX | 171

MAPS

THE LOWCOUNTRY | 8

GETTING THERE | 24

MAJOR ACCESS POINTS | 25

CHARLESTON | 31

SAVANNAH | 73

BEAUFORT | 103

HILTON HEAD | 143

INTRODUCTION

There are some places of which we have such strong impressions that, when we finally go there, they seem familiar. The Lowcountry seems to have lodged itself securely in so many imaginations that I often find, when I am asked about it, that what I have to say matters less than the opportunity for someone to focus the picture they already have.

Where these clustered impressions come from—a history lesson; interest in architecture or the natural world; or from a friend, novel, or movie—seems less important than the fact that they feel fully conceived. This isn't surprising: The Lowcountry has earned our permanent attention. It is a compelling world. Like other places that have witnessed tremendous historic upheavals and whose residents have had to adjust to changed circumstances, it evokes a natural sympathy in us for its stories.

I like listening in and locating the presence of the past: on the shores of St. Helena Sound, where I dig for clams as Native Americans might have; at Drayton Hall, where beds of lilies bloom, as they did in Jefferson's Monticello garden; at Penn Center, where descendants of formerly enslaved men and women honor their heritage in community programs and continue to educate us about African American life; on the squares of Savannah, laid out more than 275 years ago and still possessing a power of geometry that untangles nature and orders urban life. The region's physical beauty is evocative. The landscape is soft and flat, edges softened by marsh grass and sand. The air, weighted by moisture, wraps it like a package. The light changes several times a day and very dramatically from season to season.

This book is intended to introduce you to some of the long-standing pleasures and pastimes found in the Lowcountry and point you to where you might discover ones of your own as the region's cities and towns flourish in the 21st century. Your efforts may be studious or oriented to satisfy the senses: walk a beach, smell the marsh, watch a pelican dive, paddle a kayak, or taste just-caught shrimp.

THE DRAMATIC URBAN ARCHITECTURE OF THE LOWCOUNTRY REFLECTS THE WEALTH, TASTE, AND SOCIAL DOMINANCE OF PLANTERS AND MERCHANTS

ACKNOWLEDGMENTS

Many longtime friends in Charleston, Beaufort, and Savannah have helped improve each edition of the guide. Thanks to all, and to the new friends who enthusiastically answered questions and provided help at the last minute.

You could end up joining those who visit and return for good. The glossy residential resorts like Kiawah and Palmetto Bluff shine like jewels; Beaufort can't stay off "Best Small Town" lists; and ditto Hilton Head Island for its beaches. Bluffton's Old Town and the May River environment are not far behind. Savannah and Charleston keep reinventing themselves as restaurant meccas that in turn attract many other cultural activities, artists, and artisans. This dynamic new world is fastening on the old and enlarging it, just as spat fasten on oyster banks and keep them dynamic.

—Cecily McMillan, St. Helena Island, South Carolina

HISTORY: "NO FAYRER OR FYTTER PLACE"

Long before the English landed in the Lowcountry, before Jamestown and Plymouth Rock, Captain Jean Ribaut and 150 Huguenot colonists landed near Beaufort, at what is now the Marine Corps recruit depot on Parris Island. In a report he stated there was "no fayrer or fytter place" than the area of Port Royal Sound, one of the "goodlyest, best and frutfullest countres that ever was sene"; where egrets were so plentiful bushes "be all white covered with them"; where there were "so many sortes of fishes that ye may take them without net or angle."

He wrote that in 1562. Soon afterward, the French abandoned their fort site and the Spanish established the first European colonial capital there in 1566.

To a modern traveler who chances upon a rookery in Hunting Island State Park or Edisto's Botany Bay preserve, or to the youngster throwing a cast net and needing the strength of two to draw it in, little has changed. The natural resources of the Lowcountry are breathtakingly impressive. There will be schools of dolphin by your boat off Hilton Head, hundreds of loggerhead turtle nests from the ACE Basin shoreline to Port Royal Sound and the Atlantic, and thousands of terns, which—when they rise all at once off a sandbar in St. Helena Sound—appear as a cloud of smoke on the horizon. There will be late-afternoon light so intense and golden it makes the dun bark of the grayest sycamore shimmer.

And, when Ribaut called the Lowcountry a place "where nothing lacketh," Charleston, Beaufort, and Savannah had not even been conceived.

It only took about 50 years from their founding at the turn of the 17th and 18th centuries for each of these cities to develop the self-consciousness we now recognize as the spirit of place: a short time, perhaps because the raw ingredients were there all along, waiting to be shaped, tapped, and exploited. History

BONAVENTURE CEMETERY, FULL OF SCULPTURE AND HISTORY, HAS DRAWN VISITORS FOR MORE THAN 150 YEARS VISIT SAVANNAH

A PLEASING MUSIC

A beautiful green frog inhabits the grassy, marshy shores of these large rivers. They are very numerous, and their noise exactly resembles the barking of little dogs, or the yelping of puppies: these likewise make a great clamour, but as their notes are fine, and uttered in chorus, by separate bands or communities, far and near, rising and falling with the gentle breezes, affords a pleasing kind of music.

—From *Travels of William Bartram* (New York: Viking Penguin, 1988. First published in 1791)

has shown us that such loyalty, such an abiding sense of legacy and protection, can get you into trouble, and a war was fought here in part over that kind of crazy pride. And I have felt of people I know that if they ever left the city limits of Charleston or Savannah, they would vaporize.

Yet there's something to be said for deep connections, and it is interesting and worthwhile to explore a region and observe the ways place, heritage, custom, and culture resonate to this day, across racial lines and personal history. The activity of reinterpreting and understanding the past drives a new generation who have less need to be insular and more incentive to be curious.

CITY HALL © GORDONBELLPHOTOGRAPHY/ISTOCKPHOTO.COM

A HISTORIC MARKET BUILDING © PGIAM/ISTOCKPHOTO.COM

SAND HILLS

Icontinued through this forest nearly in a direct line towards the sea coast, five or six miles, when the land became uneven, with ridges of sand hills, mixed with sea shells, and covered by almost impenetrable thickets, consisting of Live Oaks, Sweet-bay (*L. Borbonia*), Myrica, Ilex aquifolium . . . This dark labyrinth is succeeded by a great extent of salt plains, beyond which the boundless ocean is seen. Betwixt the dark forest and the salt plains, I crossed a rivulet of fresh water, where I sat down a while to rest myself, under the shadow of sweet Bays and Oaks; the lively breezes were perfumed by the fragrant breath of the superb Crinum, called by the inhabitants, White Lily. This admirable beauty of the sea-coast-islands dwells in the humid shady groves, where the soil is made fertile and mellow by the admixture of seashells . . . and the texture and whiteness of its flowers at once charmed me.

—From *Travels of William Bartram*

Several distinct ecosystems make up the Lowcountry: swamps, estuaries, marshes, maritime and bottomland forests, dunes and interdune meadows, tidal creeks and sounds, alluvial and blackwater rivers. Perhaps the most common sight is the field of smooth cordgrass *(Spartina alterniflora)* that makes up the salt marsh and the muddy banks and flats that cut through it. Rimmed by wax myrtle, nandina, and cherry laurel on its banks, overshadowed by huge live oaks whose limbs are draped with Spanish

CIVIL WAR–ERA HISTORY, SUCH AS THIS MORTAR AT WHITE POINT GARDEN, ARE EVERYWHERE IN CHARLESTON
RIVERNORTHPHOTOGRAPHY/ISTOCKPHOTO.COM

moss (an air plant, member of the pineapple family), and dotted with resurrection fern, the salt marsh is nature's most productive nursery. The Lowcountry has more of it than anywhere on the Southeast coast.

What you see is this: filter feeders such as snails, crabs, oysters, shrimp, and mullet ingesting the detritus—a potent mixture of decomposed marsh grass, animal matter, algae, and fungi. Or a heron or raccoon eating its smaller prey. The fiddler crabs with their lopsided claws gather and disperse like a muddy cavalry. As the tide recedes, you will hear the marsh release oxygen and pop like 100 pricked balloons. The

THE MOCK-BIRD

This ancient sublime forest, frequently intersected with extensive avenues, vistas and green lawns, opening to extensive savannas and far distant Rice plantations, agreeably employs the imagination, and captivates the senses by scenes of magnificence and grandeur. The gay mock-bird, vocal and joyous, mounts aloft on silvered wings, rolls over and over, then gently descends, and presides in the choir of the tuneful tribes.

—From *Travels of William Bartram*

slightly sweet, sulfurous smell of "pluff mud" fills the air. Locals call that smell "puffy." If you venture to the edge of the marsh and get your sneakers wet, when they dry you'll see it's not mud at all but rather fine gray material that shakes off like dust.

Even the cities are overcome by nature's exuberance. Streets and gardens burst with azaleas and flowering dogwood in the spring. Honeysuckle, jessamine, wisteria, and trumpet vine tumble wildly over walls and race up tree trunks. And then there are the birds: the tiny, sassy Carolina wren that makes its nest in a flowerpot; mourning doves

BORN INTO SLAVERY, ROBERT SMALLS WAS A CIVIL WAR HERO AND PROMINENT RECONSTRUCTION-ERA CONGRESSMAN FROM BEAUFORT

VOLUPTUOUS CHARM

Picket life was of course the place to feel the charm of the natural beauty on the Sea Islands. We had a world of profuse and tangled vegetation around us, such as would have been a dream of delight to me, but for the constant sense of responsibility and care which came between. Amid this preoccupation, Nature seemed but a mirage, and not the close and intimate associate I had before known. I pressed no flowers, collected no insects or birds' eggs, made no notes on natural objects, reversing in these respects all previous habits. Yet now, in the retrospect, there seems to have been infused into me through every pore the voluptuous charm of the season and the place; and the slightest corresponding sound or odor now calls back the memory of those delicious days.
—From *Army Life in a Black Regiment* by Thomas Wentworth Higginson
(New York: W. W. Norton, 1984. First published in 1869)

that coo from telephone wires; chuck-will's-widows that frantically chant at dusk; the mockingbird that mimics 200 songs; and the birds of prey that soar overhead.

The first African slave was brought to the first Charleston settlement in 1670 with English settlers from Barbados, a group that would define governance, slave codes, and the establishment of a new society. The story of the Lowcountry and the narrative that draws visitors begins with this unequal racial relationship: Every historic building or landscape you see is a part of its legacy. Enslaved people, freedmen and women, and their heirs have contributed in the most essential way imaginable to its politics, economic growth, folkways, art, culture, and language. The enterprise of managing slaves as individuals and as economic assets, along with the fear of uprising, especially after the Denmark Vesey rebellion in Charleston in 1822, made for a regulation of life unknown outside the South. This was true in both the cities and the country.

In the cities, black and white residents would pass each other in the street. Black people may have been politically invisible, but their presence was known. By contrast, the plantation world that generated wealth was more isolated and self-sufficient, marked by seasonal activities: gathering marsh hay for fertilizer; harvesting, clearing, and burning the fields; building and repairing fences and dikes; growing food crops and raising cows and hogs for slaughter; moting and ginning cotton, packing it in the cotton house, and taking it to the landing for shipment. For cotton and food crops, the tool was a hoe to chop weeds and a team of oxen to dig the furrow. Cultivating rice required more knowledge about tidal flow and the operation of rice dikes. Drayton Hall and Middleton Place outside Charleston, and even modest plantation properties on the Sea Islands, are now grand and silent; they were once fantastically busy. As you tour the countryside, try to imagine it dominated by open fields punctuated by orderly windbreaks of trees, rather than the scrub you see today. The Lowcountry was a vast rice and cotton factory worked by chattel slaves, and the plantations were run like a business with as much acreage under cultivation as possible.

Within that world and responding to its demands arose the Gullah Geechee culture. It reflects a West African heritage of skills and sensitivities that survived the Middle Passage and much more. It flourished, and its legacy survives today, because slaves kept a sense of personal and community identity alive in unregulated places like plantation praise houses, brush arbors, and extended families, and later in churches and schools. Descendants' stories are continuing to be told, and they inform significant new interpretations of historic sites.

It is not possible to overestimate the way in which the Civil War disrupted the order imposed by the plantation world and the society it held in check. When recovery was to come to the Lowcountry, it would come to the countryside last.

If the Lowcountry is seen by visitors as a place rich in references to the Civil War, both physical and cultural, perhaps it is because there was such a difference in the "before" and "after." But even before the Civil War, the Lowcountry had been undergoing a slow transformation, a political and economic drift that marginalized it from the center of national opinion. As Mary Boykin Chesnut wrote in her diary at the time of secession: "South Carolina had been rampant for years. She was the torment of herself and everyone else. Nobody could live in this state unless he were a fire-eater."

In December 1860, South Carolina seceded, led by planters from Edisto and Beaufort. The following year, Georgia followed suit. Soon, the harbor forts that watched over both cities—Fort Sumter and Fort Pulaski—were battle sites. Both of the forts can be visited today, and the story of their defense is a dramatic one.

A less well-known chapter of Civil War history, having Beaufort as its center, concerns the efforts of Northern abolitionists to live among the formerly enslaved residents and prepare them for full "citizenship" after their owners had fled. The enterprise followed by several months the Union invasion of Port Royal in November 1861. This

A DEFIANT CULTURE

Secession is the fashion here. Young ladies sing for it; old ladies pray for it; young men are dying to fight for it; old men are ready to demonstrate it.

—From a dispatch to the *London Times*, April 1861, sent from Charleston by English journalist William Howard Russell

A TOUR BUS DESIGNED AFTER A VICTORIAN-STYLE STREETCAR DRIVES DOWN HISTORIC KING STREET
CRAID MCCAUSLAND/ISTOCKPHOTO.COM

A PROFOUND SENSE OF PLACE, SHARED BY ALL

To describe our growing up in the Lowcountry of South Carolina, I would have to take you to the marsh on a spring day, flush the great blue heron from its silent occupation, scatter marsh hens as we sink to our knees in the mud, open you an oyster with a pocketknife and feed it to you from the shell and say, "There. That taste. That's the taste of my childhood." I would say, "Breathe deeply," and you would breathe and remember that smell for the rest of your life, the bold, fecund aroma of the tidal marsh, exquisite and sensual, the smell of the South in heat, a smell like new milk, semen, and spilled wine, all perfumed with seawater.

—From *The Prince of Tides* by Pat Conroy (Boston: Houghton Mifflin Company, 1986)

"Gideon's Band" set up schools for young and old in front parlors and cotton houses. The occupying army converted the old houses to hospitals, barracks, and offices.

The story of the post-war Reconstruction period in the Beaufort area is now in the spotlight. Recently designated as the Reconstruction Era National Historical Park, a handful of sites and a modest interpretive museum are beginning to relate what has been an overlooked chapter of history: when liberated African Americans gained a place in social, political, and commercial worlds that had excluded them.

The region was impoverished. Older white residents hoarded their gentility as they might their last pennies, taking in sewing, teaching, and renting rooms to boarders. In the country, everyone concentrated on making a modest living. People were thrown back on their resources—fishing, hunting, and farming—and they made do. Black freedmen were able to purchase and cultivate land. Although phosphate mining, timbering, and shipyards emerged as centers of postwar activity, and the military established bases and shipyard facilities, the economy was slow to repair itself. An idea of just how poor conditions were, right up until World War II, can be glimpsed in the work of photographers sent by the Farm Security Administration to document it. Many of these images can be accessed online in the records of the Library of Congress.

The legacy of poverty was just as crucial in preserving the built environment of the Lowcountry as prosperity had been for bringing it to life. As early as the 1920s, Charlestonians were organizing to save their old buildings. In 1931, the city passed the nation's first historic district zoning ordinances; some 20 years later, the Historic Savannah Foundation was founded to oppose the demolition of the Isaiah Davenport House. Ever since, these cities' historic districts and properties in the country have been central attractions to generations of tourists, inspiring legions of architects, landscape gardeners, historians, novelists, and anthropologists.

WHAT'S WHERE IN CHARLESTON, SAVANNAH & COASTAL ISLANDS

AREA CODES 843 and 854 in South Carolina and 912 in the Savannah area. In the area covered by this book it is necessary to dial the area code even if your call is local.

AIRPORTS AND AIRLINES **Charleston International Airport** (843-767-7000; www.iflychs.com) offers service across the country on nine carriers, including American (800-433-7300; www.aa.com), Delta (800-221-1212; www.delta.com), jetBlue (800-538-2583; www.jetblue.com), United (800-241-6522; www.united.com), Southwest (800-435-9792; www.southwest.com), and British Airways (800-247-9297; www.britishairways.com)

Savannah/Hilton Head International Airport (912-964-0514; www.savannahairport.com) is located about 25 minutes from downtown Savannah and about 45 minutes from most parts of Hilton Head. Eight carriers schedule regular departures and arrivals, including American (800-433-7300; www.aa.com), Delta (800-221-1212; www.delta.com), Allegiant (702-505-8888; www.allegiantair.com), United (800-241-6522; www.united.com), and jetBlue (800-538-2583;www.jetblue.com).

Hilton Head Island Airport (www.hiltonheadairport.com) is overseen by Beaufort County and is home to three commercial carriers: American Airlines (800-433-7300; www.aa.com), Delta (800-221-1212; www.delta.com), and United (800-241-6522; www.united.com), and private planes. The airport is expanding its runway footprint and facilities to accommodate more direct flights to major cities. Most island destinations are within a 25-minute drive. Rental cars are available on-site.

Private Aviation Contact the following county or regional airports or services:

Beaufort County Airport (Lady's Island) (843-770-2003; www.beaufortcountysc.gov).

Mount Pleasant Regional (843-884-8837; www.iflychs.com/LRO/Home).

Johns Island Airport (843-559-2401; www.atlanticaviation.com).

Atlantic Aviation–Charleston International (843-746-7600; www.atlanticaviation.com).

Savannah Aviation (912-964-1022; www.savannahaviation.com).

AMTRAK (800-872-7245; http://www.amtrak.com/) travels the north–south corridor, making daily stops at North Charleston (744-8264; 4565 Gaynor Avenue), about 25 minutes from downtown; Yemassee (15 Wall Street), about 30 miles west of Beaufort; and Savannah (800-872-7245; 2611 Seaboard Coastline Drive), about 20 minutes from downtown. Cabs are available at city depots; for Yemassee you should arrange advance transportation through a Beaufort taxi company or shared-ride service. On the long hauls from cities like Boston, New York, Chicago, and Miami, there are generally two trains a day, departing morning and evening and arriving either late the same day or early the following morning. Traveling by night with sleeping accommodations is a nice option for these 10- to 18-hour trips.

BUS SERVICE **Greyhound** (800-231-2222; www.greyhound.com) serves Charleston, Beaufort, and Savannah and maintains stations in those cities. It also serves points in between, but here the stops are less formal—perhaps as simple as a crossroads store. As a result, if you're planning to do a substantial amount of traveling by bus, you should consult both a detailed map and the bus schedule. Don't expect to find a taxi or rental-car stand at every stop.

The service and price to Charleston and Savannah from various points are roughly equal; in most cases the same bus goes to both cities. Travel times on longer trips may vary up to three hours, according to the number of stops and the specific route, so it's wise to ask about arrival times and whether it's a direct trip.

Charleston Greyhound Bus Terminal (843-744-4247; 3610 Dorchester Road, North Charleston).

Savannah Greyhound Bus Terminal (912-232-2135; 610 W. Oglethorpe Avenue).

Beaufort Greyhound Bus Terminal (800-231-2222; 3659 Trask Parkway).

CLIMATE, WEATHER, AND WHAT TO WEAR There is something in bloom year-round in the Lowcountry, from April jessamine to late-summer mums to camellias to paperwhite narcissus, which scent the air at Christmas. This comes as a result of the semitropical to subtropical climate and the ever-present breezes that characterize the coastal region. There are also microclimates—as small as a yard, as wide as an acre—that make it possible to cultivate plants that are used to a warmer zone, like oranges and freesia. The annual rainfall for the region is about 51 inches.

The winters are generally mild—maybe 9 days of frost and a half-dozen hard freezes. Spring comes early. Farmers generally break ground on February 1. In the old days, the cotton crop was finished by "lay-by time" in late August, when slaves, temporarily released from heavy field work, would tend to their cemeteries and families.

By May 1 it's hot, and that heat will penetrate until the end of September. The mean summer temperature in the Lowcountry runs around 88 degrees, but with the humidity factored in it feels much hotter, especially in urban areas. The water temperature reaches the high 80s in summer and stays in the mid-70s through October. Be prepared to move slowly, wear a hat, use sunscreen, and drink plenty of liquids. Take extra precautions if you're planning athletic pursuits: The tennis court is no place to be at midday. The wild cloudbursts that drench the region in summer, and the often-spectacular thunder and lightning shows that accompany them, cool things off a bit.

Then there are the gnats, also known as flying teeth. Just when you're enjoying a beautiful spring or autumn day, they find you. Insect repellent can be effective, as is staying out of the shade or standing in a breeze.

The seasons each bring their color, their migratory birds, their harvest of fish or shellfish, duck or deer. And twice a year it seems as if there's a whole new shipment of air—in late October, when the marsh has turned golden and the clouds pull themselves into exquisitely defined cumuli; and again in late February, when the prevailing northeast winds of winter start to shift south and southwest.

But perhaps the best quality of Lowcountry weather is its subtlety and contradiction: the warm day in January that you were not expecting, the roaring fire in October that banishes the morning chill but by late afternoon seems like an inferno.

For clothing, pack more cotton shirts than you think you'll need. Take comfortable shoes for touring (high-heeled shoes are often forbidden in house museums and on tours), and a light sweater or windbreaker. An overcoat or parka may be too much in winter; sweaters and shells work better.

The hurricane season lasts from June to November, with the most recent devastating storms having come between late August and October. If you're traveling then, make sure you are aware of evacuation routes, and keep alerted to local media for hurricane watches and warning announcements. The National Weather Service (www.weather.gov/chs) provides excellent coverage of the South Carolina and Georgia area on its website.

GETTING THERE, GETTING AROUND The Lowcountry is mostly water. Perhaps this is why the old houses of the region—and the dense feeling of permanence they exude—are so venerated, above and beyond their architectural and historic status. They appear—now, as in the past—literally to triumph over their surroundings, as if daring wind, water, and the harsh storms to teach them the lessons of frailty.

The tides, which cast the riches of sea life toward shore and offered planters the possibility of power to operate rice dikes, bestowed on the Lowcountry an abundance of marine and bird life. Flat-bottomed plantation barges loaded with rice, bales of cotton, and farm produce plied the rivers and creeks to the city harbor. Eight-oared bateaux, made on the plantations and navigated by slaves, clove through the marsh from

LOWCOUNTRY WINTERS ARE MILD, WHILE SUMMERS ARE HOT AND HUMID LOWCOUNTRY & RESORT ISLANDS TOURISM COMMISSION

The only thoroughfare by Land between Beaufort and Charleston is the "Shell Road," a beautiful avenue, which, about 9 miles from Beaufort, strikes a ferry across the Coosaw River. War abolished the ferry, and made the river the permanent barrier between the opposing picket lines. For 10 miles, right and left, these lines extended, marked by well-worn footpaths, following the endless windings of the stream; and they never varied until nearly the end of the war. Upon their maintenance depended our whole foothold on the Sea Islands; and upon that finally depended the whole campaign of Sherman.

—From *Army Life in a Black Regiment* by Thomas Wentworth Higginson (New York: W. W. Norton, 1984. First published in 1869.)

one plantation to another, carrying news, goods, and passengers. The Savannah River offered both protection to an English colony in the Southern wilderness and a commercial avenue.

Quite often, what roads existed were hardly distinguishable from the water. Highways could be covered with washed-up shells, sponges, and seaweed, brought and removed by the tides each day. As time went on, people of the Lowcountry took nature one step further: They made roadbeds of oyster shell, fashioning a crown at the "center line" to facilitate drainage. These were the best roads around, and in towns like Beaufort they were in use well into the 20th century. An unimproved road common today on the Sea Islands is plowed through fine sand, perhaps a foot deep, rutted and banked. More than one elderly resident can tell a tale of pushing a Model T Ford through this sand, or of watching the ice melt through the sawdust when the iceman got stuck.

Perhaps as a result of the reliance on water travel, as well as the sheer isolation of the plantations and their rural dependencies, a thickly veined series of land transportation routes never really developed in the Lowcountry. Instead there evolved a fleet of small steamers that made their way from island to island, picking up passengers, mail, produce, and cotton to deliver to Charleston and Savannah. And ox-drawn carts, horses, or marsh "tackies" (diminutive

horses thought to have been first brought by Spanish explorers) serviced them. When, in 1894, historian Henry Adams visited St. Helena Island, he traveled first by train, then by carriage over a sand road, then on a shell road, then by foot to the ferry crossing, then over the river to board the steamer *Flora*, which carried him to his destination. These days travel is easier, but there are still plenty of unlit, two-lane roads flanked by drainage

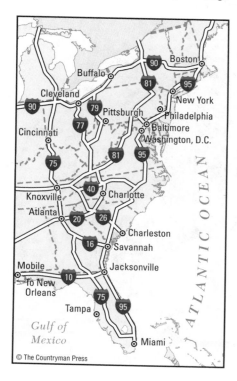

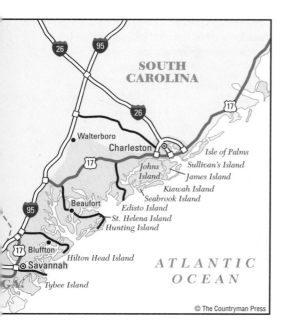

SOUTH CAROLINA

ATLANTIC OCEAN

© The Countryman Press

By Car: Unless your visit to the Lowcountry is limited to Charleston, Savannah, or a Hilton Head resort, having your own car pays off. The Lowcountry is decentralized; a lot of space separates those "points of interest." What's more, appreciating that very space by finding yourself in it lies at the heart of the Lowcountry experience. That's where you'll find some of the region's subtle treasures: the view of a marsh at sunset, the sight of feeding pelicans as they hit the water, the faded impression of an abandoned oyster-shell road strewn with wildflowers. It is in these very open spaces, in their linked geography, that the sense of times past and lives abundantly lived will catch up with you and shape your awareness of what the Lowcountry is all about. US 17, one of the region's oldest roads and still perhaps the most direct, threads its way from above Charleston to Savannah (and beyond) through marshes, old rice fields, and bottomland forests. Turnoffs that access the Sea Islands and resorts to the east and the Ashley River plantations

ditches that require extra time and careful driving. Directions to specific areas are noted near the beginning of each chapter.

MIDDLETON PLACE © AKAPLUMMER/ISTOCKPHOTO.COM

(**Drayton Hall, Middleton Place, Magnolia Gardens**) to the west (along SC 61) are well marked, as are historic sites, parks, and picnic grounds.

From Washington and points north: The approach is on I-95, which roughly parallels the coast. From there, well-marked exits direct you to downtown Charleston (via I-26), Beaufort (via US 21), Hilton Head (via US 278), and Savannah (via I-16). The coastal destinations beyond the big cities, such as Kiawah Island, Edisto Island, Beaufort, and Hilton Head, lie approximately 45 minutes east of I-95. Distance from Washington to Charleston: 512 miles; to Savannah: 616 miles.

From Jacksonville and points south: Like visitors from the north, drivers from the south approach on I-95 and then turn east to the coast. Distance from Jacksonville to Charleston: 241 miles; to Savannah: 139 miles.

From Asheville and points northwest: Take I-40 to I-26, then follow I-26 toward Spartanburg and Columbia. About an hour out of Columbia, you meet I-95. At that point either continue east to Charleston or turn south. Distance from Asheville to Charleston: 265 miles; to Savannah: 297 miles.

From Charlotte: Take I-77 south to I-20 at Columbia; follow I-20 for a few exits to link up with I-26 East. Distance to Charleston: 200 miles; to Savannah: 240 miles.

From Atlanta: Take I-75 to I-16. When it crosses I-95, go north for Charleston or continue directly to Savannah. Distance to Charleston: 286 miles; to Savannah: 259 miles.

The approximate distances and driving times to Charleston and selected cities are given in the chart below. The distance between Charleston and Savannah is 114 miles. If you're touring within the Lowcountry and stopping along the way between Charleston and Savannah in places like Beaufort, Hilton Head, Bluffton, Edisto, or Walterboro, this trip easily may take a day. In general,

traveling to specific Sea Island destinations located to the east of I-95 can add up to an hour to your trip.

To Charleston from:	Distance (miles)	Duration (hours)
Atlanta	286	5
Boston	929	17
Charlotte	200	4
Chicago	906	15.5
Knoxville	395	7
Miami	590	10.5
New Orleans	784	13
New York	768	13
Washington, DC	512	8.5

On the Water: The Intracoastal Waterway winds through creek and river, ocean and sound, from one end of the Lowcountry to the other. In Charleston, Beaufort, and Hilton Head, you can dock at a marina downtown within walking distance of restaurants and sightseeing. Savannah's marinas are about 20 minutes from downtown. Most provide repair service. If you want to make use of the charter fishing, sailing, or tour services based at marinas, see *To Do* in the appropriate chapter for some ideas. If your main mode of transportation is by boat, check those listings for details on berthing facilities and services.

In the City: In Charleston, the **Downtown Area Shuttle (DASH)** (843-724-7420; www.ridecarta.com) makes regular stops along routes in the peninsula's Historic District and is free. Board at the Visitor Center (843-724-7174; 375 Meeting Street), where you can park your car ($18 per day). There are also more than a dozen municipal parking garages ($2 per hour) downtown. City buses (check the website for fares and routes) provide bike racks on many routes.

In Savannah, there's the **dot Express shuttle** (912-233-5767; www.catchacat

.org), a free shuttle bus service within the Historic District, with 24 stops at the Visitor Center (912-944-0455; 301 Martin Luther King Jr. Boulevard), downtown inns and hotels, the waterfront, and many sites of interest. It connects to most bus routes, with additional fares for regional service throughout Chatham County. The website offers a very helpful Bike/Walk Savannah guide. For $15 visitors can buy a 24-hour pass that allows unlimited parking in any city lot, garage, or parking meter. They are available at the Visitor Center. As in Charleston, parking rules are strictly enforced.

Beaufort is experimenting with a downtown shuttle on a loop route to ease its growing downtown parking challenges as the town grows and tourism increases as a result of so much favorable press and making "Top Ten" lists.

GOLF More details are available in each chapter. The region has hosted PGA Tour and Ryder Cup events for many years, and courses on Kiawah Island and Hilton Head Island are considered world-class. Listings can be found at www.discover southcarolina.com, charlestongolfguide .com, and www.hiltonheadisland.org and cover both public and private venues.

GOVERNMENT Charleston, Beaufort, Walterboro, Ridgeland, Hampton, and Savannah are the region's county seats. The towns within the counties that you are more likely spend time in are Beaufort, Bluffton, Edisto Island, Folly Beach, Hilton Head, Isle of Palms, Port Royal, Ridgeland, and Sullivan's Island. The **South Carolina Department of Natural Resources** (803-734-3447; www.dnr.sc .gov) regulates hunting, fishing, boating, and wildlife management areas, provides maps, and issues permits and licenses. The **South Carolina Department of Parks, Recreation and Tourism** (803-734-1700; www.discoversouthcarolina.com) is a fount of information sorted by region and topic.

HANDICAPPED SERVICES Most of the region's accommodations, museums, restaurants, and touring services provide access and facilities for those with special needs, but call ahead to confirm details: Problems remain in retrofitting the older historic buildings for complete handicapped access, and this includes some house museums and inns. Your guides, hosts, or the visitor center staff in each city will gladly assist you—several offer handicap-accessibility guides, which are also available online. City buses and trolleys are handicapped friendly, and some beach access points are equipped with wheelchair mats.

HISTORIC RESEARCH There are abundant resources to help you learn more about specific properties; undertake genealogical research; examine old photographs, maps, and newspapers; and watch videos of oral histories of how neighborhoods changed over time. Some archives require an appointment for access. It would be best to start at the websites of the **Historic Charleston Foundation** (www.historiccharleston .org); **the South Carolina Historical Society in Charleston** (www.schistory.org); the **Beaufort District Collection at the Beaufort County Library** (www.beaufort countylibrary.org); the **Heritage Library** on Hilton Head (www.heritagelib.org); and the **Historic Savannah Foundation** (www.historicsavannahfoundation.org).

HOSPITALS **Beaufort Memorial Hospital** (843-522-5200; www.bmhsc.org), 955 Ribaut Road. In Charleston, **Bon Secours St. Francis Hospital** (843-402-1000; www .rsfh.com), 2095 Henry Tecklenburg Drive; **Medical University of South Carolina** (843-792-2300; www.muschealth .com), 171 Ashley Avenue; **Roper Hospital** (843-724-2000; www.rsfh.com), 316 Calhoun Street; **Trident Medical Center** (843-797-7000; www.tridenthealth system.com), 9330 Medical Plaza Drive; **Ralph H. Johnson VA Medical Center** (843-577-5011; www.charleston.va.gov),

FOLLY BEACH IN SUMMER © MARGARETW/ISTOCKPHOTO.COM

109 Bee Street; **Hilton Head Hospital** (843-681-6122; www.hiltonheadregional .com), 25 Hospital Center Boulevard. In Savannah, **Candler Hospital** (912-819-6000; www.sjchs.org), 5353 Reynolds Street; **Memorial Medical Center** (912-350-8000; www.memorialhealth.com), 4700 Waters Avenue.

PUBLIC ACCESS TO BEACHES It's not difficult to get to the beach, and you don't have to be a resort guest staying in a gated community to do so. Parking is available in lots with self-pay kiosks or in metered areas on the street or beachside. Prices range from $2 per hour to $12 per day, depending where you are and the season. Popular areas with plentiful walking access include, north to south, Isle of Palms, Sullivan's Island, Folly Beach, Beachwalker Park (on the west end of Kiawah Island, its only public access), Edisto Beach, The Sands in Port Royal, Hunting Island State Park, numerous points on Hilton Head's 12 miles of ocean and sound frontage, and Tybee Island outside Savannah. Driving is prohibited on beaches. Some are monitored by lifeguards and others are not. Rules govern leashed and unleashed pets—or

dogs at all—and permit activities in certain areas for safety reasons, but they don't detract from enjoying a beautiful asset.

READING The bibliography at the back of the book covers the region through the lenses and sensibilities of many writers, but none is as closely identified with it as the late Pat Conroy, who graduated from Beaufort High and the Citadel in Charleston, taught on Daufuskie Island, and lived and wrote later in life on Fripp Island and overlooking the marsh in Beaufort. He is buried on St. Helena Island. **The Pat Conroy Literary Center** (843-379-7025; www.patconroyliterary center.org) is located in downtown Beaufort (905 Port Republic Street) and open from noon to 4 p.m. Thursday through Sunday or by appointment. It's a modest, evocative museum filled with artifacts. His passion for writing and his legacy shine even more brightly in the annual Pat Conroy Literary Festival in the fall and through educational programming for all ages, workshops, retreats, readings, and talks by visiting writers.

OPPOSITE: AZALEAS IN MAGNOLIA PLANTATION AND GARDENS   © MARGARETW/ISTOCKPHOTO.COM

CHARLESTON

CHARLESTON

Charleston is one of the nation's oldest urban environments. It has been the site of some of the most dramatic events in American history, and scores of buildings and vistas that tell its story remain intact. Unlike many American cities, it didn't reinvent itself over time—partly because after the Civil War its leaders preferred provincial insularity to the risks of change, and partly because it was too worn down to do much but carry on in the old ways, its people too habituated to roles they inherited long after the society which had assigned them disappeared.

In the early 20th century, with the attack on Fort Sumter fresh in living memory, Charlestonians got a second chance to protect the life they knew and valued, this time with more favorable results. A group of women spearheaded the country's earliest preservation efforts, reacting strongly to demolitions and setting a vision, and it is their legacy that shapes the city today, both in structure and spirit. The environment they and later generations saved serves as the backdrop for a vibrant urban culture of restaurants, art galleries, shops, and live performances, and to accommodations ranging from an old parlor to a luxury suite. The city is neither an "authentic reproduction" nor an outdoor museum but a place with character and style.

RODMAN CANNONS, USED IN THE CIVIL WAR, AT FORT SUMTER © OVIDIUHRUBARU/ISTOCKPHOTO.COM

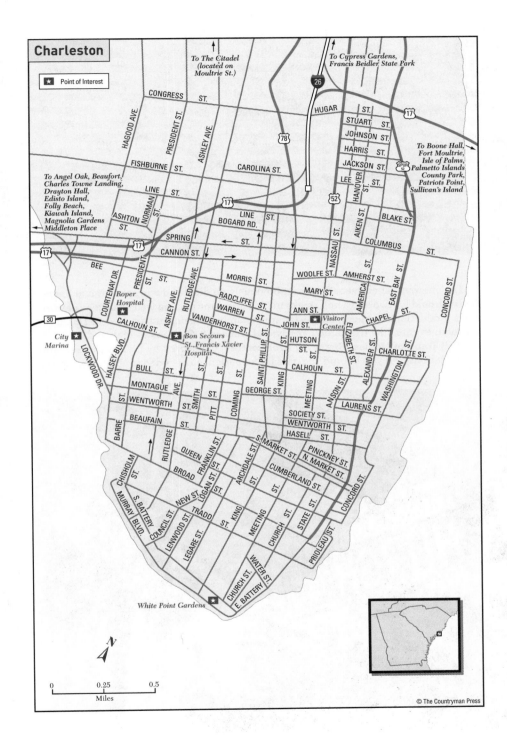

COVID-19

Due to the COVID-19 pandemic, travel in the Lowcountry, as everywhere else, requires more planning for every activity to ensure appropriate social distancing. This means that you should call or check a venue's website to confirm, among other things, if reservations are required where walk-in activity was once the norm. It also means that providers of services from hotels to restaurants or boat rides to carriage tours are likely to be running their businesses differently from in the past, with fewer visitors engaged at any one time. If you are a family group, be sure to mention that, because it may make a difference in the business owner's risk calculations. Ask if there is outdoor seating available at restaurants—many venues have changed their layouts to include more outside dining while they reduce the numbers of tables inside. Meals to go, food service delivery, and curbside pick-up options have expanded dramatically in the spring and summer of 2020; check to see if those options are still available. Annual events, including professional golf and tennis tournaments and house and garden tours, have shifted their dates and ticketing procedures. You'll have a more rewarding travel experience if you arrive prepared and flexible.

The energy that enlivens it is most obviously on display during the annual **Spoleto Festival,** held for two and a half weeks in May and June and marked by dozens of world-class productions in opera, dance, theater, chamber music, and art (see *To Do*). Other seasonal events, like the annual **Festival of Houses & Gardens** in May and June, and the **Fall Tours of Homes, History & Architecture,** sponsored by historic preservation organizations, get you behind the gates to experience the indoor and outdoor spaces

FRENCH HUGUENOT CHURCH IN THE FRENCH QUARTER © RIVERNORTHPHOTOGRAPHY/ISTOCKPHOTO.COM

KAYAKING IS A UNIQUE WAY TO BECOME ACQUAINTED WITH CHARLESTON GREATER BEAUFORT-PORT ROYAL CONVENTION & VISITORS BUREAU (BANKER OPTICAL MEDIA)

nurtured by Charleston's elite for some three centuries. You can take your history in smaller doses, too, on 90-minute walking tours that focus on ghosts, plantation life, pirates, politicians, or war (Revolutionary or Civil).

Creative newcomers and a younger generation of locals are building on traditions and introducing transformative perspectives on what it means to be "Charleston." There is a dynamic, collaborative community of chefs, farmers, and foodies who capitalize on a long growing season and easy access to fresh produce and seafood. Peers across the country envy them for a thriving, collaborative scene with diners who embrace experimentation. A food and wine festival (www.charlestonwineandfood .com) on a March weekend shows them off (see *Special Events*). Groups of galleries promote emerging and established artists and sponsor monthly tours. An appreciation for design and antiques—practically coin of the realm in the city—is newly evident in stores along 15 blocks of King Street, a greatly expanded district, and in the dozens of galleries in the French Quarter.

For all its urbanity, Charleston is deeply tied to its natural environment. Beach communities are about 30 minutes away by car to the east and south. The creeks are filled with paddleboarders and kayakers on the weekend. On the other side of the peninsula, up the Ashley River, stand the big houses at **Magnolia Plantation**, **Drayton Hall**, and **Middleton Place.** After more than 250 years, the drive to reinterpret has reached them, too, with increasing emphasis on detailing the life and work of the enslaved communities that lived there.

While there's still a nod to the past and a story on every corner, Charleston is far from what it was in 1941, when the classic *WPA Guide to the Palmetto State* noted that one "may live in Charleston, a city that competes with the New Jerusalem in his dreams; or he may live in a drafty Georgian country house," but he "recalls his past glory with a pride that surpasses his ability to appreciate thoroughly the good things of the present." That cannot be said of Charleston today.

The Carolina province, as claimed by the English, came into view during the Restoration, when Charles II gave a group of lords proprietors vast tracts of land in the New World. Sir John Colleton, who had lived in Barbados, convinced his associates that a similar plantation-based society using slaves to develop the lower coast could be profitable. Several exploratory voyages ensued, and in 1670 a ship nosed into a creek upriver from Charleston under the guidance of the cacique, or chief, of the Kiawah tribe.

The earliest years of the colony have been brought to life at **Charles Towne Landing,** a restored living history village that conveys the precariousness of periodic hostilities and the challenges of self-sufficiency. After a decade, and augmented by new arrivals, the colonists and their slaves relocated from Albemarle Point to a site on the peninsula at the mouth of the harbor, where they laid out their city.

It was all go from there. Churches and houses whose architecture recalled the classic Barbadian design of raised basements and upstairs piazzas went up along streets like Church, Broad, Meeting, Tradd, and Queen; some of them stand today. It was a

SKYLINE OVER THE ASHLEY RIVER © SEAN PAVONE/ISTOCKPHOTO.COM

time of defense and expansion, of building walls to protect residents and opening the network of creeks and rivers to the countryside, where planters put thousands of acres under cultivation with rice, indigo, and cotton.

Rice brought the first tidal wave of wealth, producing a small, landed gentry—deeply connected by marriage and property, including their slaves—that was the richest in the colonies. By 1742, when there were 7,000 people living in Charleston, Savannah's population numbered in the hundreds. Prosperous as the planters were, many became increasingly as fed up with the taxes and political tactics of the British as their Northern neighbors and joined the revolutionary cause, repelling an attack at Fort Moultrie on Sullivan's Island in 1776.

The years following brought Charleston's next phase, with an influx of entrepreneurs finding new markets for cotton while buying land and slaves. Although the profitable bounty on indigo was lost, the invention of a new cotton gin capable of removing seeds from cotton faster than slaves could drive Lowcountry expansion. The boom, which lasted until about 1820, dramatically changed the look of the city, and the Federal-style houses, with the delicately carved mantels, tapered columns, and graceful proportions you see today, were built in that period.

As Charleston emerged with its social rules and rituals, its dual devotion to piety and pleasure, Africans and African Americans created their own unique culture, known as Gullah or Gullah Geechee. Scholars have identified "Africanisms" that point to its roots on the West African coast—rice-growing techniques, folk tales, patterns of speech and dress, basketry and cooking, song, dance, and spirit belief, to name a few—but it was also shaped as a personal response to hardship and a way to preserve identity and humanity. A deepening respect for its contributions and its complexity as a culture has brought the Gullah experience, past and present, into focus for a much wider audience. The Charleston region, more than others on the coast, is the first, best place to understand it.

Some historians have said that Charleston's Golden Age was effectively over by the 1830s, battered by economic competition from cotton lands to the west and other factors. Where it had been influential, now other places held supremacy. When it came time to defend its position and attitude, it left the Union. The cost of the move was so high that it took the city nearly up until World War II to recover.

GETTING THERE **Charleston International Airport** (www.iflychs.com) is served by major airlines, with direct flights to many cities. It's easily navigated; car rental is convenient. To downtown, a 25-minute ride, a group shuttle costs about $15 and cab service about $27. The **Charleston County Aviation Authority** (843-767-7000) also runs small airports on Johns Island (Charleston Executive) and Mount Pleasant Regional to serve private aircraft.

Greyhound (800-231-2222; www.greyhound.com) and **AMTRAK** (800-872-7245; www.amtrak.com) make daily stops in North Charleston. The Greyhound depot (3610 Dorchester Road; 843-744-4247) is open daily but with limited hours according to bus schedules. The AMTRAK station at 4565 Gaynor Avenue also has limited hours, timed to arrivals and departures, usually morning and evening. Cab fare from North Charleston to downtown is about $27.

The **Charleston City Marina** (843-723-5098; www.charlestoncitymarina.com), 7 Lockwood Drive, is at Mile Marker 469.5 on the Atlantic Intracoastal Waterway. Transient fees start at $2.25/foot/night, and a courtesy shuttle departs for downtown every hour.

Public transportation is handled by **CARTA** (843-724-7420; www.ridecarta.com), and its DASH shuttle covers the downtown peninsula with stops at major sites.

✳ To See

ART **Gibbes Museum of Art** (843-722-2706; www.gibbesmuseum.org), 135 Meeting Street. Open Tues.–Sun. The permanent collection presents Charleston from the 18th century, including Charles Fraser's exquisite miniatures of prominent citizens, and interpretations of 20th-century plantation and rural life by Alice Ravenel Huger Smith, Alfred Hutty, Anna Heyward Taylor, and other members of the Charleston Renaissance school of artists. Excellent museum shop. Adults $12; seniors, students, military $10; children $6.

GALLERIES The **Charleston Gallery Association** (www.charlestongalleryassociation .com), a two-decades-long collaboration of more than 30 galleries, hosts art walks on the first Friday evening of each month, featuring work in many styles and media.

Anglin Smith Fine Art (843-853-0708; www.anglinsmith.com), 9 Queen Street, represents painter Betty Anglin Smith and her accomplished triplets—painters Jennifer Smith Rogers and Shannon Smith and photographer Tripp Smith—as well as sculptors and painters working in a realistic vein.

Gaye Sanders Fisher Fine Art Gallery (843-958-0010; www.gayesandersfisher .com), 124 Church Street, is located in an 18th-century single house with adjacent gardens and features watercolors that burst with the feeling of Lowcountry landscape and architecture. Check website for current opening information.

Helena Fox Fine Art (843-723-0073; www.helenafoxfineart.com), 106A Church Street, specializes in contemporary representational art, sterling silverware, and handcrafted gold jewelry. It maintains a strong social media presence, and you get the sense that the gallerists know the pulse of the local art scene. Open by appointment.

John Carroll Doyle Art Gallery (843-577-7344; www.johncdoyle.com), 125 Church Street. A Charleston native, Doyle was one of the painters in the "new" Charleston renaissance, capturing people in intense moments (like blues harmonica players) and teasing that intensity out of landscapes and animals.

Neema Fine Art Gallery (843-353-8079; neemagallery.com), 3 Broad Street, exhibits fine art and jewelry from African American artists with roots in the region, including ironwork by Philip Simmons, who was renowned in Charleston; the region's most celebrated and collectible painter, Jonathan Green; and sweetgrass baskets, furniture, drawings, and paintings by emerging artists.

HISTORIC HOMES, GARDENS, AND RELIGIOUS SITES A reasonable schedule, once you've made your difficult choices, would include visits to two or three city sites in a day and a tour of some kind. **Museum Mile on Meeting Street** (www.charleston museummile.org) is an orienting, first-day walk. Allow a half day for a plantation or boat tour. Visitors are welcome to enter religious sites but are asked to observe the worship schedule and related courtesies, as few of the sites offer regular tour services. Handicapped access is sometimes limited in the old buildings, and there are usually rules regarding strollers. Inquire about reduced admission fees if you choose to visit multiple properties owned by the Historic Charleston Foundation, the Charleston Museum, or the Middleton Place Foundation. Historic Charleston has a terrific free app to facilitate self-guided tours of many city sites.

Aiken-Rhett House (843-723-1159; www.historiccharleston.org), 48 Elizabeth Street. Open Mon.–Sun. Built in 1817 with Greek Revival and rococo interiors, it is preserved in a less formal way than other houses, full of atmosphere, a little worn at the edges. Its attraction is allowing a visitor to see rundown beauty and what happens when a family loves a house it can't keep up. During the fiercest shelling of Charleston in the Civil War, it was the headquarters of Confederate General P. G. T. Beauregard. The intact work yard is a compelling example of African American urban life. Adults $12; reduced admission with combination tickets to selected historic properties.

Kahal Kadosh Beth Elohim (843-723-1090; www.kkbe.org), 90 Hasell Street. Open Sun.–Fri. for tours. The country's oldest synagogue in continuous use, built in 1840 to replace an earlier building that was destroyed by fire, it is a superb example of Greek Revival architecture. Check website for current opening information.

Drayton Hall (843-769-2600; www.draytonhall.org), 3380 Ashley River Road, 13 miles northwest of Charleston. Open Thurs.–Sat. The main entrance closes at 3:30 p.m. to accommodate the last tours of the day. Built between 1738 and 1742 in the Palladian style and set on a lovely Ashley River site, it is one of the most architecturally significant dwellings in America. The house is unfurnished, with stunning examples of plasterwork and carving. It's the rare place that was never restored and provides direct insight into how the wealthiest people in the colonies presented themselves as they built rice and cotton empires with slave labor. A new gallery displays architectural fragments discovered on the site and decorative art objects of the Drayton family. A half-hour presentation focuses on the economic contribution of enslaved people and how they built the Lowcountry economy. Tours of the house, on the hour, last about 45 minutes. Not to be missed even if it's raining. Adults $32, youth $15; admission paid online only.

Edmonston-Alston House (843-722-7171; www.edmondstonalston.com), 21 E. Battery. Open Tues.–Sat. First built in 1825 by one wealthy man, and later enlarged by another, its location overlooking Charleston Harbor, structure, lavish decoration, documents, family furnishings, silver, and china reveal the lifestyle some Southerners

A HORSE-DRAWN CARRIAGE RIDE IN THE FRENCH QUARTER © TRIGGERPHOTO/ISTOCKPHOTO.COM

fought to protect. Adults $12, children $8; reduced admission with combination tickets to selected historic properties.

Mother Emanuel African Methodist Episcopal Church (843-722-2561; www.mother emanuel.com), 110 Calhoun Street. The Free African Society, composed of free Blacks and slaves, was formed in 1791, and by 1818, under the leadership of Morris Brown, this independent congregation built a small church for its services. Denmark Vesey planned his slave insurrection there. The current building was built in 1891. Known as Mother Emanuel, it is the oldest AME church in the Southern United States and was the target of a white supremacist who killed nine church members at a prayer service in 2015.

French Protestant (Huguenot) Church (843-722-4385; www.huguenot-church.org), 136 Church Street. French Huguenots fleeing religious persecution worshiped in Charleston as early as 1687. This church, built on the site of earlier ones, dates from 1845 and reflects the Gothic Revival style.

Heyward-Washington House (843-722-2996; www.charlestonmuseum.org), 87 Church Street. Open daily. Built in 1772 by a rice planter and home of Thomas Heyward Jr., signer of the Declaration of Independence, it was George Washington's headquarters in 1791. Its furniture collection, including several 18th-century Charleston-made pieces and the magnificent Holmes bookcase, is unmatched in colonial-era craftsmanship. A formal garden with plants of the period and a kitchen house complete the

DRAYTON HALL IS KNOWN FOR ITS STUNNING ARCHITECTURAL DETAILS EXPLORE CHARLESTON

property. Adults $12, youth $10, children $5; discounted admission with a ticket to other Charleston Museum properties.

Joseph Manigault House (843-722-2996; www.charlestonmuseum.org), 350 Meeting Street. Open daily. The outside of this structure is three stories of brick; the inside is something like shaped light. Designed by native son Gabriel Manigault for his brother and completed in 1803, it exudes a beauty-loving sense of detail by an artist educated in Europe and exposed to sophisticated design ideas and decorating schemes. The furniture is of the period: English, American, and French. Adults $12, youth $10; discounted admission with a ticket to other Charleston Museum properties.

Magnolia Plantation and Gardens (843-571-1266; www.magnoliaplantation .com), 3550 Ashley River Road, 10 miles northwest of Charleston. Open daily; shorter hours in winter. The current building was floated here by barge in 1873, but the entire tract dates back to the time of the Barbadian planters and the Drayton family. The gardens and their design

THE FLYING STAIRCASE AT THE NATHANIEL RUSSELL HOUSE EXPLORE CHARLESTON

reflect three centuries of horticulture, including 250 varieties of *Azalea indica* and 900 varieties of *Camellia japonica*. Family friendly with self-guided paths, a zoo, boat and tram tours, and the Audubon Swamp Garden. A recently developed tour addresses the experience of enslaved families and the cabins they lived in. Basic admission is adults $20, children $10, with additional fees for interpretative tours.

Middleton Place (843-556-6020; www.middletonplace.org), 4300 Ashley River Road, 14 miles northwest of Charleston. Open daily. The formal gardens, laid out in 1741 and constructed by 100 slaves over a decade, feature terraces, camellia allées, butterfly lakes, and hillside drifts of azalea. The strong landscape design can be appreciated even when little is in bloom. Adjacent stables and a farmyard evoke the plantation era, with artisan demonstrations and a 60-minute interpretative walk examining African American life. The main house was sacked by Union forces; a remaining wing honors the Middletons, but the real reason to come here is what's outside. A good restaurant serves lunch and dinner. Adults $29, students $15, children $10; house tours cost an additional $15 per person. Several options for combination tickets are available.

Nathaniel Russell House (843-722-3405; www.historiccharleston.org), 51 Meeting Street. Open daily. A circa-1808 brick townhouse, it represents the epitome of the Adam style in the city—its stairway appears to float, a lovely combination of function and fantasy—and it is one of the most thoroughly conceived and exquisitely executed neoclassical dwellings in the nation. House admission is $10 for adults, and tickets to other Historic Charleston Foundation properties can be combined in a discount package.

St. Michael's Church (843-723-0603; stmichaelschurch.net), Meeting Street at Broad Street. Open daily. This Episcopal church and its bells are still the center of

THE CITADEL © SAILAWAY46/ISTOCKPHOTO.COM

many lives, as they have been since 1761. It is part of the famous "Four Corners of Law," an intersection that represents religious, civic, judicial, and federal order. There is a tranquil walled churchyard to explore.

St. Philip's Church (843-722-7734; www.stphilipschurchsc.org), 142 Church Street. Constructed in 1835–38, facing a central park, and flanked by its gravestones, St. Philip's seems out of the Old World of Europe. The building is sheathed in a mottled, tan stucco material that reflects the gradual shifting in light over the course of a day.

MILITARY MUSEUMS AND SITES **The Citadel Museum** (843-953-2569; www.citadel .edu), 171 Moultrie Street. The museum is open daily, with abbreviated hours on the weekends. Located on the campus of the Military College of South Carolina, founded in 1842, it tells the history of the school and the Corps of Cadets. Dress parades take place most Fridays at 3:45 during the academic year. Free admission.

Fort Lamar Heritage Preserve (www.dnr.sc.gov), Fort Lamar Road, James Island (take SC 171 to Battery Island Road; left for about 8 miles to Fort Lamar Road; right for about 5 miles to small parking lot on left). Open daily dawn–dusk. The site of the **Battle of Secessionville,** waged in the predawn darkness of June 16, 1862, when federal troops attacked this Confederate earthwork fort. The self-guided walking tour directs you across what was an open field rimmed by marsh and woods, around the simple M-shaped field fortification, and then past the magazines, dry moat, earthworks, and the likely mass grave of federal wounded.

Fort Moultrie (843-883-3123; www.nps.gov/fosu), 1214 Middle Street, Sullivan's Island, 10 miles east of Charleston. Open daily; shorter hours in winter. The base of Charleston's seacoast defense system, from its first test in the American Revolution. The palmetto-log fort that repelled the British fleet is gone, but buildings and earthworks dating from 1809 convey the sense of fragility and isolation the early patriots must have felt. A 20-minute film in the visitor center provides an excellent introduction.

It is also the burial site of the Seminole warrior Osceola, who, meeting under a flag of truce, was imprisoned here in 1838. Adults $10.

Fort Sumter National Monument (843-883-3123; www.nps.gov/fosu or www.fort sumtertours.com for boat tour information). Cruises depart from a National Park Service interpretative center at 340 Concord Street by the Charleston Aquarium and Patriots Point. Trips run three to four times each day, but fewer in winter months, to the place where the Civil War began. National Park Service rangers answer your questions, but you can explore at your own pace. The entire tour lasts just over two hours. A bonus is the view of peninsular Charleston from the water. Adults $23, seniors $21, children ages 4–11 $15.

H. L. Hunley Exhibit (843-743-4865 for information; www.hunley.org), Warren Lasch Conservation Center, 1250 Supply Street, Building 255, North Charleston. Open Sat. and Sun. The *H. L. Hunley* was the forerunner of a modern submarine, most famous for its sinking of the USS *Housatonic* outside Charleston Harbor. Its last voyage ended in disaster; all eight men aboard died. The 40-foot submersible, powered by men pedaling a crankshaft, is undergoing restoration, a fascinating process that, along with the *Hunley's* story, is well explained by docents. Adults $16, kids and teens $8.

Patriots Point Naval and Maritime Museum (843-884-2727; www.patriotspoint.org), 40 Patriots Point Road, Mount Pleasant. Open daily. Visit the aircraft carrier *Yorktown*, the World War II sub *Clamagore*, and the destroyer *Laffey*, and examine aircraft, guns, missiles, and quarters in a fun and interactive experience. The view of peninsular

FORT MOULTRIE WAS A SIGNIFICANT PRESENCE IN THE REVOLUTIONARY AND CIVIL WARS EXPLORE CHARLESTON

THE USS *YORKTOWN* BERTHED AT PATRIOTS POINT EXPLORE CHARLESTON

Charleston from the platform of the *Yorktown* is unbeatable. Adults $24, seniors $19, and discounted admission for military and first responders.

MUSEUMS **Avery Research Center for African American History and Culture** (843-953-7609; avery.cofc.edu), 125 Bull Street. Housed in one of the first schools dedicated to educating freed slaves, the center is an archive and library of printed materials, photographs, and objects related to the heritage of the region's African Americans. It's affiliated with the College of Charleston. Check the website for current opening conditions and hours.

Charleston Museum (843-722-2996; www.charlestonmuseum.org), 360 Meeting Street. Open daily. Founded in 1773, this is the oldest museum in America and reflects more than two centuries of the city's self-consciousness. Exhibits interpret subjects like flora and fauna, fashion, the art of silversmithing, Native American life, and plantation culture. The section on slavery is superb. If you're traveling with kids, this will capture their attention in a way a historic house might not. Adults $12, children $5, and youth $10; combination tickets to the museum and its historic properties available at a discount.

Charles Towne Landing (843-852-4200; www.southcarolinaparks.com), 1500 Old Towne Road (SC 171 between I-26 and US 17). Open daily. This 664-acre park is an outdoor living history museum that documents lives of the first settlers in a village; on a

17th-century replica of a typical coastal trading vessel; and in "wilderness," as found in the Animal Forest, where birds and beasts common to the area in 1670 roam in a secured habitat. A visitor center offers expanded interpretation of first contact with the Kiawah tribe and of ongoing archaeological investigations. Great place for a family picnic. Admission charged.

Old Slave Mart Museum (843-958-6467; www.oldslavemart.org), 6 Chalmers Street. Open Mon.–Sat. This moving museum, on an original slave auction site, has dramatically improved the portrait of the domestic slave economy that enabled Charleston's growth. One section focuses on the slave trade at large, which forcibly relocated some 1 million American-born slaves throughout the South between 1789 and 1861; the other highlights individual stories, letters, and documents related to African Americans, slave traders, and the way the slave market complex functioned. There's a lot to read and a great deal of information to absorb, so kids might get restless. Admission charged.

South Carolina Aquarium (843-577-3474; www.scaquarium.org), 100 Aquarium Wharf. Open daily. You'll find displays of the state's aquatic habitat, from the mountain streams of the up-country to Lowcountry marshes. More than 5,000 creatures reside here in the 385,000-gallon Great Ocean Tank, in living habitat exhibits, and in the hands-on water tables and touch tanks. You can watch scuba divers in the tank, observe daily feedings, and visit the sea turtle care center, which rescues and rehabilitates loggerheads and other turtles that nest on South Carolina beaches. Highly kid friendly. Adults $29.95, children 3–12, $22.95.

RANDOLPH HALL AT THE COLLEGE OF CHARLESTON © LEAMUS/ISTOCKPHOTO.COM

SALT MARSH IN SOUTH CAROLINA'S LOWCOUNTRY © GINGER WAREHAM/PICKLEJUICE.COM

✳ To Do

Joining a tour led by a licensed guide is an efficient way to learn about Charleston, and, especially in the summer, air-conditioned vans, open-air carriages, or boats are welcome options. Assume that the tours will last at least 90 minutes to two hours; carriage rides are shorter. They depart from various locations downtown, usually one in the morning and one in the afternoon. For a good overview of all the options, visit www .charlestontours.com. Doing a bit of research is worth it because many tours are organized around a topic that may particularly interest you, like architecture, art, gardens, food, Gullah history, the Civil War, ghost stories, and so on. With sufficient advance notice, some private guides will craft a unique tour for your group or offer bilingual service. Reservations can be booked online but are not required.

BY FOOT **Bulldog Tours** (843-722-8687; www.bulldogtours.com). They provide the broadest and deepest selection of offerings, including strolls on history, art and culture, the food scene, and the city's haunted side. Prices for adults start at around $29, for those under 17 about $19.

    Old Charleston Walking Tours (843-568-0473; www.oldcharlestontours.com). The Pleasing Terrors Ghost Tour takes place twice daily, led by a Charleston native who has been guiding for nearly two decades. Adults $20, kids $10.

Old South Carriage Co. (843-723-9712; www.oldsouthcarriage.com). Options include walking, walking/carriage tours (they also do carriages separately), and other combinations, starting at about $25 for adults and $15 for kids.

BY CARRIAGE These companies leave from stables in the City Market area, and prices for an hour tour start at about $28 for adults. It's evident that the employees care not only about the visitors' experience but the horses' experience, too, in making sure they are rested and watered in the summer. The most comfortable times to ride beginning in about May and through the summer are early morning or in the evening.

Classic Carriage Tours (843-853-3747; classiccarriage.com).

Palmetto Carriage Works (843-723-8145; www.palmettocarriage.com).

BY BUS OR MINIVAN The audio is high quality, and extra-large windows offer great views. These tours also travel to sites out of the city limits; larger vehicles are restricted in some neighborhoods with narrow streets. They are a good choice for handicapped passengers, the eager visitor who wants to see a lot in a day, and groups of six or more. They're probably not the best option for fidgety kids. Motorized tours generally pick up and deliver passengers from the Visitor Center at 375 Meeting Street. Prices vary depending on the itinerary.

Adventure Sightseeing (843-762-0088; adventuresightseeing.com). You can cover a lot of ground by selecting a combined plantation and city tour that lasts several hours.

Gullah Tours (843-763-7551; www.gullahtours.com). Alphonso Brown is kind of a legendary guide on his 25-passenger bus, a former schoolteacher who tells great stories about the African American Gullah culture and the artisans who built Charleston. He speaks Gullah, which he will also translate for you when the patois gets hard to decipher. Visitors don't usually get the opportunity to hear it.

BY BOAT **Sandlapper Water Tours** (843-849-8687; www.sandlappertours.com). History, nature, and sunset cruises with a cash bar aboard a 45-foot motorized catamaran

TOURS ON THE WATER CAN GIVE A SPECTACULAR VIEW OF 19TH-CENTURY HOMES LINING THE CHARLESTON BATTERY EXPLORE CHARLESTON

depart three times a day from the Charleston Maritime Center, 10 Wharfside Street. The two-hour sunset cruise is stunning (adults $40, 12 and under $30), and prices range for daytime options where naturalists and historians serve as your guides.

Spirit Line Harbor Tour (843-722-2628; www.spiritlinecruises.com). The 90-minute harbor tour is led by a licensed guide who fills you in on maritime, trade, and military history while you relax (beer available to purchase) and enjoy breathtaking views of ship traffic and sites like Fort Sumter and the Battery.

BY BICYCLE Discovering the nooks and crannies of the historic districts under your own steam is an intimate way to imagine the past. There is a wide selection of bikes available for adults and kids, high performance and hybrid, tag-along and tandems. Rental rates of beach cruisers or geared bikes are around $7–$10 per hour and $28–$40 per day. Bikes can be delivered to your lodgings. Shops have maps and ideas for longer rides, and they also can service your bike. Helmets, child seats, and locks are provided at low or no cost.

Affordabike (843-789-3281; www.affordabike.com), 534 King Street.

The Bicycle Shoppe (843-722-8168; www.thebicycleshoppe.com), 280 Meeting Street.

✳ To Do

OUTSIDE THE CITY

CANOEING, KAYAKING, AND PADDLEBOARDING Exploring the natural environment during a day trip has never been easier. Guided ecotours, instruction, and equipment rentals are available from **Coastal Expeditions** (843-884-7684; www.coastalexpeditions.com) and **Nature Adventures Outfitters** (843-568-3222; www.kayakcharlestonsc.com). For example, a day trip to the Francis Marion National Forest or a sea kayak expedition on the Kiawah River costs about $95 per person; two- and three-hour group kayak trips start at $45. The options, prices, and destinations, including many in the creeks and rivers of the ACE Basin, are too numerous to list but are designed to accommodate your stamina, expertise, and goals. Rentals are available by the hour, half-day, day, and longer.

The Edisto River, thought to be the nation's longest free-flowing blackwater stream, offers calm waters and great bird and wildlife observation, like great blue herons wading by the oak-lined riverbank or hummingbirds feeding at wildflowers. The trail follows an ancient waterway used by Native Americans and early settlers. **Colleton State Park** (843-538-8206; www.southcarolinaparks.com), US 15, Canadys, 12 miles north of Walterboro, and **Givhans Ferry State Park** (843-873-0692; www.southcarolinaparks.com), SC 61, 16 miles west of Summerville, are along the route.

FISHING Opportunities are endless and year-round: fly-fishing in the inland flats, fishing from a pier, fishing with bait from small (15 to 26 feet) and large (up to 54 feet) craft, fishing off an artificial reef, surf casting from the beach, trolling in the Gulf Stream. Charter fees include equipment, instruction, fuel, bait, licenses, and food or drink if applicable. For small craft, the price is generally based on two people, $50 for each additional person (size of party limited by size of boat). You can get from a basic trip for two for three hours at around $350 to twice as much pretty quickly. Have a conversation with the captain about your group and what you hope to get out of the experience.

JUST OVER THE RAVENEL BRIDGE FROM CHARLESTON, THE MEMORIAL PARK IN MOUNT PLEASANT IS A FAVORITE PLACE TO FISH, WATCH OUTDOOR MOVIES, AND ENJOY AN INCREDIBLE VIEW EXPLORE CHARLESTON

Avid Angling Fishing Charters (843-566-3433; www.avidangling.com), 10 Wharfside Street. Inshore, nearshore, fly-fishing and fly-casting lessons; surf fishing; and cobia and tarpon trips for all levels of anglers and ages. They also offer crabbing and shark-teeth hunting for the younger set.

Bohicket Marina (843-768-1280; www.bohicket.com), 1880 Andell Bluff Boulevard, Seabrook Island. Large selection of boats from 14 to 55 feet for inshore bass and trout fishing, jetty fishing, and offshore fishing for shark, mackerel, tuna, and marlin. Full- and half-day trips, on your own or with a guide.

Headshaker Charters (843-810-0495; www.headshakercharters.com). Captain Legare Leland grew up fishing here and arranges trips in Charleston Harbor and nearby estuaries to troll for redfish, trout, flounder, and other species. Very family-friendly fishing in safe, maneuverable boats.

GOLF The first golf course in America was built in Charleston, and courses take advantage of its ocean vistas and forest boundaries. Charleston Area Golf Guide (www.charlestongolfguide.com) is a central listing service where you can scan course descriptions and book tee times online.

Fees vary according to seasonal categories. Lowest rates are usually December through February and after 3 p.m. Carts are required at peak playing times on many courses. For resort play, golf privileges are sometimes extended to nonresort guests; check with your concierge or call the resort directly. Reservations are often made three months in advance at the resorts. Club rentals and instruction are available at all courses. Weekday rates generally assume play Monday through Thursday only.

PUBLIC AND SEMIPRIVATE COURSES Charleston Municipal Golf Course (843-795-6517; www.charleston-sc.gov), 2110 Maybank Highway, about 10 minutes from downtown on James Island. Six sets of tees make the course flexible for players of all skill levels. Par 72, yardage 3,628 to 6,432 yards. Greens fees during the week start around $20 if you walk, $40 with cart rental. Rates increase on weekends. Check website for current opening information.

Charleston National (843-884-4653; www.charlestonnationalgolf.com), 1360 National Drive, Mount Pleasant. Par 72, yardage 5,086 to 7,064 yards. Fees $60–$85 with significant discounts after 4 p.m. Rees Jones design.

Coosaw Creek Country Club (843-767-9000; www.coosawcreek.com), 4110 Club Course Drive. Par 71 on 5,064-yard forward course to 6,619-yard champion course. Fees: $69–$79. An Arthur Hills design.

Dunes West (843-856-9000; www.duneswestgolfclub.com), 3535 Wando Plantation Way, Mount Pleasant. Par 72 on 5,208-yard forward course to 6,859-yard champion course. Fees in six seasonal categories range from $45–$80 (weekdays) to $50–$96 (weekends).

Patriots Point Links (843-881-0042; www.patriotspointlinks.com), 1 Patriots Point Road, Mount Pleasant. Par 72. Range: 5,100-yard forward course to 7,000-yard championship course with panoramic views of the harbor and Fort Sumter. Fees: $69–$89 with discounts after 3 p.m.

Shadowmoss Plantation Golf Club (843-556-8251; www.shadowmossgolf.com), SC 61. Par 72. Range: 5,169-yard forward course to 6,701-yard championship course. Fees: $46–$59 (weekdays) and $50–$60 (weekends).

GOLF AT CHARLESTON AREA RESORTS Kiawah Island (800-654-2924; www.kiawahresort.com), One Sanctuary Beach Drive. Five championship courses have been carved out of Kiawah's gorgeous Sea Island landscape by the game's top designers: Pete Dye and Alice Dye, Jack Nicklaus, Gary Player, Tom Fazio, and Clyde Johnston. The Ocean Course features 10 holes hard by the Atlantic Ocean, and significant winds challenge even the top players. *Golf Digest* has cited it as the toughest resort course in the country. Osprey Point is consistently ranked in the country's top 75 courses, with a landscape that includes four lakes, a maritime forest, and creeks. Cougar Point and Turtle Point make good use of Kiawah's unique geography—bracketed by the Atlantic and the Kiawah River. Oak Point is part of the resort but located on nearby Haulover Creek. There are golf packages galore that include luxury accommodations and dining.

Seabrook Island (843-768-2529; www.discoverseabrook.com), 130 Gardener's Circle, Seabrook Island, offers two courses: Crooked Oaks, designed by Robert Trent Jones Sr., and Ocean Winds, a Willard Byrd design. They won the resort a silver medal commendation from *Golf* magazine. Both of these courses are certified members of the Audubon Cooperative Sanctuary Program for Golf. Note that Ocean Winds will be closed for renovations for part of 2020.

Wild Dunes (866-359-5593; www.destinationhotels.com), Isle of Palms, boasts two courses designed by Tom Fazio. The Links (par 72; range: 4,907-yard forward course to 6,709-yard championship course) offers oceanfront golf at its best. The Harbor (par 70; range: 4,689-yard forward course to 6,359-yard championship course) features challenging holes that are, in some cases, an island apart.

TENNIS The Family Circle Tennis Center (843-849-5300; www.ltpdanielisland.com) is a beautiful public facility on Daniel Island with 13 Har-Tru and 4 hard courts, 13 lighted, and a clubhouse. Fees are $10–$15 per hour, with $2 for lights. Books courts online. Its 10,000-seat stadium hosts the annual Volvo Car Open in April (formerly the Family Circle Cup), a premier event on the women's tour. Area resorts (See *Golf* above) also have complete tennis layouts and offer similar packages for vacationers.

WIND SURFING/SURFING Folly Beach is the surfing hub, with the best conditions at The Washout. Shops provide lessons, rental gear, repairs, and tips. Several surfing schools cater to kids and adults with daily or weekly sessions. **McKevlin's Surf Shop** (843-588-2247; www.mckevlins.com), 8 Center Street, Folly Beach, and **Ocean Surf Shop** (843-588-9175; www.oceansurfshop.com), 31 Center Street, Folly Beach, publish daily surf reports online.

✳ Green Space

BEACHES In addition to lots of public access and metered street and public lot parking at Isle of Palms and Folly Beach, Charleston County Parks (www.ccprc.com) manages three beaches with lifeguards, designated swimming areas, restrooms, and changing facilities and other amenities. Some are wheelchair accessible. There's a daily fee for parking, $5–$15 depending on the season and $20 for RVs. Check with individual beach parks on the website about rules concerning dogs. County parks are open daylight hours in the summer and limited hours in the off-season. They include **Isle of Palms County Park** (843-762-9957), 1st through 14th Avenues and Palm Boulevard; **Folly Beach County Park** (843-795-4386), 1100 W. Ashley Avenue; and a bit farther south, off US 17 at the gate to Kiawah Island, **Beachwalker Park** (843-762-9964), 8 Beachwalker Drive. This site is beautiful and popular, and the parking lot can fill up early on the weekends.

   Sullivan's Island (www.sullivansisland.sc.gov), about 25 minutes from Charleston, is a lovely, low-key community whose 2.5 miles of beach is accessible by several footpaths and boardwalks. Handicap paths are located at Stations 18, 21, and 26. You may park in the public right of way, with all wheels off the pavement. No lifeguards on duty.

BIRD-WATCHING The barrier islands mentioned above provide the least-disturbed habitats for birds and wildlife, but if you can't make it there, other places are accessible. Because of its location on the North American flyway and its diverse natural environment, the Lowcountry attracts scores of wading, shore-, and songbirds, some of them as unusual as the roseate spoonbill and parasitic jaeger. Woodcocks flock in plowed fields, owls hover in roadside forests, and hawks soar over open grassland. Sites recommended by local birders include:

   Bear Island (843-844-8957; www2.dnr.sc.gov/managedlands), south of Charleston off US 17 at Green Pond. Bear Island is an extensive habitat characterized by old rice fields, meandering creeks and rivers, marshes, and all sorts of woodlands. Open daylight hours in designated areas February to October. Expect to see abundant waterfowl, wading birds, song birds, eagles, and wood storks.

   I'on Swamp (www.sctrails.net), 15 miles north of Mount Pleasant off US 17 on US Forest Service Road 228. Spring brings warblers—possibly even the shy Bachman's—and also resident upland birds, including red-cockaded woodpeckers, who make their homes here. It is famous for the variety of birds that land during their spring and fall migrations. The 2-mile loop trail is easy to navigate.

   In **Mount Pleasant**, sightings of marbled godwits, oystercatchers, grebes, and mergansers have been reported in the area leading to the Old Pitt Street Bridge. Activity is best at half tide, especially in fall and winter. A spotting scope is useful. On **Sullivan's**

Island, around the beach behind Fort Moultrie, you might see peeps or an occasional purple sandpiper. Along

On US 17, by the Ashepoo and Combahee river crossings, anhinga, rails, and gallinules nest in the remnant rice fields.

NATURE PRESERVES If you are interested in the ecology of the Lowcountry, the life cycle of the marsh, the effects of tidal flow on vegetation, and the interdependence of plant and animal life, these sites will give you a feel for the rhythms beneath the surface.

Ernest F. Hollings ACE Basin National Wildlife Refuge (843-889-3084; www.fws .gov/refuge/ace_basin). South off US 17, take SC 174 through Adams Run and follow signs to headquarters. A consortium was formed to preserve some 350,000 acres of diverse habitat, including several islands, creating one of the largest estuarine sanctuaries on the East Coast. ACE takes its name from the area it embraces: the lands and waters amid the Ashepoo, Combahee, and Edisto Rivers on both sides of St. Helena Sound, a fishery so rich and pristine it accounts for nearly 10 percent of the state's shellfish harvest. Open year-round, daylight to dusk; you may park and walk in. Extensive trail maps online.

Caw Caw Interpretive Center (843-762-8015; www.ccprc.com), 5200 Savannah Highway, Ravenel, 20 miles south of Charleston. Elevated boardwalks overlook the wetlands and rice fields that originally marked this plantation, which is now a low-impact wildlife preserve. There are 6 miles of trails and exhibits that highlight the contributions of the African Americans who worked here long ago. A good stop if you're heading down the coast to Edisto, Beaufort, or Savannah. Closed Monday. Admission $2.

Francis Beidler Forest in Four Holes Swamp (843-462-2150; sc.audubon.org/visit/ beidler), 336 Sanctuary Road, Harleyville. An 18,000-acre sanctuary contains the largest remaining virgin stand of bald cypress and tupelo gum trees in the world. It feels ancient and otherworldly. There's a self-guided 1.75-mile boardwalk that is handicapped accessible. Open Tues.–Sun. Adults $10, seniors $8, kids $5. Kayak and canoe tours led by an Audubon naturalist are offered March, April, and May. Four-hour trips leave at 1 p.m. Friday and Saturday, with a two-hour trip at 9 a.m. Saturday. Fees are $25–$40 for adults, $10–$15 for kids.

SHORE REFUGES **Cape Romain National Wildlife Refuge** (843-928-3264; www.fws .gov/refuge/cape_romain), 5801 US 17 N, Awendaw. It covers 22 miles of coast consisting of numerous landscapes and habitats: **Bulls Island,** a 5,000-acre barrier island; **Cape Island,** a favorite spot for loggerhead turtles to nest; **Garris Landing,** the site of ferry services and an observation pier just right for birders; and **Raccoon Key Island,** a popular spot for shelling. Check website for current opening information.

Coastal Expeditions (843-884-7684; www.coastalexpeditions.com) offers exclusive ferry service to Bulls Island, weather permitting. Ticket prices are $40 for adults and $20 for children under 12 for a day trip to explore 16 miles of trails and 7 miles of beach, especially the Boneyard, where hundreds of weathered oaks, cedars, and pines have been left behind in the surf due to beach erosion. From March through November, the ferry makes two round-trips every Tuesday, Thursday, Friday, and Saturday. From December through February, there's one trip only, on Saturday. Book online. You can take a fat-tired bike on the ferry, but you must reserve a spot for it.

Capers Island is a classic, undisturbed barrier island managed by the South Carolina Department of Natural Resources (843-953-9001; www.dnr.sc.gov/mlands). You can get there in a sea kayak from Coastal Expeditions or on a 40-foot boat with **Barrier**

Island EcoTours (843-886-5000; www.nature-tours.com). A 3½-hour tour led by a naturalist and marine biologist costs $45 for adults, $35 for children. Once-daily trips occur Monday to Saturday from May through September and weekends September through November, with limited midweek trips September through May. They offer many other tours and fishing expeditions, too.

✳ Lodging

President George Washington toured the Lowcountry in 1791, staying with planters and in "public houses" with messengers, small farmers, and merchants. The modest but attentive hospitality they offered existed well into the 20th century. It was a custom, like most, that had its roots in necessity: during the years of poverty following the Civil War, taking in guests provided income for families or Confederate widows who still lived in the commodious houses.

These days, if you stay in an old home or its dependencies that have been transformed into a glossy bed-and-breakfast, the only Confederate widow in evidence will be a portrait on the wall. Many are elegant places, with Jacuzzi tubs and fireplaces, where you are likely to be served with old silver and overlook walled gardens dense with flowers, fragrant olive trees, camellias, and azaleas.

Charleston also has luxury hotels; inns renovated from former commercial buildings; its share of attractive options from national name brands; and upscale beach resorts. If you intend to spend most of your time in the city, consider the 25- to 35-minute travel time to the beach. Alternatively, if golf, tennis, boating, and being on the ocean are at the center of your trip, or especially if you're traveling with children, you could make a resort or rental home your base. Some hotels and inns have on-site babysitting services and explicitly offer family packages. Deposit/cancellation policies are strictly followed in smaller inns and bed-and-breakfasts. High (expensive) season is March through June; September and October; and during the summer at the beaches. In many establishments,

parking costs extra. Most have online videos of the rooms and property so you can see exactly what you're getting.

HOTELS **Belmond Charleston Place** (843-722-4900; www.belmond.com), 205 Meeting Street. Its construction some 30 years ago created a unique luxury microclimate with its own elegant boutiques, piano bar and restaurant, a rooftop pool and European spa, and grand decorating gestures like a spectacular curved staircase and a huge chandelier, massive pots of flowers, shiny marble floors, and rooms of polished furniture. It's centrally located at the intersection of Market and King Streets, and a shopping district on upper King Street grew up around it. Special rate packages, which include tickets to Spoleto performances and reasonable off-season rates, are worth looking into. $$$$.

Embassy Suites by Hilton Charleston Historic District (843-723-6900; www .hilton.com/en/embassy), 337 Meeting Street. Located in a fine makeover of the 19th-century Citadel building where generations of Southern boys attended military school, it has a massive, theatrical feel with lit palm trees, a courtyard, and crenellated turrets, but the outdoor pool and sundeck soften the institutional edges. Suites allow for flexible arrangements for families or work. On Marion Square near the Visitor Center, where many tours originate. $$$.

Francis Marion Hotel (843-722-0600; www.francismarionhotel.com), 387 King Street. This old chestnut with 200-plus rooms from the 1920s was overhauled, redecorated, and placed on the National Register of Historic Places. There are wide stairs and hallways, wood paneling, plaster moldings covered in gold leaf, a lobby with big windows and club chairs, and high ceilings. It also offers a full-service spa. Overlooking Marion Square, with great views of Charleston from rooms on the upper floors, and the most convenient place to stay during the annual Wine and Food Festival (see *Special Events*). It offers several special lodging and tour packages throughout the year. $$$.

Harbour View Inn (843-853-8439; www.harbourviewcharleston.com), 2 Vendue Range. Just steps from Waterfront Park, it features many rooms with stunning views and harbor breezes, and a great rooftop bar. The right mix of elegance and understatement characterizes the best of Charleston design: seagrass/rush carpeting, cream-colored walls, big windows (some with broad, slatted plantation shutters), perhaps one framed print, and an armoire made by a local artisan. Many of the rooms

have fireplaces, some have balconies or whirlpool baths. A good deal of attention is paid to detail here, even in the choice, framing, and hanging of art in the hallways. $$$–$$$$.

The Mills House (843-577-2400; www .millshouse.com), 115 Meeting Street. Completely renovated in 2008 to better recall its 1853 origin, you can imagine what it was like when cotton planters, politicians, and brokers roamed the first floor and terraces. If you're walking the city, it's about a half mile to East Bay Street, the City Market area, the South of Broad neighborhood, two historic house museums, the Gibbes Museum of Art, and the French Quarter Art District. Nice pool, adjacent (for a fee) parking, and a few handicapped-accessible rooms. $$$.

Renaissance Charleston Historic District (843-534-0300; www.marriott.com),

MARION SQUARE AT DUSK © SEAN PAVONE/ISTOCKPHOTO.COM

THE HISTORIC MILLS HOUSE © LISA-BLUE/ISTOCKPHOTO.COM

68 Wentworth Street. A large hotel (162 rooms) in the Marriott chain with an outdoor heated pool and fitness center in a good location just north of Market Street and the hipper sections of upper King Street. The decor is modern, with lots of graphic prints. The staff makes a point of concierge service and helping you with itineraries and suggestions based on what you like. $$$.

SMALLER INNS **Ansonborough Inn** (800-723-1655; www.ansonboroughinn .com), 21 Hasell Street. This circa-1901 stationer's warehouse two blocks from the City Market was given new life as a boutique inn, but reminders of its past use—including huge beams, plank floors, and walls of exposed brick—remain. Forty-five suites, from small split-level loft rooms to two-room kings, generally feature a wet bar and microwave/mini refrigerator. The rooftop patio offers a terrific view across the river. A nice touch is a continental breakfast that has fresh pastries and a hot bar. $$$–$$$$.
  Fulton Lane Inn (843-720-2600; www .charminginns.com), 202 King Street.

Located in the heart of the downtown antique and gallery district, the two dozen rooms and suites have a refreshing, airy look: sisal, wicker, and chintz decorating accents; louvered shutters; wall coverings and paint in soft, liquid colors like celadon, pale peach, and lemon. The feel is summer in the Lowcountry. You can go simple or deluxe, with canopied beds and fireplaces, kitchens, and whirlpool baths. They are tuned into accommodating families in connecting rooms. It's part of a local consortium of inns with knowledgeable concierge service. $$$–$$$$.
  John Rutledge House Inn (843-723-7999; www.johnrutledgehouseinn.com), 116 Broad Street. George Washington did visit this house, which dates from 1763 and whose 19 guest rooms, including several spacious suites, are decorated with antiques, sumptuous fabrics, and carved mantelpieces. It's a National Historic Landmark. You can stay in the main house or in two carriage houses set in a charming courtyard. Suites in the main house include an additional sitting room and fireplace; some have Jacuzzi

tubs. It's a minute's walk to get to South of Broad. This is probably the closest you'll get to feeling what it was like to live in 18th- and 19th-century Charleston. Welcoming to families and not a bit stuffy. $$$$.

Planters Inn (843-722-2345; www .plantersinn.com), 112 N. Market Street. The inn exemplifies low-key elegance and quality in its suites and king and queen bedrooms, and in the back courtyard. It is probably the hippest inn in the city, in the sense of setting a tone and aesthetic of simplicity, with nods to historic reproduction pieces and a modern palette of whites and creams. It is relaxing. It's within walking distance of practically every Charleston asset. The acclaimed Peninsula Grill (see *Where to Eat*) is perennially on national "Best of" lists. It's very expensive and worth it. $$$$.

Wentworth Mansion (843-853-1886; www.wentworthmansion.com), 149 Wentworth Street. This Second Empire–style mansion (built in 1886 for a cotton baron) will turn your head with its carved plasterwork ceilings, marble fireplaces, Tiffany glass, mahogany paneling, intricately tiled floors, and a cupola, accessed by a stairway for the brave, which yields a panoramic view of the city. There are 21 rooms with king-sized beds, whirlpools, and fireplaces. You start the day with a full breakfast and end it with sherry, port, or brandy in the stately library. It's about a 10- to 15-minute walk to downtown. Circa 1886 in the Carriage House is another of Charleston's best restaurants (see *Where to Eat*). $$$$.

BED-AND-BREAKFASTS A central listing service, **Historic Charleston Bed and Breakfast** (843-722-6606; www.historicc harlestonbedandbreakfast.com) offers accommodations as small as single- or two-room rentals in carriage or kitchen houses. Call weekdays, to inquire about cost and bookings. Airbnb has made this service seem a bit outdated, but there are budget choices.

Governor's House Inn (843-720-2070; www.governorshouse.com), 117 Broad Street. Once home to Governor Edward Rutledge, who at 26 years old signed the Declaration of Independence and at 30 was a patriot under arrest. The stunning restoration of this grand home suggests he appreciated the finer things in life. The nicest rooms have 12-foot ceilings and their own veranda access, with views of Charleston's fanciest neighborhood. A kitchen house with an original 1760 fireplace has two suites. It's an excellent spot for an indulge-yourself weekend. $$$$.

Two Meeting Street Inn (843-723-7322; www.twomeetingstreetinn.com), 2 Meeting Street. A massive Queen Anne mansion that looks like a picture on a postcard, with its wraparound porches and rocking chairs overlooking the Battery, oak-paneled sitting rooms, and nine guest rooms filled with Oriental rugs and period family accessories. Some have Victorian-style tubs or private balcony access. Honeymooners and celebrating couples book a year in advance, especially for those rooms with canopied four-posters needing a special set of stairs to reach. All reservations are taken over the phone, not online. A gourmet breakfast and an elaborate tea is included. $$$–$$$$.

21 East Battery Bed & Breakfast (843-722-6606; www.21eastbattery.com), 21 E. Battery. A handsomely renovated carriage house (one bedroom and bath and large sitting room with sleeper sofa) and adjacent two-story former slave quarters (two bedrooms and two baths) are tucked in the historic Edmonston–Alston House museum complex in a spectacular location on the High Battery by White Point Gardens. A complimentary tour of the house is included. Taken together, the properties can accommodate 10 but can be rented independently. Full breakfasts to order and off-street parking are included. $$$–$$$$.

27 State Street (843-722-4243; www .27statestreet.com), 27 State Street. Enter

OAK TREES IN WHITE POINT GARDEN © PGLAM/ISTOCKPHOTO.COM

your private suite (with kitchenette) through the courtyard or veranda of a foursquare, circa-1800 house in the French Quarter, a block off East Bay Street and its wonderful restaurants and close to the Waterfront Park for morning jogging. $$–$$$.

CHARLESTON ENVIRONS

The Inn at Middleton Place (843-556-0500; www.theinnatmiddletonplace .com) is sited on a bluff adjacent to the astonishing Middleton Place Gardens (see *To See*) about 25 minutes from downtown. For serenity, long walks along the Ashley River or in the gardens (admission waived for guests), kayaking, and horseback riding, come here. It's handsomely modern on the outside, splendidly minimalist inside. There are 55 rooms in four buildings, each with working log fireplaces, custom-made furniture, soft colors, and large bathrooms.

Some are handicapped accessible. Floor-to-ceiling windows with louvered shutters filter the light and air in the woodland setting. The restaurant at Middleton Place serves lunch and dinner daily, featuring farm-and-fish-to-table entrées. $$$$.

FOLLY BEACH

Tides Folly Beach (843-588-6464; www .tidesfollybeach.com), 1 Center Street, Folly Beach. The transformation from an oceanfront Holiday Inn to the current incarnation took great advantage of its central location (everything is walkable), and a new, contemporary bar and restaurant, Blu, has received raves for its small plate menu and fresh seafood. Folly Beach is a down-to-earth, lively mecca for surfers and families, and dances on the nearby pier are a summer draw. Handicap access; pets OK for a fee. $$$–$$$$.

MUST SEE

For a long weekend, consider visiting at least one historic house in the city, one Ashley River Plantation, and one service to get on the water (a cruise tour or a half-day kayak adventure). You also must walk through the residential neighborhood south of Broad Street, down King Street, Meeting Street, Tradd Street, Church Street, and along Rainbow Row (83–107 East Bay Street), a stretch of pastel-colored houses dating from the 18th century. Find details at *To See* and *To Do* in this chapter. Take a break on benches in the Battery (easy to park and walk from here) or in Waterfront Park. You will have the time to do all of these things and you'll see Charleston as a living city, not a museum. On your mind should be which among the sites intrigue you the most. For example, I would choose Drayton Hall for its architecture (no furniture here) and location, but Middleton Place and its gardens are a source of amazement and a testament to the work of enslaved laborers for years and years. As far as house tours, the Aiken-Rhett House revels in its lightly restored condition and its several dependencies. That is, you get a sense of space and how people worked even more than the objects and wealth that activity produced. I would not leave without visiting the Old Slave Mart Museum and absorbing its knowledge and exhibits about the African and African American experience.

Relax and indulge by eating at one fine restaurant that's put Charleston on the map as a culinary destination. The chefs' creative use of the freshest local ingredients and the attention to service will leave you with the impression that one of the qualities that distinguishes Charleston is that it has managed to bring a fairly insular culture forward pretty darn seamlessly. It's not necessary to visit during the Spoleto Festival, the house and garden tours, or the Wine and Food Festival to savor Charleston. There's not an off-season where seeing, doing, and tasting are not available. As for the resorts, Kiawah Island is the most luxurious. It would be easy to have a golf weekend there and spend one day in Charleston.

COLORFUL WINDOW BOXES ALONG RAINBOW ROW © RIVERNORTHPHOTOGRAPHY/ISTOCKPHOTO.COM

BROAD STREET IN SUMMER © JOEL CARILLET/ISTOCKPHOTO.COM

MIDDLETON PLACE ON THE ASHLEY RIVER EXPLORE CHARLESTON

ISLE OF PALMS

The Palms Hotel (888-484-9004; www
.palmscharleston.com), 1126 Ocean
Boulevard, Isle of Palms. There are 57
recently renovated rooms, some with
views or partial views, in a great location
with all the beach and pool amenities.
$$–$$$.

RESORTS AND RENTALS

CHARLESTON AREA SEA ISLANDS

The Sea Island resort areas are popular year-round, with golf and tennis
every day and ocean swimming for all
but about four months. Each resort has
a well-supervised children's activity
program. For longer stays of a week or
more, you may want to contact some of
the rental agents who specialize in private beach properties, including villas
and houses located within and outside
the resorts. Note that rental rates for
some high-end private homes within the
resorts can be as much as twice the average rates quoted below.

Rental accommodations are fully
furnished, including washer and dryer.
Check on special features like handicap
access or if a fee for cleaning after your
departure is included. Deposits are necessary, and during summer months minimum stays are usually required.

Typical summer rental prices for a
two-bedroom, oceanfront house generally start from $2,500 per week, but
properties by a lagoon or in the woods
are less expensive. November through
February are low-season months. The
resorts offer numerous packages covering a long weekend or week's stay to
attract golfers, honeymooners, Thanks-
giving get-togethers, and visitors coming for the tours of historic homes in the
fall and spring.

**Kiawah Island Golf Resort and
The Sanctuary** (800-654-2924; www
.kiawahresort.com). Kiawah is a world-
class resort with hundreds of villa
accommodations in several sizes and
grand homes you can rent that aren't
anything like a sandy house on stilts.
The beach is private and 10 miles long;
30 miles of paved bike trails wind around
five golf courses and recreational areas,
ultimately linking two distinct resort
villages. The Sanctuary, a luxury hotel
complex, has 255 guest rooms, a spa and
fitness center, and two oceanfront restaurants. If you book lodgings through the
resort (as opposed to a rental agency),
you are eligible for discounts, preferred
tee times, and use of all Kiawah amenities. $$$$.

Seabrook Island (843-768-2500; www
.discoverseabrook.com) is a 2,200-acre
private country club community. Visitors rent cottages, villas, or homes. Its
unique asset is its equestrian center
and miles of riding trails, but it also
has golf and tennis, a beach and beach
club, and a fitness center. Pam Harrington Exclusives (843-768-3635; www
.pamharringtonexclusives.com) is one
real estate agent who has handled rent-
als for more than 30 years. $$$–$$$$.

Wild Dunes (888-778-1876; www
.destinationhotels.com), 5757 Palm
Boulevard, Isle of Palms. A small resort
located on the northeast end of the mod-
est Isle of Palms and the closest of the
resorts to Charleston. Guests choose
accommodations in the 93-room **Board-
walk Inn** (843-886-2260) or in villas,
townhouses, and cottages. Island Realty
(800-707-6421; www.islandrealty.com)
has a deep and varied inventory of rent-
als on the island. $$–$$$$.

CAMPING OPTIONS **James Island
County Park** (843-406-6990; www.ccprc
.com), 871 Riverland Drive. Has 116 full
RV sites, 10 three-bedroom cottages on
the marsh, primitive camping area, shuttle service to downtown Charleston ($10
fee), paved trails, fishing and crabbing
docks, playgrounds, and picnic shelters.
Rates for overnight stays range from
$33–$61.

Lake Aire RV Park and Campground
(843-571-1271; www.lakeairerv.com),

ANGEL OAK PARK ON JOHNS ISLAND © PGLAM/ISTOCKPHOTO.COM

4375 SC 162, Hollywood. The full-service park about 20 minutes south of downtown Charleston includes nearly a hundred RV sites, including full hook-ups, and 26 primitive and electrified tent sites. Seven-acre fishing lake, swimming pool, paddleboat and canoe rentals, showers, laundry, recreation area, and bike and foot trails. Rates are $22–$52 nightly.

Oak Plantation Campground (843-766-5936; www.oakplantation campground.com), 3540 Savannah Highway, Johns Island. Full hook-ups with 30- and 50-amp service; 200 RV sites, propane, laundry, groceries, bathrooms. Rates are $59–$67 nightly.

✻ Where to Eat

Dining was an important Lowcountry ritual and celebrated the resourcefulness of the cooks who brought African and West Indian traditions to the meal. As the extraordinary Southern chef Edna Lewis said: "The birds are just the beginning. In the South you put everything you have on the table." In Charleston that means an incredible harvest of seafood, game, rice and grits, and heirloom vegetables. The city is a mecca for creative chefs, many of whom were and are winners of James Beard Awards. Reservations are recommended for higher-end restaurants.

WASHINGTON SQUARE IN DOWNTOWN CHARLESTON © BKAMPRATH/ISTOCKPHOTO.COM

These choices, listed alphabetically, reflect all price ranges and cuisines, including smaller or more informal places where takeout might also be an option. The general price range is meant to reflect the cost of a single meal, usually dinner, featuring an appetizer, entrée, dessert, and coffee. Cocktails, beer, wine, gratuity, and tax are not included in the estimated price. Good picnicking spots are found at Waterfront Park at the foot of Queen Street, in the shady grove of Washington Square, or on a bench at the Battery.

Amen Street Fish and Raw Bar (843-853-8600; www.amenstreet.com), 205 E. Bay Street. Open for lunch and dinner daily, with full bar until 2 a.m. A favorite among locals, with an extensive raw bar and late-night crowd that comes for a half dozen or dozen with a glass of wine or craft beer. The emphasis is on fresh American-style cooking, focused on Lowcountry seafood, and unencumbered by too much sauce. $$$–$$$$.

Basil Thai (843-724-3490; www .eatatbasil.com), 460 King Street. Open for lunch weekdays and dinner daily.

Closed Mondays. Gallery owners, creative types, and professors flock here. Thai standards include crispy red curry duck and spicy noodle soups, vegetarian

LOCAL FARM AND SEAFOOD CROPS AND CREATIVE CHEFS WHO BUY THEM DAILY HAVE MADE CHARLESTON A CULINARY DESTINATION EXPLORE CHARLESTON

dishes, and plentiful peanuts and coconut and curries. The grill is open, with seating at the chef's counter, or at tables, booths, or a tiny bar. No reservations. $$–$$$.

Caviar & Bananas (843-577-7757; caviarandbananas.com), 51 George Street. Open for breakfast, lunch, and dinner in a popular historic neighborhood. It reflects its eclectic, loyal customers who love a splurge and depend on the ordinary; hence the name. It's a gourmet market and café, so you can eat in or order online and have your food delivered or prepared for pickup. $$–$$.

Charleston Grill (843-577-4522; www .charlestongrill.com), 224 King Street at Belmond Charleston Place. Open daily for dinner. Very polished but not stuffy, excellent service, and tables that shine like little jewels against the wood paneling of a large room. Very small combos of guitar, piano, and horn talents perform soul, blues, and jazz seven nights a week. Chef Michelle Weaver, a 20-year veteran of the restaurant, is committed to farmers. Her menus are arranged by theme—like "Roots & Stems" or "Waves & Marsh"—and have a French inflection. $$$–$$$$.

Circa 1886 (843-853-7828; www .circa1886.com), 149 Wentworth Street. Open for dinner except Sunday. Deluxe and cozy, tucked into a beautifully renovated carriage house at Wentworth Mansion. Once common local ingredients like conch, quail, venison, and oxtail turn up with fruit and sweet accents and spices. There are vegetarian and gluten-free entrées and always a sturdy beef selection. Notable wine list and chef's tasting menu. $$$–$$$$.

Cru Café (843-534-2434; www.crucafe .com), 18 Pinckney Street. A local favorite for lunch, with homemade soups, salads and wraps, wine and beer, and seating inside—sometimes you share a larger table—and on the porch of the 18th-century house near the City Market. Also open for dinner. The café sources from more than a dozen local purveyors and is very much part of the restaurant

scene, albeit more "gourmet casual." Closed Sunday and Monday. $–$$.

FIG (843-805-5900; www.eatatfig .com), 232 Meeting Street. Open for dinner except Sundays. James Beard Award–winning chef Mike Lata has made this a destination restaurant. The menu changes weekly and seasonally, and he and his staff have assembled a group of local food purveyors they trust to provide extraordinary ingredients. There's a story behind every menu item if you'd like to know, but there's no pretension in service or quality. It's still a favorite among Charlestonians for special occasions. Reservations are accepted a month in advance. $$–$$$$.

OUTDOOR DINING ON EAST BAY STREET © JOAL CARILLET/ ISTOCKPHOTO.COM

HANK'S SEAFOOD RESTAURANT © JOEL CARILLET/ISTOCKPHOTO.COM

Fulton Five (843-853-5555; www
.fultonfivecharleston.com), 5 Fulton
Street. Open for dinner except Sundays. It's said Gian Carlo Menotti chose
Charleston for his Spoleto Festival USA
because it had a Mediterranean feel, a
serene charm as easy to appreciate and
as softly worn as stucco walls. That's
what it feels like here. The Northern Italian menu includes lamb, veal, risotto and
pasta, and fresh seafood specials. $$–$$$.

Gaulart & Maliclet (843-577-9797;
www.fastandfrenchcharleston.com), 98
Broad Street. Open for lunch, dinner,
and Sunday brunch. It's the most popular, enduring little place in the Historic
District for lunch specials—cheese plate,
soup, a glass of wine, a prosciutto melt—
or drop by for an early dinner. It's informal and a Charleston favorite. $–$$.

Hank's (843-723-3474; www
.hanksseafoodrestaurant.com), 10 Hayne
Street. Open daily for dinner. A good-
natured, festive throwback to family
seafood houses of the 1950s, except
there's no sawdust on the floor and the

grilled fish entrées could come with
roasted tomato beurre blanc. The extensive menu doesn't give short shrift to the
fried entrée favorites, but they're done
up in style here. $$–$$$$.

SHRIMP FRESH FROM THE CREEK LOWCOUNTRY & RESORT
ISLANDS TOURISM COMMISSION

SPOLETO

For 18 days at the end of spring, a time of budding oleander, fading azalea, and unapologetically fragrant magnolias, Spoleto comes to Charleston and Charleston becomes the artistic city it loves to be with first-rate international performances and art. Founded in 1977, each season offers more than 100 scheduled events, including premieres of opera and dance as well as dozens of chamber music, choral, jazz, and orchestral shows. Performances take place indoors and out—in parks, plantation gardens, amphitheaters, and auditoriums. Spoleto Festival USA (843-722-2764; box office 843-579-3100; www.spoletousa.org),14 George Street.

Start planning early; the website is best. Tickets go on sale in January and quickly sell out, as the festival draws visitors from around the world. Order by a ticket package or by individual performances, which take place in several venues. You can try your luck at the last minute for standing room, or order on the phone, often up to the morning before the performance.

More than 600 Piccolo Spoleto Festival performances, readings, art and craft exhibitions, concerts, and loads of community events (often free) run concurrently and are organized by the Office of Cultural Affairs (843-724-7305; www.piccolospoleto.com), 180 Meeting Street.

High Cotton (843-724-3815; www.highcottoncharleston.com), 199 E. Bay Street. Open daily for dinner; brunch Saturday and Sunday. Glossy, unabashed, and high energy, it's an especially fun place to have a drink or go for the jazz brunch. Although seafood takes up most of the menu, the filet mignon, rack of lamb, and strip steaks are outstanding, and smaller plates like grits with ham gravy or local clams with sausage are unabashedly down home. $$$–$$$$.

Peninsula Grill (843-723-0700; www.peninsulagrill.com),112 N. Market Street. Open daily for dinner. A high-end culinary and visual experience is in the top 10 of the city's most expensive restaurants. The light is suffused with soft gold overtones, as if the color had been rubbed on the air. Jell-O would taste good here. You can also eat in the rear courtyard, lit with gas carriage lanterns, or have foie gras and oysters and at the champagne bar. Entrées include seafood, duck, and steaks, but the reductions and sauces, which you can order separately, really set them apart. $$$$.

Saffron (843-722-5588; www.eatatsaffron.com), 333 E. Bay Street. Open daily for breakfast, lunch, and dinner, it has a spacious, airy interior and patio seating. The food is inflected with a Middle Eastern touch; the racks of fresh bread and the glass cases filled with daily specials like chocolate chip scones and pastries could top off a gourmet picnic if you don't want to eat here. $–$$.

Virginia's on King (843-735-5800; www.virginiasonking.com), 412 King Street. In a nod to its downhome Southern cooking, it's open for daily for breakfast, dinner (as lunch is called here), and supper. You'll find passed-down family recipes lovingly served: Frogmore stew, greens, okra, country fried steak, smoked pork chops, and fried tomatoes are featured. Located a block north of King Street's intersection with Calhoun Street, it's a great destination after shopping. $$.

✳ Entertainment

Find the most comprehensive listings at the weekly *Charleston City Paper* (www.charlestoncitypaper.com), which has been a reliable source of news, features, and reviews for 20 years. Contact the venue to learn about social distancing requirements.

THE DOCK STREET THEATRE IN HISTORIC DOWNTOWN © PGLAM/ISTOCKPHOTO.COM

For dancing and concerts, a younger crowd, and college kids from out of town head to **Music Farm** (843-577-6969; www.musicfarm.com), 32 Ann Street.

AN ANCIENT CYPRESS GARDEN IN THE SWAMP EXPLORE CHARLESTON

Charleston Grill (843-577-4522; www.charlestongrill.com), 224 King Street at Charleston Place (see *Lodging*) is the classiest option, with incredible desserts and live jazz. Check website for current opening information.

Dock Street Theatre (843-577-7183; www.charlestonstage.com). Located at 135 Church Street, the theater hosts a local professional theater company year-round and many touring events in a historic space that was first carved out of a 19th-century hotel, renovated again as a federal Works Progress Administration project in the 1930s, and then again by the City of Charleston about 10 years ago to improve seating, sight lines, and acoustics. It is a premier destination for Spoleto events in May and June.

For a fun summer evening, locals go to watch the **Charleston RiverDogs,** a Class A Minor League affiliate of the New York Yankees, at Joe Riley Jr. Park (843-577-3647 for tickets; www.riverdogs.com), 360 Fishburne Street. Ticket prices are generally $10–$25.

SHRIMP BOATS AT REST

✳ Selective Shopping

The main locales are **King Street** north of Broad Street, where antiques stores have long reigned, but newer neighbors include home and furniture storefronts offering unique designs, as well as high-end clothing boutiques; **Queen Street and Church Street** (for art, especially); and around the old three-block **City Market** (North and South Market Streets east of Meeting Street). The Market area is touristy, and the most notable items for sale in and around the handsome brick-and-lattice sheds are

CITY MARKET © KRUCK20/ISTOCKPHOTO.COM

the sweetgrass baskets hand-woven by African American women. Weavers also work on the sidewalks of Broad and King Streets. The baskets are expensive because of the work that goes into collecting the raw materials and the weaving, but they are unique works of art and durable baskets for use on the table.

ANTIQUES **Carolina Antique Maps and Prints** (843-722-4773; www.carolina antiqueprints.com), 91 Church Street. Deep inventory and a knowledgeable staff; early botanicals, 19th-century maps, woodblocks, and hand-colored pieces. Check website for current opening information.

George C. Birlant & Co. (843-722-3842; birlantantiquescharleston.com), 191 King Street. In business for more than 80 years, selling brass, silver, crystal, and small and large English antiques, which they import directly. Big, old-fashioned picture windows open onto the street, and there's lots of room

to walk around inside. Reproductions of Charleston's own cypress-and-iron Battery Bench available.

Julia Santen (843-534-0758; www .juliasantengallery.com), 188 King Street. Here is a collection of original vintage posters, including many from Europe, that will make a room pop out of its dreariness.

Moore House American Antiques (843-722-8065; www.moorehouse antiques.com), 143 King Street. Fine 18th- and 19th-century American pieces where styles from England show through, as in Sheraton side tables and Chinese export porcelain.

Terrace Oaks Antique Mall (843-795-9689; www.terraceoaksantiques.com), 2037 Maybank Highway. A short drive from Charleston, this well-known hodgepodge houses 60 dealers who sell an amazing assortment of rugs, glassware, silver, large pieces, and accessories.

The Silver Vault (843-722-0631; www.silvervaultcharleston.com), 195

THE SHOPS ON HISTORIC KING STREET © CRAIG MCCAUSLAND/ISTOCKPHOTO.COM

CHARLESTON IS A DESTINATION FOR COLLECTORS OF FINE ANTIQUES FROM THE SOUTH, EUROPE, AND ASIA EXPLORE CHARLESTON

King Street. Historic silver objects and tableware from America, England, and the Continent, as well as decorative art and antique jewelry. Currently open by appointment only.

The Old Charleston Joggling Board Company (www.oldcharleston jogglingboard.com). This long, springy board or bench (10 feet or 16 feet) that rests on rocking trestles is common in many Charleston gardens and has been a staple piece of outdoor furniture since the early 19th century. It can be ordered online from the company, which has been making reproductions for 50 years.

BOOKS **Blue Bicycle Books** (843-722-2666; www.bluebicyclebooks.com), 420 King Street. A committed independent bookstore that supports local writers and whose staff knows what's come in—new, used, rare, and of regional interest. They offer readings and participate in many community events.

Historic Charleston Foundation Shops (843-724-8484; www.historic charleston.org), 108 Meeting Street. If you want to know more about Low-country history and the decorative arts, preservation efforts, architecture, and related topics, stop in. The shops feature many volumes about historic properties here and elsewhere, as well as an excellent children's section, home

THE INTERSECTION OF MEETING STREET AND MARKET STREET IN HISTORIC DOWNTOWN CHARLESTON © CRAIG MCCAUSLAND/ISTOCKPHOTO.COM

goods, and many reproduction decorative items.

Preservation Society of Charleston (843-723-2775; www.preservationsociety.org), 147 King Street. The society's headquarters has an unhurried, Old World feeling, a very special place with many books on Charleston history, art, architecture, and culture. It's expanded a gift line of accessories that represent Charleston's blend of fashion and quirkiness.

CLOTHING Menswear in Charleston is still a funny combination of casual hunting/outdoorsy preppy, along with sharp bow ties, fedoras, and stylish eyeglasses. Women, however, have more to choose from in stylish cuts that wouldn't look out of place in New York City.

Ben Silver (843-577-4556; www.bensilver.com), 149 King Street. This shop is the epitome of the classic Charleston look for men and women, with lots of English hunting overtones. Check website for current opening information.

Half-Moon Outfitters (843-853-0990; www.halfmoonoutfitters.com), 280 King Street. The most durable and fashionable outdoor wear (like Patagonia) is here, plus coats, tents, packs, camping supplies, and the best advice on local outdoor adventuring to be found in the city.

Kids on King (843-720-8647; www.kidsonking.com), 310 King Street. The old smocked dresses and seersucker suits of yesteryear are mixed in with European styles for kids of all ages and sizes.

M. Dumas & Sons (843-723-8603), 294 King Street. Even the wallpaper here is riding to hounds. Since 1918, the go-to store for outdoor wear and now more updated fashion lines.

RTW (843-577-9748; www.rtwcharleston.com), 186 King Street. A boutique for women who delight in gorgeous fabrics, sweaters that tumble with color, one-of-a-kind shirts, hats, scarves, and accessories, and for those who like to dress with a sense of individuality and esprit. Longtime owner Janyce McMenamin's curator's eye for fashion and workmanship is a rare find in any city.

Worthwhile (843-723-4418; www.shopworthwhile.com), 268 King Street. This wonderful, crazy store defies easy categorization: It's ironic (it could be a 5&10 for yuppies, with lots of small, beautiful objects for the house) but sweet (flax and linen clothes for women, goofy baby hats, cotton sweaters, and leggings). Check website for current opening information.

FARMS AND FARMERS' MARKETS Several outdoor markets convene between April and November, selling everything from bull grapes and greens to tomato pie and pepper jelly. Due to their increased popularity during the COVID-19 outbreak, they may extend their weekly presence into the earlier months of 2021; they have been successful in providing community support to both farmers and customers who prefer the outdoor social distancing practices to shopping in conventional grocery stores. Many offer prepared foods, food cooked on-site, and coffee. The **Charleston Farmers Market** (843-724-7305; www.charlestonfarmersmarket.com) is in Marion Square (Calhoun Street at King Street). Near Charleston on Johns Island, on the way to the resorts, are **Stono Market** (843-559-9999; www.stonofarmmarket.com), 842 Main Road, and **Rosebank Farms** (843-768-0508; www.rosebankfarms.com), 4362 Betsy Kerrison Parkway. They are working farms and collaborate with others—fishermen, bakers, cooks, and gardeners—to provide an abundance of fresh foods.

✳ Special Events

SPRING *March:* **Charleston Wine and Food Festival** (843-727-9998; charlestonwineandfood.com). This 5-day event includes demonstrations, tasting areas featuring Charleston's best cooks, visiting chefs, winemakers and authors, and special events staged throughout the city. Hotels offer packages and tickets are available online, all-inclusive, or by event.

Festival of Houses & Gardens (843-722-3405; www.historiccharleston.org), 108 Meeting Street. The Historic Charleston Foundation's tours of private homes, plantations, gardens, and churches usually start toward the end of the month and last 4 weeks. A tradition for more than 50 years, they will enrich your understanding of the city's unique urban geography. Neighborhood streets and sidewalks, where laughter and conversation drift from gardens and homes, are crowded and warmly accommodating.

April: **Cooper River Bridge Run** (www.bridgerun.com) is a 10K race that starts in Mount Pleasant, takes runners up and over the Ravenel Bridge, and then through two of Charleston's main streets. It's grown every year and is a joyful marker of spring for local and regional runners and families. To participate, check the website for registration.

Volvo Car Open (www.volvocaropen.com; 843-856-7900) is a top WTA Tour event, formerly called the Family Circle Cup, and is known for a relaxed atmosphere where you can watch match play or warm-ups from a small stadium or by the outer courts. The draw usually includes several of the highest-ranked women in the field. Held on Daniel Island, a nongated community near Charleston, it lasts a week and offers day and nighttime play with tickets at a variety of price points and hotel packages, including for finals weekend.

May: **Spoleto Festival USA** (843-579-3100; spoletousa.org), 95 Calhoun Street. For 17 days more than a dozen venues in and around Charleston present concerts, chamber music, plays, dance, opera, solo performances, and multimedia art pieces. Some are classic; some are cutting-edge interpretations; many are premieres. Ticket prices are so varied and packages with hotels and restaurants so numerous that as soon as possible after the first of January, when tickets go on sale, you should check the website and design your trip. **Piccolo Spoleto** (www.piccolospoleto.com) runs at the same time and offers many free events. Both festivals run into the first week of June.

SUMMER *July:* **The Mount Pleasant Sweetgrass Festival** (www.sweetgrassfestival.com) is held in the Memorial Park at the foot of the Ravenel Bridge in Mount Pleasant, usually the first or second Saturday of July. It is designed to showcase and heighten awareness of the traditional Lowcountry art perfected by members of the Gullah Geechee community. Baskets and woven artwork are for sale, and artisans demonstrate their work and talk about its design and use. There is free programming that highlights singers, storytellers, and dancers who bring to life their interpretations of the Gullah Geechee experience.

FALL *September:* **Moja Arts Festival** (843-724-7305; www.mojafestival.com), Office of Cultural Affairs, 180 Meeting Street. This is a celebration of the African American and Caribbean heritage in the Charleston area, where influence on Southern culture is traced through music, dance, art, food, stage performances, and more.

October: **The Fall Tours of Homes, History & Architecture** (843-405-1050; www.preservationsociety.org), 147 King Street. Self-guided walking tours of private homes and gardens are offered over a period of about 4 weeks by the city's oldest preservation organization. Docents greet and guide you at the sites. A new addition is curated garden tours for those who want to learn about horticultural history, design in this urban environment, and modern practice in Charleston, and

THE WATERFRONT PARK PINEAPPLE FOUNTAIN © SEAN PAVONE/ISTOCKPHOTO.COM

take advantage of an opportunity to visit very private gardens. Tickets are $125 per person and are limited.

WINTER *February*: **Southeastern Wildlife Exposition** (843-723-1748; www.sewe.com). A comprehensive, multisite exhibition presents wildlife art in various media and programs promoting habitat conservation and wildlife appreciation. Tickets ($50 for three days; kids under 10 free) sell out early to this national event, which draws collectors, artists, hunters, and birdwatchers.

SAVANNAH

SAVANNAH

It's no secret that the preservation of the Lowcountry's great places occurred less as a result of enlightened social policy than from post–Civil War impoverishment. Decades of stalled expectations treated Savannah as they did Charleston, and the cities do share similar assets, including vibrant, architecturally intact, downtown historic districts; a heritage that reflects the diverse contributions of generations of residents; and a culture enriched by unique African American musical, religious, culinary, and artistic contributions.

Yet Savannah is a more modern city and evolving differently from Charleston on a smaller scale. It is edgier and funkier, enlivened by art students, film festivals, and hip restaurants that would not be out of place in San Francisco. There's a more detached air about it. Behind every bold statement about its history or beauty lurks sarcasm. During the cotton boom, Savannah madly envied New York City for its commercial muscle; 170 years later, the two cities share a liking for attitude and being hip.

This trait was evident during the Civil War. Legend has it that General W. T. Sherman spared Savannah because the city was beautiful, the women were gracious, and the parties were just what he needed at the end of his blazing "March to the Sea" campaign. He took up residence, was feted, and, in a remarkable telegraph of 1864, offered the unmolested city to President Lincoln as a Christmas gift.

Well, Savannah is still beautiful . . . and still partying. This quality, and the world it describes, is revealed with great skill in the best book on Savannah's downtown culture, John Berendt's 1994 best-seller, *Midnight in the Garden of Good and Evil*. The blend of reverence and hilarity, of high-mindedness and getting by, gives the city its character. When the local minor league baseball team renamed itself the Sand Gnats (the top choice in a citywide poll), it chose for its slogan "Bite Me." The city shuts down every St. Patrick's Day to accommodate 24 hours of revelry. There's less standing on ceremony here than in Charleston, for Charleston is an iconic Southern place, a city with such a significant, unique presence in American history that it must meet all sorts of expectations. The feeling in Savannah is more along the lines of the church lyric "brighten the corner where you are," and the vibe is more laissez-faire.

Savannah is defined by 21 handsome squares that function as vest-pocket parks. They are embowered and rimmed with native flowering species, crossed with internal sidewalks, and are linked by one-way cross streets along their sides, which, in turn, feed a few broad parkways divided by banks of trees and shrubs. It is one of the largest National Historic Landmark Districts, simply called the Historic District by locals, containing some 1,200 notable buildings. It includes blocks of magnificent town houses, many 19th-century places of worship, and several examples of Regency architecture popularized in this country by an Englishman, William Jay. The best way to see them and to feel the roots of American urbanism is on foot or on a carriage or trolley tour (see *To Do*).

The restoration and adaptive reuse of private and institutional buildings continues. The **Savannah College of Art and Design** (www.scad.edu) has redone more than 40 sites and sponsors or populates numerous art galleries. Its students are ubiquitous and bring with them a sense that imaginative things are happening, like an old filling station on one main artery that became an upscale market selling fresh produce such

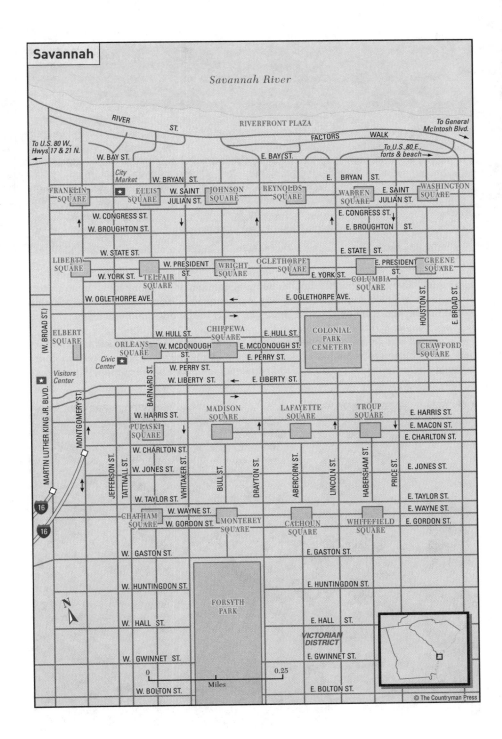

COVID-19

Due to the COVID-19 pandemic, travel in the Lowcountry, as everywhere else, requires more planning for every activity to ensure appropriate social distancing. This means that you should call or check a venue's website to confirm, among other things, if reservations are required where walk-in activity was once the norm. It also means that providers of services from hotels to restaurants or boat rides to carriage tours are likely to be running their businesses differently from in the past, with fewer visitors engaged at any one time. If you are a family group, be sure to mention that, because it may make a difference in the business owner's risk calculations. Ask if there is outdoor seating available at restaurants—many venues have changed their layouts to include more outside dining while they reduce the numbers of tables inside. Meals to go, food service delivery, and curbside pick-up options have expanded dramatically in the spring and summer of 2020; check to see if those options are still available. Annual events, including professional golf and tennis tournaments and house and garden tours, have shifted their dates and ticketing procedures. You'll have a more rewarding travel experience if you arrive prepared and flexible.

as arugula. Even the staid Telfair Museum accommodated a makeover by architect Moshe Safdie, who convinced city leaders and preservationists that a modern addition would not detract from neither the beauty or scale of the original Regency-style mansion nor the views from nearby squares.

Savannah has developed in several distinctive sections. **City Market** is a touristy pedestrian streetscape with shops, galleries, and restaurants. Many carriage tours originate here, and visitors will be drinking sweet tea in one of the outdoor cafés before

THE GREAT HALL AT CHARLESTON CITY MARKET © JOEL CARILLET/ISTOCKPHOTO.COM

or after their ride. On **River Street,** 19th-century brick warehouses are filled with bars, restaurants, gift shops, and the hubbub that attracts people to other American cities that have revived waterfront estate into festival-style marketplaces. From here, ferries zip across the Savannah River to Hutchinson Island, the International Trade & Convention Center, and Westin Savannah Harbor resort. By night and on weekends, jugglers and street musicians entertain the crowds.

Broughton Street is once again a central downtown artery where national retailers and new restaurants exist side by side. Residents in the **Victorian District** are tackling renovations in their neighborhood of large, fancifully designed houses and gingerbread bungalows. Entrepreneurs in smaller areas, like **Wright Square** and blocks of **Whitaker Street,** have joined together to make their address a destination for design or home and garden shops.

Savannah began as an idea in the mind of several enlightened Englishmen who came to be known as the Trustees. They petitioned for a grant in the colonies where land would be held communally and liquor, slavery, and speculation forbidden. Settlers would be

SAILBOATS IN CHARLESTON HARBOR © JOEL CARILLET/ISTOCKPHOTO.COM

selected from "impoverished classes" and under the Trustees' direction would develop exports like wine and silk and defend the region from Spanish encroachment. The group of 114 that arrived in 1733 was led by General James Oglethorpe, and such was his sense of mission that when his ship *Anne* eased into Charleston Harbor to meet the royal governor, the passengers were required to remain aboard and fish for their supper so as not to have their heads turned by the newly prosperous city. Continuing south, the *Anne* stopped at tiny Beaufort. Here passengers were allowed to fraternize with residents, whose standard of living probably appeared to be more in line with what they envisioned.

Oglethorpe chose a settlement site where "the river forms a half-moon, along the south side of which the banks are about 40 feet high, and on the top a flat, which they call a bluff." He was assisted by Colonel William Bull, an engineer with surveying experience, and guided by Tomochichi, a friendly Yamacraw chief. It was a port sufficiently deep for ships drawing up to 12 feet to navigate within 10 yards of the shore.

Oglethorpe and Bull immediately started planning the city in the wilderness. The basic form consisted of blocks of five symmetrical 60-by-90-foot lots encompassing 24 squares. Space was designated for public buildings and market areas, as well as for secure retreats for settlers living outside the city limits. Tomochichi supported the colonists' work, was instrumental in winning the trust of area tribes, and backed Oglethorpe in sporadic skirmishes with the Spanish. The existence of a trading post nearby—run by John Musgrove of South Carolina and his wife, Mary, who was part Creek Indian—also smoothed the way.

It was up to the settlers to clear and build, hunt and farm, and establish the Trustees' Garden. This they did, on the grants of 50 acres received by heads of families (5 acres in the city, 45 outside it for farming). By 1741, buoyed by gifts of livestock, horses, and rice from South Carolina neighbors, and growing with Irish, Scottish, Swiss, German, Italian, and Jewish settlers, the original settlement was poised for change. There were 142 homes, a courthouse, jail, storehouse, market building, and a 10-acre fenced public garden. By 1742, the liquor ban was repealed; in 1749, the ban on slavery was lifted. In 1750, the Trustees relinquished their hold on the land.

Released from Oglethorpe's idealism, the colonists proceeded to develop plantations like their neighbors to the north, and Savannah began to flourish as a colonial seat and trading port serving the Georgia backcountry and the coastal islands. In 1776, four South Carolinians and three Georgians signed the Declaration of Independence. They were indeed on the same page: The Lowcountry had pulled together, united by shared commercial and social goals, regular trade and communication, and a culture deeply affected by slavery.

GETTING THERE **Savannah/Hilton Head International Airport** (912-964-0514; www .savannahairport.com) is the gateway, with some 40 stops each day from East Coast and Midwestern cities. Rental cars from all major agencies are available at the airport, as are courtesy shuttles if you are staying at a big hotel. If you are staying elsewhere, ask the proprietor for advice or select a cab service or shared service like Uber or Lyft. Expect to pay $30 to Savannah. For private flights, contact **Savannah Aviation** (912-964-1022; www.savannahaviation.com).

AMTRAK (800-872-7245; www.amtrak.com) travels the north–south corridor, making daily stops at Savannah (912-234-2611; 2611 Seaboard Coastline Drive), about 20 minutes from downtown. From Boston, New York, Chicago, and Miami, there are generally two trains a day, departing morning and evening and arriving either late the same day or early the following morning.

BUS SERVICE (800-231-2222; www.greyhound.com) serves Savannah, and the station is located downtown.

BY CAR I-95 is just 10 miles from the Historic District, with an exit at I-16 that goes directly into town. Savannah is 252 miles from Atlanta, 105 miles from Charleston, 195 miles from Charlotte, 140 miles from Jacksonville, and 467 miles from Knoxville.

In the city, the **dot Express shuttle** (912-233-5767; www.catchacat.org) is a free shuttle bus service within the Historic District, with 24 stops at the **Visitor Center** (912-944-0455; 301 Martin Luther King Jr. Boulevard.), downtown inns and hotels, the waterfront, and many sites of interest. It connects to most bus routes, with additional fares for regional service throughout Chatham County. The website offers a very helpful Bike/Walk Savannah guide. For $15 visitors can buy a 24-hour pass that allows unlimited parking in any garage and electronic city meter.

✳ To See

Savannah's architectural inventory includes Federal-period mansions and town houses; buildings designed by William Jay, the Regency-period architect who delighted in fancy scrollwork and a freehand imposition of Greek motifs; grand antebellum homes; and a district of Victorian homes made of wood and masonry. Whatever their specific style, the older buildings downtown share a formal and restrained design that makes a cohesive whole. Their colors come from a muted palette of grays, greens, and tans, and the end result is that they resonate with the geometry of Savannah's squares.

ART **The Savannah College of Art and Design** (www.scad.edu) greatly raised the profile of the city as an arts center. Frequently changing exhibitions of work are on display in college buildings throughout the city and in private commercial galleries. In addition, graduates stay in the region and many have started arts-related businesses in film and digital media production, framing, and restoration; their work stretches the boundaries of two-dimensional representation. The increasing number of artists who teach at SCAD and wish to exhibit has expanded gallery space, including innovative "pop-up" shows in shared spaces or alternative venues, like hotel lobbies and warehouses. A glance at *Connect Savannah* (www.connectsavannah.com), a free weekly, will turn up undiscovered or short-run shows—as will another site, www.savannahoffthebeatenpath.com.

Beach Institute African American Cultural Center (912-335-8868; www.beachinstitute.org), 502 E. Harris Street is open Tues.–Sat. noon–5 p.m. Established in 1867 by the American Missionary Association to educate the newly freed slaves of Savannah, the Beach is now an African American cultural center that features permanent and revolving exhibits focused on arts, photography, and documents by and about the Gullah Geechee and African American experience. Of unique interest is the collection of 238 hand-carved wooden sculptures, including likenesses of presidents, by acclaimed folk artist and Savannah barber Ulysses Davis. Adults $10, students and seniors $7.

Ray Ellis Gallery (912-234-3537; www.rayellis.com), 205 W. Congress Street. Paintings, prints, watercolors, books, and prints of golf and traditional maritime scenes by Ray Ellis, perhaps the best known of traditional Lowcountry artists.

John Tucker Fine Arts (912-231-8161), 5 W. Charlton Street. This handsome gallery on Madison Square features several yearly shows of established artists whose work usually reflects Southern themes, along with an inventory of 19th- and 20th-century portraits, still lifes, genre scenes, and folk art.

Kobo Gallery (912-201-0304; www.kobogallery.com), 33 Barnard Street. A contemporary artists' cooperative with shows by members and invited guests displaying a range of work from the very best artists working in Savannah.

SAVANNAH'S FIRST AFRICAN BAPTIST CHURCH VISIT SAVANNAH

Pei Ling Chan Garden for the Arts (800-869-7223; www.scad.edu), 322 Martin Luther King Jr. Boulevard. At W. Harris Street. This walled garden, with individual sections reflecting African American, English, French, and Asian cultures, is the backdrop for sculpture exhibits. There is also a small amphitheater used during theatrical productions. You can have a quiet moment here in the thick of downtown. Check website for current opening information.

shopSCAD (912-525-5180; www.shopscad.com), 340 Bull Street. Featuring work by students, faculty, and occasional guests each month, it selects work of the college's best students and has expanded into a terrific shop. Check website for current opening information.

SCAD Savannah Film Festival (912-525-5051; filmfest.scad.edu). SCAD hosts this eight-day event each fall at downtown venues, including the Lucas Theatre and Trustees Theater, it draws independent filmmakers from around the world and offers screenings, workshops, and lectures. Admission varies according to event.

HISTORIC HOMES, GARDENS, AND RELIGIOUS SITES **Andrew Low House** (912-233-6854; www.andrewlowhouse.com), 329 Abercorn Street. Open daily. A city house in the high style, although adapted to Savannah's summer heat by means of jalousied rear porches. By 1849, when the house was built, Savannah was in its prime: This is how the wealthy cotton merchants lived, and there is a large collection of furniture to tell their story. It was from this house that Juliette Gordon Low founded the Girl Scouts and where she died in 1927. Adults $10, students $9; discounts for Girl Scouts.

First African Baptist Church (912-233-6597; www.firstafricanbc.com), 23 Montgomery Street. Tours Tues.–Sun. Built in 1788 and believed to be the oldest continuously active church for black worshippers in North America, it was built by slaves for slaves. Many original pews remain intact. It was the birthplace of the civil rights movement in

Savannah and a refuge on the Underground Railroad. Adults $10, students and seniors $9. Check website for current opening information.

Green-Meldrim House (912-233-3845; www.stjohnssav.org), 14 W. Macon Street. Open Tues., Thurs.–Sat. Used as headquarters by General W. T. Sherman during his 1864 Christmas occupation of Savannah, this Gothic Revival mansion on Madison Square was the city's most expensive house when it was built in 1850. The exterior ironwork and porches are the best example of the style in the city. Adults $10, students $5.

Isaiah Davenport House (912-236-8097; www.davenporthousemuseum.org), 324 E. State Street. Open daily. The proposed demolition of this landmark—built circa 1820 by a master builder from Rhode Island for his family—to salvage the brick and make way for a parking lot galvanized Savannah preservationists. That was in 1954, and the effort marked the birth of the Historic Savannah Foundation. Today it's a museum adorned with furnishings and decorative arts of the Federal period and reflects the lifestyle of a successful entrepreneur in a city that was growing quickly. There's a lovely garden out back and an excellent museum shop. Adults $9, children $5. Combination tickets are available with the Andrew Low House and the Ships of the Sea Museum.

Juliette Gordon Low Birthplace (912-233-4501; www.juliettegordonlowbirthplace .org), 10 E. Oglethorpe Avenue. Open Mon.–Sat.; hours change seasonally. A Regency town house decorated in postbellum period style, this building commemorates the childhood of the founder of the Girl Scouts, who was born here in 1860. There's a gift shop with special things for Scouts. Adults $15, Scouts $12, children $10. Check website for current opening information.

King-Tisdell Cottage (912-335-8868; www.beachinstitute.org), 514 E. Huntingdon Street. This charming, original Victorian cottage (circa 1896) houses a museum of the Black history and culture of Savannah and the Sea Islands. It represents the achievement of African American entrepreneurs. Admission charged.

Laurel Grove South Cemetery (www.savannahga.gov/498/Cemeteries), 2101 Kollock Street, located at the western end of 37th Street. Open daily. Laurel Grove South was dedicated in 1852 for the burial of "free persons of color" and enslaved people. Many of the city's most famous African Americans are buried here. **Laurel Grove North** and **Bonaventure Cemetery** are also well known for their cemetery architecture and 150-year-old landscaping. Descriptive information can be found on the website.

Mercer Williams House (912-236-6352; www.mercerhouse.com), 429 Bull Street at Monterey Square. Open daily. Construction on this Italianate mansion began in 1860 and was completed in 1868. While it was built for the great-grandfather of Savannah's favorite son, Johnny Mercer, no member of the Mercer family ever lived here, and the house is most famous for its association with the late preservationist and antiques dealer Jim Williams, depicted as a main figure in *Midnight in the Garden of Good and Evil*. Mr. Williams finished his two-year restoration of the house in 1971, and many pieces of his private collection are on display in the house, including 18th- and 19th-century portraits. Admission charged.

Owens-Thomas House & Slave Quarters (912-790-8800; www.telfair.org), 124 Abercorn Street. Open daily; last tour at 4:20 p.m. Designed in 1816 by Englishman William Jay and considered the best example of an urban villa in his Regency style in the United States, this house contains a collection of European and American decorative art objects, many from family collections, and has a formal garden. The Carriage House is the site of one of the few discovered slave quarters in the Historic District, and it offers the best insight into the lives of urban African American slaves in Savannah. Adults $20, seniors $18, students $15, children $5. Discount tickets are available with admission to the Telfair Academy and Jepson Center.

Second African Baptist Church (912-233-6163; www.visit-historic-savannah.com), 123 Houston Street. Call ahead to arrange a visit. The church, established in 1802, was the site of two historic occurrences: General W. T. Sherman's reading of the Emancipation Proclamation to the newly freed slaves and, nearly a century later in a rebuilt sanctuary, Dr. Martin Luther King Jr.'s presentation of his "I Have a Dream" sermon prior to its delivery in Washington, DC.

Temple Mickve Israel (912-233-1547; www.mickveisrael.org), 20 E. Gordon Street. Docent-led tours occur weekdays. The Gothic-style synagogue was built in the 1870s, more than 100 years after the congregation was established. The museum and library house the two oldest Torah scrolls in America, as well as letters, books, and historical documents. Check website for current opening information.

Wormsloe State Historic Site (912-353-3023; www.gastateparks.org), 7601 Skidaway Road, Isle of Hope. Open daily. The tabby ruins, an avenue of oaks, and artifacts excavated from the site are all that remain of the colonial plantation built by Noble Jones, a physician and carpenter who came with the first settlers on the ship *Anne* and established the Georgia colony. An audio-video presentation and costumed interpreters of colonial life make the period vivid for visitors. Adults $10; seniors $9; children 6–17, $4.50; children under 6, $2.

Annual tours of private homes and gardens are sponsored by preservation organizations. They usually take place in **March,** last all day or all weekend, and include six to nine homes and gardens on a self-paced tour where docents greet you on-site. Tickets are generally $25–$45. Contact the **Savannah Tour of Homes and Gardens** (912-234-8054; www.savannahtourofhomes.org) or **The Garden Club of Savannah** (912-447-3879; www.gcofsavnogstour.org) about its **Annual NOGS Tour** (that is, gardens "North of Gwinnett Street").

MILITARY MUSEUMS AND SITES The island forts and lighthouses recall the sense of isolation felt by soldiers stationed there and the effort they made to create a community.

Fort Jackson (912-232-3945; www.chsgeorgia.org), 1 Fort Jackson Road, 3 miles from downtown. Open daily. The oldest standing fort in Georgia, first established in 1809 on an earlier fortification, it was central to the Confederate network of river batteries during the Civil War. A self-guided tour leads you to military exhibits in the fort's casemates. Special military history programs enliven the fort several times each year, and interpreters and interactive experiences introduce kids to its history. Adults $9; children $5.

Fort McAllister Historic Park (912-727-2339; www.gastateparks.org), 3894 Fort McAllister Road, Richmond Hill (24 miles south of Savannah on I-95). Open daily. The fall of Fort McAllister, on the Ogeechee River, signaled the end of Sherman's March to the Sea. By that time it had outlasted other forts due to its earthen walls, which, unlike the popular masonry equivalent, could be swiftly repaired after a bombardment. There are self-guided tours, rangers on hand, and a good, small museum. Picnicking in the park is popular but bring insect repellent. There are biking trails and canoe/kayak rentals. Adults $9, seniors $8, children $5.

Fort Pulaski National Monument (912-786-5787; www.nps.gov/fopu), Cockspur Island, US 80 East, about 30 minutes from Savannah. Open daily. A young officer named Robert E. Lee had his first military assignment here, soon after the fort was built. It's a masterpiece of engineering, a huge and heavy brick building, surrounded by a moat, sitting on an unstable marsh. And yet during the Civil War, cannons blasted holes in the masonry of such forts, and they became obsolete. Interpretive programs explain life at the fort during the Civil War, and you are free to roam its ramparts.

An excellent selection of books is available at the gift shop. Adults $10, ages 15 and younger free. Check website for current opening information.

National Museum of the Mighty Eighth Air Force (912-748-8888; www.mightyeighth .org), 175 Bourne Avenue, Pooler (take I-95 Exit 102 to US 80 East, then go left on Bourne Avenue). Open daily. The museum is dedicated to the men and women who served in the "Mighty Eighth" (formed in Savannah in 1942) during World War II. Exhibits also track later engagements, such as operation Desert Storm, supplemented by photos and film presentations. Adults $10; children 6–12, $8; discounts available for seniors and military families.

Tybee Island Museum and Lighthouse/Fort Screven (912-786-5801; www.tybee lighthouse.org), 30 Meddin Drive, Tybee Island, 18 miles east of Savannah. Open daily, except Tues. Ticket sales stop at 4:30 p.m. Located within Fort Screven, which was acquired by the federal government in 1808 and used as a post through World War II, the museum and lighthouse, and its adjacent cottages, offer visitors a glimpse of life at a beach outpost. The museum has an assortment of objects, Native American and Civil War weaponry, as well as memorabilia and illustrated newspaper accounts of the Civil War. A lighthouse has marked this site since 1736. Today you can climb this 19th-century version (more than 150 feet tall) for a wonderful view of the river. Adults $10, seniors and children $8.

MUSEUMS **Georgia State Railroad Museum** (912-651-6823; www.chsgeorgia.org), 655 Louisville Road. Open daily. This National Historic Landmark is a collection of structures first built in 1838 and used as a railroad manufacturing and repair facility. Today you can see the roundhouse and turntable, a 125-foot brick smokestack, antique steam engines, diesel locomotives, and rolling stock. There are guided tours and train rides. Adults $11, children $7.

Ralph Mark Gilbert Civil Rights Museum (912-777-6099; rmgilbertcivilrights museum.com), 460 Martin Luther King Jr. Boulevard. Open Tues.–Sat. Dr. Gilbert, who died in 1956, was a leader in early efforts to gain educational, social, and political equality for African Americans in Savannah. This museum features state-of-the-art interactive exhibits on three floors, focusing on the history of Jim Crow and the civil rights movement in the city. Adults $10, seniors $8, students $6. Check website for current opening information.

Ships of the Sea Maritime Museum (912-232-1511; www.shipsofthesea.org), 41 Martin Luther King Jr. Boulevard. Open Tues.–Sun. Ship models, a magnificent dollhouse-style construction of a huge 19th-century ship, and ships-in-bottles tell the exciting story of maritime adventure, war, commerce, and exploration in the world's oceans from the time of the Vikings forward. Located in the William Scarbrough House, which is a Regency jewel with a lovely garden carefully curated with native and historic plantings. The gift shop has an excellent collection of books on art, architecture, maritime history, and Savannah. Adults $9, students and seniors $7, with discounts for families.

Telfair Academy/Jepson Center for the Arts (912-790-8800; www.telfair.org), 121 Barnard Street. Open daily. The Telfair, Savannah's premier art museum, housed in a Regency-style mansion, hosts a permanent collection of American and European impressionist paintings, drawings, prints, and sculpture. The Jepson displays more contemporary art from the 20th and 21st century augmented by traveling exhibitions. A single admission fee allows access to three sites: Telfair Academy, Jepson Center, and the Owens-Thomas House & Slave Quarters (see *To See*). There's also an interactive space for kids and a café. Adults $20, seniors $18, students $15, children $5.

✳ To Do

You might as well decide whether you want to concentrate on ghosts, the Civil War, "The Book" (*Midnight in the Garden of Good and Evil*), gardens, or old houses; and whether you want to go on foot, by carriage, trolley, or air-conditioned bus or van; and whether you prefer to tour by daylight or moonlight. Most tours last one to two hours, and the services operate daily. Reservations are suggested. You can also pick up self-guided tours (apps are also found online) at the **Visitor Center** (912-944-0455; www.visitsavannah.com), 301 Martin Luther King Jr. Boulevard. Some motorized tours allow you to step off and catch up with them at a later stop. For tours that are more specifically nature-oriented or may require equipment such as a kayak or canoe, see below. Expect tour prices to start at $20–$25 for adults and $10–$15 for children. Handicapped accessibility or the ease with which wheelchairs can navigate the old sidewalks is variable. Often buses and trolleys require advance notice for passengers who need assistance.

BY CARRIAGE Several companies offer narrated horse-drawn tours of the Historic District during the day and in the evening. They last about an hour and usually board at City Market; West Street, Julian Street, and Jefferson Street; and Ellis Square. The rates start at $22 for adults and $12 for children. Walk-ups are welcome but reservations (online or by phone) secure your spot.

Carriage Tours of Savannah (912-236-6756; www.carriagetoursofsavannah.com).

Historic Savannah Carriage Tours (912-443-9333; www.savannahcarriage.com).

Plantation Carriage (912-659-9005; www.plantationcarriagecompany.com).

BY TROLLEY The Historic District "on/off" tour, where you can get off and reboard at a different stop at any time during the day, is widely offered. The rates are about $30 for adults and $13 for children, with discounts for booking online. The central embarkation points are the Visitor Center at 301 Martin Luther King Jr. Boulevard or the Savannah Welcome Center at 214 W. Boundary. Both locations offer free parking.

Old Savannah Tours (912-234-8128; www.oldsavannahtours.com). Historical reenactors may jump on your trolley from time to time. They are usually locals who have worked with the company to craft their own interpretations and scripts, and they're eager to engage your curiosity.

Old Town Trolley Tours (855-245-8992; www.trolleytours.com) also offers a variety of custom touring packages.

CARRIAGE TOURS ARE A POPULAR AND HISTORIC WAY OF SEEING THE SIGHTS © JOEL CARILLET/ISTOCKPHOTO.COM

BY FOOT Architectural Tours of Savannah (912-604-6354; www.architectural savannah.com). A graduate of SCAD with a master's degree in architecture leads one 90-minute tour a day, usually in the morning, and highlights the impact of Savannah's unique built environment. Check website for days when tours are not offered. $30 per person.

Footprints of Savannah (912-695-3872;www.footprintsofsavannah.com). Once-daily tours begin at Wright Square and focus on the African American experience in Savannah, from slavery and the cotton business, with a focus on Factors Walk and City Market, to illuminate how enslaved and formerly enslaved people worked and lived in the city. Adults $20, seniors $14, children $7.

Ghost Talk Ghost Walk (912-233-3896; www.ghosttalkghostwalk.com). Ninety-minute tours have various schedules. Some of them are oriented to Girl Scouts and their troops who often visit the city. $10 adults, $5 children.

Savannah Ghosts & Folklore Tour and Haunted Pub Crawl Tour (912-604-3007; www.ghostsavannah.com) offers 90-minute candlelit walking tours daily.

Savannah Walks (912-385-0577; www.savannahwalks.com) has the most extensive menu of walks, from gardens to ghosts.

BY BIKE Savannah Bike Tours (912-704-4043; www.savannahbiketours.com), 41 Habersham Street. Twice-daily bike tours cover about 3 miles of flat landscape and let you see close-up the modern and historic sides of Savannah. Bikes and safety equipment provided. Adults $30, children $10.

BY BUS OR MINIVAN Freedom Trail Tour (912-398-2785; www.visitsavannah.com). The guide focuses on African American history.

Savannah Grayline (912-964-8989; www.savannahgrayline.us) offers van tours in the Historic District, and combination tickets are available to pair the tours with a Savannah Riverboat cruise. Tickets start at $35.

Savannah Heritage Tours (912-224-8365; www.savannahheritagetours.com) offers curated tours or step-on services to buses.

OUTSIDE THE CITY

BY BOAT Bull River Marina (912-897-7300; www.bullrivermarina.com), 8005 US 80, East Savannah. The marina has a broad assortment of dolphin watch and nature tour cruises and opportunities to be dropped off and picked up to explore beaches in the area. Fees start at $25 for adults.

Captain Mike's Dolphin Tours (912-786-5848; www.tybeedolphins.com) is at Lazaretto Creek Marina, Old Highway 80, Tybee Island. Adults $15, children $8.

Dolphin Magic Tours (912-897-4990; www.dolphin-magic.com). Tours depart from River Street and last about two hours. They head down the Savannah River toward Tybee Island and Fort Pulaski, depending on the weather and where the dolphins are. Adults $30, children $15.

CANOEING, KAYAKING, AND PADDLEBOARDING If you are traveling with your own boat, access points along the Savannah River and boat landings at Isle of Hope, Skidaway Island, and Tybee Island allow you to launch into tidal creeks throughout the area. For outing ideas, instruction, ecotours, maps, and expedition opportunities, **Sea Kayak Georgia** (912-786-8732; www.seakayakgeorgia.com) and **Savannah Canoe and Kayak** (912-341-9502; www.savannahcanoeandkayak.com) are the experts. They have fully equipped shops and rental equipment, including many types and sizes of kayaks and paddleboards. No experience necessary for many excursions. Trips that last three hours leave Tybee Island daily in the morning and afternoon, and longer camping expeditions can be arranged. Lessons and specialized skills workshops start at $95 per person with a minimum of two participants and last three to four hours. A three-hour guided trip starts at $65 per person. Other providers include:

East Coast Paddleboarding (912-484-3200; www.eastcoastpaddleboarding.com). Three launching locations on Tybee Island.

North Island Surf & Kayak (912-786-4000; www.northislandkayak.com), Old Highway 80, Tybee Island.

FISHING Inshore, there are fish in shallow water and narrow creeks when the tide is right; offshore, there are bigger game fish in the Gulf Stream. Some guides specialize in the art of saltwater fly-fishing.

A good place to plan a fishing trip is at a marina. Charters usually take care of required licenses, but the state Wildlife Resources Division (800-366-2661; www.georgiawildlife.com/fishing) is a source of abundant information. A listing of some of the many charter boat services follows. Most boats are fully outfitted with supplies and bait, but check in advance, especially if you have questions about bringing your favorite rod—an option for fly-fishing—or if the length of the trip requires food. Always bring sunscreen, a hat, and a windbreaker. The cost does not include gratuity for the mate(s). The 2020 prices for half-day trips (generally up to four passengers for inshore fishing, four to six for offshore fishing) start at $350. A 12-hour trip can cost $1,400, and a 14-hour trip to the Gulf Stream costs about $2,100.

Bull River Marina (912-897-7300; www.bullrivermarina.com), 8005 US 80 East, located halfway to Tybee.

Coastal River Charters (912-441-9930; www.coastalrivercharters.com) offers inshore fishing and sightseeing tours of barrier islands and secluded creeks. They have a number of packages, including family fishing adventures where two adults and two kids can spend three hours on the water for $300 or two experienced anglers can fish for four hours for $400.

Miss Judy Charters (912-897-4921; www.missjudycharters.com), 124 Palmetto Drive. Captain Judy Helmey guides deep-sea fishing and trolling outings, Gulf Stream trips, and inshore fishing. There are 12 options for offshore fishing and nine for inshore, depending on the number of passengers and length of time.

Sundial Nature and Fishing Tours (912-786-9470; www.sundialcharters.com), 142 Pelican Drive, Tybee Island. Inshore fishing, crabbing, and net casting are on the menu. Also ask about naturalist-led outings to Little Tybee and Wassaw Islands and overnight camping possibilities.

Tybee Island Charters (912-786-4801; www.fishtybee.com), 1 US 80 East, Tybee Island. Fish inshore and offshore or arrange for nature cruises.

GOLF The most varied opportunities for golf exist on Hilton Head and Bluffton, about 45 minutes away depending on where you go (see *Hilton Head*), but here are some local options.

Bacon Park Golf Course (912-354-2625; www.baconparkgolf.com), 1 Shorty Cooper Drive. Par 72; 27 holes across three layouts; 6,700 yards. Putting green and lighted driving range. Fees for 18 holes: $22 plus $22 cart fees.

Wilmington Island Club (912-897-1615; www.wilmingtonislandclub.com), 501 Wilmington Island Road. Par 71; 18 holes; 6,876 yards. Driving range and putting green. Fees start at $70.

TENNIS Seven city parks in and around Savannah have a total of 47 courts, and nearly all are lighted for night play. The custom at public parks is first come, first served. The locations are: **Bacon Park** (6262 Skidaway Road); **Daffin Park** (1001 E. Victory Drive); **Forsyth Park** (Gaston and Drayton Streets); **Lake Mayer Park** (Montgomery Crossroad and Sallie Mood Drive); **Stell Park** (Bush Road); **Tybee Memorial Park** (Butler Avenue); and **Wilmington Island Community Park** (Lang Street and Walthour Road).

✳ Green Space

Savannah's squares offer abundant shady green space. **Forsyth Park,** in the center of the city, is the site of the **Saturday Farmers' Market.**

BEACH ACCESS The only beach accessible by car on Georgia's northern coast, Tybee Island (www.visittybee.com) lies 18 miles east of Savannah on US 80. Strictly enforced "No Dogs Allowed on Beach" policy. Check beach rules and regulations before you go.

Wassaw Island (912-652-4415; www.fws.gov/wassaw), located east of Savannah and Skidaway Island, can be reached by private or charter boat or by guided kayak tour (see *Canoeing, Kayaking, and Paddleboarding*). It is a National Wildlife Refuge managed by the US Fish and Wildlife Service. Within its 10,000 acres are more than 20 miles of inland island trails and a 7-mile beach to explore.

Oatland Island Wildlife Center (912-395-1212; www.oatlandisland.org), 711 Sandtown Road. Open daily. Children will love walking the nearly 2 miles of wooded trails in this 175-acre preserve, where they can watch for animals and experience the salt marsh, forest, and wetland habitat of the Lowcountry. Sheep, goats, ponies, and swans may cross your path while bald eagles and hawks soar overhead. There is a farmyard, too. Adults $5, children $3.

BIRD-WATCHING The best spots for birding around Savannah are part of the Savannah National Wildlife Refuge System, a complex of seven coastal parks that provide habitat on the beach and dunes as well as in abandoned rice fields, swamps, creeks, and estuarine systems.

Tybee Island North Beach by parking at the **Tybee Island Museum** (see *Military Museums and Sites*).

Skidaway Island State Park (912-598-2300; www.gastateparks.org), 52 Diamond Causeway, is separated from the Atlantic by salt marsh to the east and Wassaw Island to the south. This unique geography attracts a wide variety of songbirds as well as large ospreys and bald eagles. To get there, take Exit 164 off I-16 west of Savannah and head south. It will become Diamond Causeway.

Harris Neck National Wildlife Refuge (912-832-4608; www.fws.gov/harrisneck) supports a large colony of wood storks and dozens of nesting wading birds in a 2,700-acre area of freshwater impoundments and marsh, river-bottom hardwood swamp, forest, and field. Take US 17 south to Harris Neck Road, then travel 6.5 miles to the refuge entrance. There is an interpretive kiosk near the entrance gate, providing a brief description, and you can bike or drive along the 4-mile Laurel Hill Wildlife Road.

NATURE PRESERVES AND REFUGES Some of the most accessible and user-friendly preserves in the Lowcountry are located within 30 minutes of Savannah. They include:

Coastal Georgia Botanical Gardens at the Historic Bamboo Farm (912-921-5460; coastalbg.uga.edu), Canebrake Road off US 17, 15 miles southwest of Savannah. Open daily. A 46-acre educational and research center that started more than 100 years ago

GLIDING IN THE REGION'S HUNDREDS OF MILES OF ESTUARIES AND CREEKS PUTS YOU AT EYE LEVEL WITH AN AMAZING NUMBER OF BIRDS VISIT SAVANNAH

when a local bamboo fancier was given three giant Japanese timber bamboo plants. Today there are more than 100 types of plants, flowers, and trees growing here and more than 70 species of bamboo. The gardens of camellias, irises, and roses bloom seasonally, but the crepe myrtle allées and formal parterre garden show their architectural structural form all year. A relatively new addition is a miniature replica of the plantings found in Savannah's original Trustees' Garden in 1734. Adults $5, youth $3.

Pinckney Island National Wildlife Refuge (843-784-2468; www.fws.gov/pinckney island), US 278, a half-mile west of Hilton Head Island, approximately 35 minutes from Savannah. A 4,053-acre complex of small islands and hammocks set in the marsh with 14 miles of trails. Open dawn to dusk.

Savannah National Wildlife Refuge (843-784-2468; www.fws.gov/savannah), I-95 Exit 5 to US 17 South; 6 miles south of Hardeeville on SC 170. The refuge consists of 25,608 acres spread across land once used for growing rice. The visitor center is located on US 17 (6 miles north of Savannah and 7 miles south of Hardeeville), and is open Mon.–Sat. Get a map at the visitor center. There's a loop road in this diverse environment, and 39 miles of hiking trails are well marked, many of them following the path of the old rice dikes.

Savannah-Ogeechee Canal (912-748-8068; www.savannahogeecheecanal.org), 681 Fort Argyle Road, Savannah. Open daily. Located on a barge canal created in the 1820s by enslaved African Americans and Irish laborers to transport local crops and goods to the shipping port of Savannah, the park's 6 miles of footpaths thread through rice fields and swamps. Adults $2, children $1.

Victoria Bluff Heritage Preserve (803-734-3886; www.dnr.sc.gov), on Sawmill Creek Road off US 278, 3 miles from Hilton Head. Open dawn to dusk daily. This beautiful parcel of nearly 1,000 acres on the Colleton River was long eyed for residential or industrial development, but local residents secured its protection as a passive recreation area.

✱ Lodging

Savannah and its Sea Island neighbor, Tybee Island, offer accommodations from upscale inns to funky beach houses and condos. The caveats of Charleston hold true: Reservations are recommended, especially in the "high season" of spring or fall, when a two-night minimum stay is common; cancellation policies and room deposits are standard; and smoking takes place outside if it is allowed at all. Access for the handicapped can be problematic outside the large hotels; carriage houses with ground-floor access are often a good bet. Ask about these and other restrictions, including whether children are welcome and a fee for pets if they are allowed. Not all hotels offer parking, which starts around $30 per night. Not all offer shuttle service from the airport. At random I researched hotel discounts available when booking online and found there were more opportunities for them in Savannah than in Charleston. As in Charleston, Airbnb has taken a big share of the market for good accommodations for one or two guests on a budget. **Visit Savannah** (877-SAVANNAH; www.visitsavannah .com) provides information, a printed guide, and links.

HOTELS AND LARGER INNS **Andaz Hotel** (912-233-2116; www.hyatt.com), 14 Barnard Street. A chic, boutique hot spot with 151 rooms, including 68 suites that have good city views. Heated pool, fire pit, and a restaurant featuring an extensive wine list are on-site. All of the rooms and suites feature luxury bedding.

Located across the street from the newly restored Ellis Square. $$$–$$$$.

Bohemian Hotel Savannah Riverfront (912-721-3800; marriot.com), 102 W. Bay Street. A prime location on Savannah's riverfront offers 75 rooms, including 12 suites. British and Colonial furniture with wood, brass, and leather elements evokes the 18th century. Its rooftop bar, Rocks on the Roof, overlooks the Savannah River with fantastic views and is the go-to place for the city's professional beau monde. $$$$.

Hampton Inn Savannah Historic District (912-231-9700; savannahlodging .com), 201 E. Bay Street. Heart pine flooring, Savannah gray bricks, a rooftop pool, and an atmosphere that is both cozy and simple take the chain-hotel feeling off this renovated brick low-rise. Located across Bay Street from the riverfront, it's convenient and welcoming to families. $$$.

Kimpton Brice (912-238-1200; www .bricehotel.com), 601 E. Bay Street. A new hotel that many think wins the prize for modern decor and service in a big place of 145 rooms, including 26 suites. It's upbeat. Surprisingly, if you're not a rewards member you may have to pay for WiFi, but check. $$$$.

The Marshall House (912-644-7896; www.marshallhouse.com), 123 E. Broughton Street. A classic example of decline and rebirth on Broughton Street, where an old gem (circa 1850) is back with panache. The streetscape is bustling again with theaters, upscale restaurants, and shopping, a definite plus, but it can be noisy to stay here. Its bar draws an older, cool, local crowd. There are 68 rooms, some suites among them with separate sleeping areas. Modernized with all the amenities and putting out a high-gloss sheen. $$$–$$$$.

Westin Savannah Harbor Golf Resort & Spa (912-201-2000; marriott.com), 1 Resort Drive. A luxury resort complex is located on Hutchinson Island, 90 seconds by water taxi across the Savannah River from the Historic District or a brief car trip over the Talmadge Bridge. From here the views of Savannah and the river traffic are stunning and the proximity to downtown Savannah, plus the resort amenities, are unusual in the Lowcountry, where you often have to drive 35 minutes out of town to a resort destination. $$$$.

SMALLER LUXURY INNS **Ballastone Inn** (912-236-1484; www.ballastone.com), 14 E. Oglethorpe Avenue. At Christmas, this looks like a scene out of Dickens— holly, magnolia leaves, native mistletoe, and garlands of smilax carry its grand front parlor back in time to 1838, when this townhouse was built and English taste influenced the city. The decor echoes this high-style period in rich colors (like chocolate-toned walls), drapes, and furnishings. It's very comfortable, but to some it may be a little too full of fabric and stuff. There are 16 rooms, including three deluxe suites—many of them with Jacuzzis and fireplaces—and a courtyard you may not want to leave. A handsome bar on the first floor is a wonderful amenity, one of the coziest nooks in the city. A full Southern breakfast, afternoon tea, and hors d'oeuvres are included. $$$–$$$$.

Eliza Thompson House (912-236-3620; www.elizathompsonhouse.com), 5 W. Jones Street. This 25-room inn gives off a sense of family warmth amid beautiful old objects. It was one of Savannah's first luxury inns, and while it may be outclassed in luxury these days, it maintains its sense of hospitality. Its spacious courtyard and fountain, and its location on a brick-paved street embowered by oaks and lined with iron-balconied townhouses, still fulfill the expectations of visitors who come in search of the

SAVANNAH'S MANSIONS HAVE BECOME LUXURIOUS INNS VISIT SAVANNAH

MUST SEE

The historic layout of Savannah, with its squares, makes it unique and provides a sense of place that is different from what you get from visiting one historic house or site. There's cumulative pleasure in experiencing Savannah. The option of buying a ticket on a trolley that you can hop on and off at your leisure, and then shopping or eating in a neighborhood (see *Where to Eat* and check the less expensive options), makes a tourist feel embedded. The Historic District is small enough to experience most of it, or its highlights, in a day. My favorite sites to visit are the Owens-Thomas House (www.telfair.org), 124 Abercorn Street, a Regency-style urban villa designed by William Jay in 1816, and Fort Pulaski (www.nps.gov/fopu) on US 80, a masonry fort that is a great place for a picnic or a bicycling destination. Suggestions in *To See* round out my choices; for example, the folk art sculpture that celebrates the talent of Ulysses Davis and other African American artists at The Beach Institute (www.beachinstitute.org), 502 E. Harris Street. I've characterized Savannah as a modern city relative to its historic roots, and what that means to a visitor is that you can have a late-afternoon bite and drink in a wonderful, often gardenlike setting, before you have a fancy meal. It's relaxed and there are a lot of options. Given that Tybee Island is close and informal, I would definitely carve out a day there for the beach, the food, or a half-day kayak tour, an inshore fishing experience, or a dolphin excursion (see *To Do*).

cities of the Old South. Many extras like breakfast in the courtyard, evening wine, coffee, and desserts. $$$.

Forsyth Park Inn (912-233-6800; www.forsythparkinn.com), 102 W. Hall Street. A modest, quiet place with 11 rooms, including a courtyard cottage that can accommodate up to four, this inn might best be used for a romantic weekend getaway for a busy couple, or the cottage can accommodate families. The main house, a Victorian-era mansion with inlaid hardwood floors, is furnished with period antiques, reproductions, and four-poster beds. It's directly across from a beautiful urban park, which would appeal to joggers and families. $$$.

The Gastonian (912-232-2869; www.gastonian.com), 220 E. Gaston Street. This Regency/Italianate residence complex dating from 1868 has lost little of its imposing feel. Period-appropriate decor and muted colors take visitors back to the post–Civil War era, when the Old South was becoming the New South. Each of the 17 guest rooms and suites has a gas fireplace; many have four-poster beds, and some have Jacuzzi tubs or Japanese soak tubs. The side garden has been restored to its fragrant, secret self. Local people often reserve months in advance for special occasions. It's

part of the **Historic Inns of Savannah** (www.historicinnsofsavannah.com), a group of six inns, and can recommend other sites if they are full. Full Southern breakfast. $$$$.

The Kehoe House (912-232-1020; www.kehoehouse.com), 123 Habersham Street. This restored Victorian mansion has had several lives; this is its grandest. There are 13 guest rooms (many with private balconies) and several opulent public rooms adorned with huge urns of fresh flowers in the main building, as well as three additional rooms in the townhouse across the courtyard. Everything here is scaled to *fin de siècle* oversize: the ceiling moldings, the valances, the draperies, the armoires, the library tables, even the banisters and paneling. Confirm age restrictions for guests in advance. $$–$$$$.

Mansion on Forsyth Park (912-238-5158; www.kesslercollection.com), 700 Drayton Street. After the initial tourist rush in the mid-'80s that put Savannah on the map, the industry matured, and some of the quainter bed-and-breakfasts faded. Chocolates on the pillows were not enough. The Mansion may be over the top even for Savannah—a tricked-out car among the classics. It's not about a touch here, a touch there, a nice oil painting or a fondly told Civil War story/myth. This is seriously deluxe, with 126 rooms, a massive gallery with hundreds of paintings and sculptures, a spa, a cooking school, and a 150-seat restaurant (700 Drayton) composed of six dining rooms. Showmanship and glamour: it's rocking Savannah's world. $$$$.

SMALLER ACCOMMODATIONS AND OFFBEAT LODGINGS These are alternatives to the full-blown, fancy places and can be a budget choice or an option for extended families or friends traveling together.

Bed & Breakfast Inn (912-238-0518; www.savannahbnb.com), 117 W. Gordon Street. A mid-1850s townhouse sitting at Chatham Square that is closer to Forsyth Park than the river but in an old neighborhood. This inn has been around for years and has many fans. $$.

Thunderbird Inn (912-232-2661; www.thethunderbirdinn.com), 611 W. Oglethorpe Avenue. Renovated to a retro/motor lodge vibe, pet friendly, and 42 rooms. If you're an urban hipster it will definitely appeal. They are greener than other places in business operations and are making a big effort to reduce the waste generated by the tourism industry. You will find bargains even if you book online at the last minute. $$.

RESORTS AND RENTALS

TYBEE ISLAND

Savannah's beach is Tybee Island, the opposite of a gated resort. While there are some new luxury homes, it's mostly raised houses with latticed skirts hiding the pilings and a deck out back. There is a refreshing lack of the need to monetize every piece of one's property or view. The beach is broad and public, with a pier and plenty of access points. There are shops for beachwear and boogie boards, a couple of good restaurants, some fine bed-and-breakfasts, ocean-front hotels, and a campground and RV park. It's also the best place to get on the water in a kayak or paddleboard (see *Canoeing, Kayaking, and Paddleboarding*). Condo complexes and inexpensive motels are typical lodgings, but some other options are listed here. **The Tybee Visitor Center** (912-786-5444; www.visittybee.com), 802 First Street, Tybee Island, is open daily.

Beachview Bed & Breakfast (912-786-5500; www.beachviewtybee.com), 1701 Butler Avenue. Ten rooms in a circa-1910 house at the beach, one block from the water, 30 minutes from downtown Savannah. $$.

Dunes Inn and Suites (912-786-4591; www.dunesinn.com), 1409 Butler Avenue. An upscale version of a chain hotel where some of the 54 rooms have kitchenettes, some have king beds and Jacuzzis. It's simple, clean, close to the beach, and has a swimming pool. $$.

AZALEAS IN SAVANNAH'S FORSYTH PARK VISIT SAVANNAH

17th Street Inn (912-208-3732; www
.17thstreetinn.com), 12 17th Street. Eight
rooms with kitchenettes, along with a
back deck for all guests and plenty of
room for families, distinguish its appeal.
Recently renovated in a beach-simple
style, it's less than one block from the
southern Tybee beach. Kids accommodated with beds at modest additional
cost. $$–$$$.

Tybee Island Inn (912-786-9255;
www.tybeeislandinn.com), 24 Van Horn
Avenue. Once part of the Fort Screven
infirmary, this seven-room inn is located
one block from the beach on the quieter
north end of the island (closer to Savannah) amid live oaks, palmettos, and
many places to walk or jog. $$$$.

RENTAL AGENTS

TYBEE ISLAND

Oceanfront Cottage Rentals (800-786-
5889; www.oceanfrontcottage.com), 717
First Street. Listing dozens of condos
and homes on the ocean or with an ocean
view. Many welcome pets and usually
provide boogie boards, bikes, and beach
chairs. Some have pools and hot tubs.

Tybee Vacation Rentals (786-5853;
www.tybeevacationrentals.com). They
list hundreds of properties, including
houses that can sleep 10 and smaller villas and condos. Pet-friendly properties.
Online reservations.

CAMPING **River's End Campground
and RV Park** (912-786-5518; www
.riversendcampground.com), 5 Fort Avenue, Tybee Island. A hundred sites
located a half mile from the beach, with
full hook-ups that cost $49–$99 nightly;
small campers and tent sites from $29–
$79 nightly; and bare bones cabin rentals
from $70–$175 for up to six-person occupancy. Free WiFi.

Skidaway Island State Park (912-598-
2300; www.gastateparks.org), 52 Diamond Causeway. A 533-acre park with
87 tent, trailer, and RV sites and three
camper cabins; laundry; bathhouse;
nature trail; and interpretative walks

TYBEE ISLAND'S BROAD BEACH AND FRIENDLY, NONRESORT ATMOSPHERE SUM UP THE SIMPLE LIFE   VISIT SAVANNAH

and programs represent another budget option. Rates are $23–$50 for campsites; $75–$250 for cabins; and on a sliding scale for RVs.

✳ Where to Eat

SAVANNAH

The art and pleasure of dining stayed home-based in Savannah well into the 20th century. There were few places to dine out and few reasons to do so. You could conduct your business in a restaurant, but not your social life. Savannah's many restaurants show how that has changed. Today, the city is filled with plain and fancy places to eat that are listed alphabetically below. The local population, including thousands of students, is eager to dine out, and late-night delivery is noted. There are many informal cafés, coffee bars, and bistros to sample. The general price range is meant to reflect the cost of a single meal, usually dinner, featuring an appetizer, entrée, dessert, and coffee. Cocktails, beer, wine, gratuity, and tax are not included in the estimated price.

Betty Bombers (912-272-9326; www .bettybombers.com), 1108 Bull Street. It's situated inside American Legion Post 135. Burgers, tacos, wings, chili, fries, and assorted sandwiches are available from lunch to midnight, later on weekends, and can also be delivered. A younger demographic of visitors might choose this fare and its availability, but the restaurant is an excellent example of how creativity is landing in the city. $.

Cha Bella (912-790-7888; www.cha -bella.com), 102 E. Broad Street. Open for dinner, closed Mondays. Organic and locally sourced food from sustainable farms is the theme. The menu changes every day, according to what's growing and at the fish market, truly farm-to-table. American Southern cuisine with a twist, Italian risottos, and herbs of Provence flavor the meals.

This exuberant, modern restaurant has uniquely hit the tone for 21st-century Savannah with its space in a former industrial building and outside seating. $$–$$$.

Circa 1875 (912-443-1875; www.circa 1875.com), 48 Whitaker Street. Open daily except Sundays for dinner or for drinks and appetizers at the bar. Excellent French bistro cuisine and an extensive wine list with many wines by the glass. The pub and adjacent dining room are handsome and have high ceilings, but the white-tablecloth feel is as cozy and welcoming as a known-only-to-locals country inn in the Loire Valley. Grilled meats and poultry, the full array of local vegetables and seafood, and wonderful desserts, which many patrons take at the bar after a performance or gallery walk. $$–$$$.

Clary's Café (912-233-0402; www .claryscafe.com), 404 Abercorn Street. Open daily for breakfast and lunch. A bacon-and-egg sandwich on wheat and coffee is a typical order at Clary's, a downtown eatery where your cup stays filled and breakfast waffles can set you up for the day. At lunch, the Greek salad is big enough to share. *Midnight in the Garden of Good and Evil* fame sent the crowds here, but the traditional "diner" food of burgers, sandwiches, and beverages makes it worth the trip. $.

Crystal Beer Parlor (912-349-1000; www.crystalbeerparlor.com), 301 W. Jones Street. Open daily for lunch and dinner. Located at the end of one of Savannah's prettiest residential streets on the edge of the Historic District, the Crystal is a bar with leather booths and frosted mugs that serves bar food and a legendary crab stew. I'd go at, say, 2 p.m. after a day on your feet, with some exploring left to do before a bigger meal at the end of the day. $–$$.

Foxy Loxy (912-401-0543; www.foxy loxycafe.com), 1919 Bull Street. Besides extra-strong coffee, you can sample Tex-Mex cuisine or cheese boards and indulge in weekend brunch as well as daily meals. Visit the print gallery or hear local musicians in informal evening jam sessions. Indoor and outdoor seating around a firepit, where you can have a wine or beer and feel like a part of the local arts scene. $.

Gallery Espresso (912-233-5348; www.galleryespresso.com), 234 Bull Street. Artists, students, neighborhood residents, and regulars come here for coffee concoctions and many kinds of tea, as well as homemade muffins, bagels, soups, salads, and sandwiches. The gallery supports the work of dozens of artists in the community and features regular shows. $.

Little Duck Diner (912-235-6773; www.littleduckdiner.com), 150 W. Saint Julian Street. Just like any old diner, it's open daily for three meals a day; you can sit in banquettes, on stools, or at stand-alone tables; and there's a tile floor and retro design details. However, what makes the Little Duck Diner unusual is the range of mid-priced meals with upscale additions (avocado toast or vegan options come to mind) and a welcoming atmosphere that doesn't classify you as a tourist or a local, art student or grandparent of said student. They have found a niche where everyone seems content and are enjoying each other's company, which no other place in Savannah or Charleston has managed to capture. $$.

Lulu's Chocolate Bar (912-480-4564; www.luluschocolatebar.com), 42 Martin Luther King Jr. Boulevard. Open daily from midafternoon until midnight, later on weekends. You could go for the happy hour, champagne cocktails, or the specialty martinis, but they're nothing compared to the incredible desserts downtown partygoers savor on their last stop of the evening. It's also a very worthy stop after a Saturday of sightseeing. $.

Mrs. Wilkes' Dining Room (912-232-5997; www.mrswilkes.com), 107 W. Jones Street. Lunch is served on weekdays. The line starts to form well before 11 a.m. This is cooking and serving as it would be at home: diners seated around large tables with heaping platters of fried chicken, baskets of biscuits, and bowls of

OUTDOOR DINING IS POSSIBLE NEARLY YEAR-ROUND AT SAVANNAH'S CITY MARKET VISIT SAVANNAH

slaw, vegetables, red rice, and black-eyed peas or green beans placed before them. If you've ever been grateful for the kindness of strangers, the one who gives you the last chicken leg could be your friend for life. No credit cards. $$.

Olympia Café (912-233-3131; www.olympiacafe.net), 5 E. River Street. Open daily for lunch and dinner. River Street is not subtle, with bars, gift shops, and crowds, but it's fun, and this family-friendly, reliable restaurant honors the heritage and contributions of Savannah's Greek community. There are Mediterranean appetizers like dolmadakia, gyros and kabobs; traditional Greek dishes like lemon chicken and moussaka; as well as vegan options and a large selection of desserts. $$.

The Grey (912-662-5999; thegreyrestaurant.com), 109 Martin Luther King Jr. Boulevard. Open for dinner except Mondays, with extended hours at its Diner Bar and for take-out at The Grey Market. Chef Mashama Bailey spent her youth in and around Savannah, where she learned and loved the cooking of her extended family, and then had classical training and stints in New York restaurants. She knows farm-to-table cuisine and the people who provide the harvest. Her restaurant celebrates fresh, local ingredients in dishes that are sorted by categories like pantry, dirt, water, and pasture. She's been nominated for James Beard Awards, and she and her partners radically restored a 1938 bus station where Southern food meets modern flair. $–$$$.

The Olde Pink House (912-232-4286; www.theoldepinkhouserestaurant.com), 23 Abercorn Street. Open for lunch and dinner Tues.–Sat. Arches, its bar that opens into a garden, is a wonderful spot to relax starting in midafternoon. It offers a limited, less expensive menu and signature cocktails and is also a lively place to drop in after dinner. The elegant Georgian mansion was restored in 2019. A beloved local place, its most popular dishes include she-crab soup, crispy

scored flounder with apricot glaze, and grilled pork tenderloin with bourbon molasses. $–$$$.

Rancho Alegre (912-292-1656; www.ranchoalegrecuban.com), 402 Martin Luther King Jr. Boulevard. Open daily for lunch and dinner, when live jazz is played at a comfortable volume. The menu is Cuban, Caribbean, and Spanish and features 27 entrées and combinations, which include yucca, plantains, and, of course, rice and beans and mojo sauce. There are long tables to seat multigenerational families, for which this restaurant is a joyous favorite. $$.

Wright Square Café (912-238-1150; www.wrightsquarecafe.com), 21 W. York Street. Open Mon.–Sat. for breakfast and into the late afternoon. Lunch is popular, to eat in or take out, and features paninis, salads, and wraps. Chocolates, books, and gifts line the shelves. Located on a square with several shops for antiques, upscale clothing, and home furnishings. $.

TYBEE ISLAND

The Breakfast Club (912-786-5984; www.thebreakfastclubtybee.com), 1500 Butler Avenue. Here is the kicked-back lifestyle of Tybee, sitting among locals at booths and tables set close together. You might run into the shrimpers coming in or the early anglers and birders just setting out. If you want to get a jump on the day or take a quiet walk on a deserted morning beach, this is a great place to start, with menu selections and combinations that run four pages. There will be a line on weekends or by midmorning. $.

Crab Shack at Chimney Creek (912-786-9857; www.thecrabshack.com), 40 Estill Hammock Road (second right past Lazaretto Creek Bridge). The setting couldn't be more informal—it used to be a fish camp—and welcoming, which is good, because there's usually a line and no reservations are accepted. There are three bars, indoor and outdoor seating, a water feature where you can feed

BREAKFAST ON THE PORCH IN SAVANNAH VISIT SAVANNAH

baby alligators, a gift shack, and an aviary with rescued birds. Daily lunch and dinner menus offer seafood done several ways as well as barbecue pork, ribs, and grilled chicken. The Crab Shack is pet friendly, and they also love families. $–$$.

Gerald's Pig and Shrimp (912-786-4227; www.tybeebbq.com), US 80 at McKenzie Street. This roadside restaurant is undergoing renovations, so check the website for hours, but if you like pig and shrimp and hushpuppies, it is for you and your family. It's the height of informal, and the owner and servers are accommodating and just plain nice. The surf-and-turf baskets, pulled pork sandwiches, ribs, fried oysters, and peel-your-own shrimp draw the most discriminating locals. $–$$.

North Beach Bar & Grill (912-786-4442; www.northbeachbarandgrill .net), 33 Meddin Drive. Set very modestly by the Tybee Lighthouse, it serves Cuban- and Caribbean-styled pork, fish, plantains, and rice for lunch and dinner. Sandy feet and flip-flops are typical, and

local bands play regularly. The beer is cheap, the portions are large, and, if you have to wait, the service is laid-back. It's in a beautiful spot. $–$$.

Sundae Café (912-786-7694; www .sundaecafe.com), 304 First Street. Open Mon.–Sat. for lunch and dinner. Don't let the strip mall exterior fool you: this is a small gem. The owners have transformed a former ice cream parlor into a destination for those in the know. Their menu is inspired Southern, focusing on steaks and seafood. The crispy scored flounder, filet mignon, and shrimp and grits inspire a loyal following. Call ahead for reservations. $$$.

✳ Entertainment

For comprehensive entertainment listings, see *Connect Savannah* (www .connectsavannah.com), a weekly arts and entertainment paper.

Jazz'd (912-236-7777; www.jazzd savannah.com), 52 Barnard Street. Live music performed Tues.–Sun. in a downstairs venue. The food is served tapas style, with more than two dozen small plates to choose from, accompanied by selections from an extensive bar.

Lucas Theatre for the Arts (912-525-5051; www.lucastheatre.com), 32 Abercorn Street. An old movie palace features films and musical performances from symphony repertoire to rock and theatricals. It's one venue for the fall SCAD Savannah Film Festival. Check website for current opening information.

Savannah Music Festival (912-525-5050; www.savannahmusicfestival.org). A terrific jazz, blues, classical, and world music festival that takes place for about two weeks in March and April at churches, halls, clubs, and auditoriums around the city. It's a mini-Spoleto that draws music aficionados from all over.

Savannah Stopover (www.savannahstopover.com). A 3-day festival designed for 50-plus bands heading to SXSW in Austin every March, it brings buoyancy and big energy to the city through more than 80 performances.

The Jinx (912-236-2281; thejinx912.com), 127 W. Congress Street. By City Market, this is most popular bar and music venue to hear local, regional, and national rock and alternative bands.

✳ Selective Shopping

There's not much you can't buy in Savannah, from collard greens to a gilded armoire to edgy art. Concentrate on Whitaker Street, Broughton Street, Abercorn Street, Wright Square, and Ellis Square. River Street is the most generic and geared toward tourists. Parking meters are checked regularly. Walk, take the free trolley service, or purchase a parking pass.

ANTIQUES There are antiques of every period and style available, or a dealer will find what you want, whether you live in a sleek, minimalist apartment or a farmhouse, or want to create a look for a second home. My experience is that

SHOPPING ON RIVER STREET VISIT SAVANNAH

Savannah demonstrates a greater capacity of imagination than Charleston about how to decorate and accessorize a home. The axiom that residents love old things because they don't have to like the new ones is an argument that Savannah challenges in interesting ways.

Bull Street Estate Sales & Consignments (912-443-9353; www.bull streetestatesales.com), 2819 Bull Street. Open Thurs.–Sat. and Mon., the shop has a constantly revolving stock of furniture, rugs, decorative items, art, and collectibles that appears on consignment or from their estate sales.

Alex Raskin Antiques (912-232-8205; www.alexraskinantiques.com), 441 Bull Street. If the setting in the Noble-Hardee mansion on Monterey Square isn't enough to get your attention, then the inventory will. Among the big, older antique vendors, it's a little more laid-back in that the furniture, rugs, paintings, and light fixtures simply overflow the space.

Pinch of the Past (912-232-5563; www.pinchofthepast.com), 2603 Whitaker Street at 43rd Street. Open Tues.–Sat. Architectural fragments and vintage house parts, including antique ironwork, doorframes, columns, mantels, lighting fixtures, hardware, and salvaged pieces, constitute an incredible inventory.

V & J Duncan (912-232-0338; www .vjduncan.com), 12 E. Taylor Street. You could browse for hours through the files and piles of prints, maps, old advertising art, etchings, botanicals, and illustrations.

BOOKS **The Book Lady** (912-233-3628; www.thebookladybookstore.com), 6 E. Liberty Street. Open daily and selling new, used, and antique or collectible volumes in every genre you can imagine.

E. Shaver, Bookseller (912-234-7257; www.eshaverbooks.com), 326 Bull Street. It's the best general bookstore in the region, sponsors readings and events, and has sustained its independent business for more than 40 years.

Ex Libris (912-525-7550; www.bkstr .com/savannahstore/home), 228 Martin Luther King Jr. Boulevard. This three-story bookstore provides course books and art supplies for students at the Savannah College of Art and Design, as well as general fiction and nonfiction. They also sell laptops and new and used tech products.

CLOTHING **Custard Boutique** (912-232-4733; www.custardboutique.com), 422 Whitaker Street. The boutique caters to women of all sizes who are looking for casual/fashionable outfits, accessories, jewelry, and shoes that suit their personalities. They carry some men's and children's clothing, too.

Rivers & Glen (912-349-2352; www .riversandglen.com), 24 Drayton Street. A seller of high-end outdoor brands for active hunters and fly fishermen, like Orvis and Barbour, the store also sells casual wear and accessories for men and women who want to look good in the outdoors.

Terra Cotta (912-236-6150; terracottasavannah.com), 34 Barnard Street. Elegant, soft cottons for the bed and bath. Also, simply cut, stylish casual wear, including some vintage.

FARMS AND FARMERS' MARKETS **Forsyth Farmers' Market** (forsyth farmersmarket.com) is located at the entrance of Forsyth Park and E. Park Avenue downtown. Open Sat., it attracts food purveyors of all kinds and also serves as a place where the community gathers. **Brighter Day** (912-236-4703; www.brighterdayfoods.com), 1102 Bull Street, a short walk away, is a health-food store and organic deli featuring a full line of breads, produce, natural foods, juices, and supplements as well as fresh sandwiches that you could buy and eat while you stroll the market.

HOME GOODS Two sections of the city have emerged as centers of home furnishing/decoration. One is the **Downtown Design District,** located on

Whitaker Street between Charlton and Gordon Streets, and the other is the **Starland Design District**, just south of downtown between 37th and 41st Streets, from Whitaker to Habersham. The furnishings can be sleek and modern, hand-painted, antique, rustic, or representing the best in modern lighting fixtures.

ARCANUMmarket (912-236-6000; www.arcanummarket.com), 346 Whitaker Street. The designers here have a way of mixing the old with the contemporary.

One Fish Two Fish (912-447-4600; www.onefishstore.com), 401 Whitaker Street. Painted chairs, benches, floor cloths, and household accents are mixed with antiques, jewelry, and custom furniture.

The Paris Market & Brocante (912-232-1500; www.theparismarket.com), 36 W. Broughton Street. A curatorial eye that presents everything from fragrances, linens, and candles to country antiques, paper goods, and garden decorations animates this store, which is probably the city's broadest and best in terms of inventory. Tucked in a restored commercial space is a little café with pastries, coffee, and wine. Worth it to browse and get ideas for your home, even if all you buy is French milled soap.

24e Design Company (912-233-2274; www.24estyle.com), 24 E. Broughton Street. Modern, distressed, re-created, and whimsical furniture fills the floors in an old brick building. A changing group of smaller pieces by local and regional artists is also on sale.

✳ Special Events

SPRING *March*: **St. Patrick's Day Parade** Savannah claims a substantial Irish heritage and celebrates it with abandon. Mobs of people turn out to watch the downtown parade, which starts at 10 a.m. and dominates all other city activity for the day and night.

Savannah Music Festival (912-525-5050; www.savannahmusicfestival.org), 216 E. Broughton Street. Fifteen days of jazz, blues, folk, international, and classical music performances are held in the Historic District at multiple venues. It's another example of how lots of genres or styles thrive side by side in the city.

Savannah Stopover (478-254-0888; www.savannahstopover.com). More than 50 acts, some up-and-coming and others traditional favorites, flow through Savannah for a weekend in early March on their way to the South by Southwest Festival in Austin. They perform in venues throughout the Historic District and outdoors. Check the website for schedules and tickets.

Savannah Tour of Homes and Gardens (912-234-8054; www.savannah tourofhomes.org), 2020 Bull Street. Each day of the three-day tour features a different neighborhood to explore at your own pace, with guides and docents on hand to answer questions. You can expect to cover about eight sites, including churches and museums, in a three-hour period. Homes and gardens are not generally handicapped accessible.

Hidden Gardens of Savannah (912-447-3879; www.gardenclubofsavannah .org). A small gem, usually featuring fewer than 10 walled gardens, but all treasures, located north of Gwinnett Street and informally called the NOGS Tour.

May: **Savannah Scottish Games and Highland Gathering** (www.savannah scottishgames.com). The community celebrates its Scottish heritage in reenactments, games, piping parades, highland dancing, traditional competitions, and farming and food presentations. Nominal admission.

FALL *September*: **Savannah Jazz Festival** (912-228-3158; www.savannahjazz.org). All styles of blues and jazz played for several days throughout the city, including two dozen free concerts. Hotels and

RIVER STREET IS KNOWN FOR SPONTANEOUS LIVELINESS

THE FAMOUS ST. PATRICK'S DAY PARADE IN SAVANNAH VISIT SAVANNAH

restaurants offer special discounts to visitors in ticket packages.

October/November: **SCAD Savannah Film Festival** (912-525-5051; filmfest .scad.edu). Screenings, lectures, panels, workshops, and receptions last for a week. Basic passes start at $75, and more expensive passes scale up to $500 or more.

This premier event showcases emerging filmmakers and veterans in every genre, selected through competition. If you're interested in film artistry, check the website to purchase tickets before they sell out; if that's not your focus, note that many places to stay and eat in Savannah will be booked at that time.

OPPOSITE: THE DOCKS ON DAUFUSKIE ISLAND LOWCOUNTRY & RESORT ISLANDS TOURISM COMMISSION

BEAUFORT, EDISTO
& BLUFFTON

BEAUFORT, EDISTO & BLUFFTON

The fields, creeks, sandy roads, and spreading marshes of the rural Lowcountry, the place where its history began, have once again become a center of attention. Along the coast from Charleston to Savannah, there is an increasing awareness of what the culture of the countryside, expressed in a lifetime of habits and rituals, has meant to the two great cities that bookend the region and present themselves like magnificent finished products. It is most clearly seen in the areas around Beaufort—Lady's Island, St. Helena Island, and Port Royal—on Edisto Island, and in the Old Town village of Bluffton.

It took years for them to recover from the Civil War, the boll weevil, and a broken agricultural economy, but recover they have, as places where vistas and fields are valued as much as brickwork, porches, and Palladian windows. Although Beaufort, in particular, is a destination itself, driving or bicycling on Edisto Island or St. Helena Island—through the landscape of small homes and churches, across narrow creeks, by "rabbit-box" stores, farm and fish stands, and packing houses—puts the cities and the wealth that produced them in context.

Beaufort

Beaufort has been a small town for a long time. Spanish and French explorers came to the area 100 years before the Pilgrims landed at Plymouth Rock; English and Scottish settlers followed. The city of Beaufort is itself on Port Royal Island, one of more than 65 islands that make up Beaufort County. Other islands accessible by car with points of interest include St. Helena, Lady's, Dataw, Harbor, Hunting, Fripp, Cat, Parris, Bray's, Lemon, and Pinckney.

Formally founded in 1711, Beaufort was a frontier settlement and trading center, attacked at times by Yemassee Indians, beset with illness, and populated by the scrupulous and unscrupulous. Resources were plentiful: Beaufort's outlying lands sustained dense forests, which gave up shipbuilding timber and naval stores; vast tracts of land suitable for raising cattle and crops like corn, potatoes, indigo, rice, and cotton; and rich marshes to feed fowl and game. The maze of waterways provided fish and shellfish in abundance.

Beaufort was bustling before the American Revolution, although the first boom came immediately after the war. The stability of the newly independent country; the increase in population (both enslaved and free); the migration of New England merchants and families; and the successful cultivation of highly marketable long staple Sea Island cotton and the development of the cotton gin near Savannah lit the fuse. An explosion of wealth launched Beaufort's heyday. It was a time of building houses and churches in town and developing cotton plantations and plantation households on the islands.

A visitor can see the legacies of this period throughout Beaufort, particularly in a neighborhood called The Point, an astonishing collection of houses and gardens

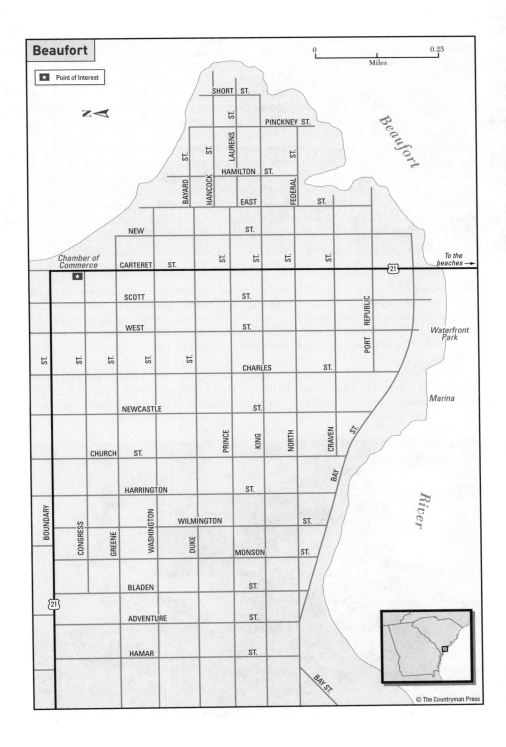

Beauufort

0   0.25

Miles

★   Point of Interest

N

SHORT ST.

PINCKNEY ST.

LAURENS ST.

BAYARD ST.

HANCOCK ST.

HAMILTON ST.

FEDERAL ST.

EAST ST.

NEW ST.

Chamber of Commerce

CARTERET ST.

★

SCOTT ST.

WEST ST.

ST.

CHARLES ST.

NEWCASTLE ST.

PRINCE

KING

NORTH

CRAVEN

PORT REPUBLIC

CHURCH ST.

HARRINGTON ST.

BAY ST.

BOUNDARY

CONGRESS

GREENE

WASHINGTON

DUKE

WILMINGTON ST.

MONSON ST.

BLADEN ST.

ADVENTURE ST.

HAMAR ST.

BAY ST.

Beauufort

River

Waterfront Park

Marina

To the beaches →

21

21

© The Countryman Press

COVID-19

Due to the COVID-19 pandemic, travel in the Lowcountry, as everywhere else, requires more planning for every activity to ensure appropriate social distancing. This means that you should call or check a venue's website to confirm, among other things, if reservations are required where walk-in activity was once the norm. It also means that providers of services from hotels to restaurants or boat rides to carriage tours are likely to be running their businesses differently from in the past, with fewer visitors engaged at any one time. If you are a family group, be sure to mention that, because it may make a difference in the business owner's risk calculations. Ask if there is outdoor seating available at restaurants—many venues have changed their layouts to include more outside dining while they reduce the numbers of tables inside. Meals to go, food service delivery, and curbside pick-up options have expanded dramatically in the spring and summer of 2020; check to see if those options are still available. Annual events, including professional golf and tennis tournaments and house and garden tours, have shifted their dates and ticketing procedures. You'll have a more rewarding travel experience if you arrive prepared and flexible.

embowered by live oaks. Standing in Beaufort's Waterfront Park, it is easy to imagine a 19th-century scene come to life as dozens of schooners, bateaux, and cotton box barges, brimming with crops, timber, mail, cotton, animals, passengers, produce, and the latest in English fashion and furniture, load or unload goods. There was a lot of activity, for like other societies made newly rich, Beaufort's had a taste for luxury and indulged it.

That changed abruptly. In another time and place, the shelling of a nearby federal fort (in this case Fort Sumter in Charleston Harbor), and the response to it, might have produced a shred of hesitation as to the wisdom of the secessionist rebellion.

A 42-POUND CANNON AT FORT SUMTER NATIONAL MONUMENT © VISIONSOFMAINE/ISTOCKPHOTO.COM

Not so in Beaufort: With great surprise on November 7, 1861, white residents took flight—leaving hot food on the table, the story goes—from Yankee troops who swiftly demolished the Confederate port defenses at Bay Point and on Hilton Head Island at the mouth of Port Royal Sound.

Thus the occupation began. Soon the grand old houses were being used as hospitals and headquarters. The area was under military command. Pickets were posted at the outskirts of town and along creeks and boat landings: Some on guard duty watched the smoke of rebel campfires across the water. Plantations were turned over to Union regiments, who appropriated the livestock and horses, and the liquor, furniture, wagons, and food crops.

By April 1862, the first wave of Northern abolitionists had arrived with a mandate to live in and manage the plantations and teach the former slaves to read and write, to "prepare them for freedom." Their enterprise, which was funded by private missionary societies in the North and carried out with the approval of the federal government, came to be called the Port Royal Experiment. In a sense this was an early Peace Corps, in which idealistic, mostly young men and women volunteered to assist a cause they believed in under conditions they were not used to in a culture they were unfamiliar with. Their efforts affected opportunities for freedmen that resonate today, in particular at Penn Center on St. Helena Island, an important institution for education and empowerment for more than 150 years.

In the years following the Civil War, promises made were usually promises broken. Some former slaves were given land; some bought tracts individually and communally; some worked the old fields under a new owner. A nascent phosphate mining industry provided jobs for a while but eventually collapsed. The terrible hurricane of 1893, in which some 5,000 islanders died, soured Sea Island soil for fine cotton plants. The scourge of the boll weevil in the 1920s dimmed the last hope of large-scale cotton production. Commercial truck farming and a seafood processing industry eventually took its place. Photographs from the early 1900s and those taken even as late as 1936 by employees of the federal Farm Security Administration—Walker Evans and Marion Post Wolcott among them—showed islanders dressed in rags and living in shacks with matted palmetto fronds for roofs, and the large houses in town on the far side of shabby gentility. These were the years of unpaved roads, bare feet, and few cars, when white people were "too poor to paint, too proud to whitewash." In 1969, Beaufort County was still one of the poorest counties in the United States, the focus of a "hunger tour" by several US senators.

It is hard to believe that today's downtown Beaufort ever suffered reverses. The paint doesn't dare peel. The town has been discovered and lands on "Best of" lists every year, including recognition as having a strong gallery scene that supports local artists and an annual film festival in February that is highly regarded and often sells out. Yet it retains a small-scale charm. On your own by foot or carriage makes an easy day of touring; with a car you could include St. Helena Island sites or Hunting Island State Park as well (see *To See*).

A CHAPTER ENDS IN 1862

There is something very sad about these fine deserted houses. Ours has Egyptian marble mantels, gilt cornice and centerpiece in parlor, and bathroom, with several wash-bowls set in different rooms. The force-pump is broken and all the bowls and their marble slabs smashed to get out the plated cocks. . . . Bureaus, commodes, and wardrobes are smashed in, as well as door panels, to get out the contents of the drawers and lockers, which I suppose contained some wine and ale, judging by the broken bottles lying about. The officers saved a good many pianos and other furniture and stored it in the jail for safe-keeping. But we kindle our fires with chips of polished mahogany, and I am writing on my knee with a piece of flower stand across them for a table, sitting on my camp bedstead.
— Edward S. Philbrick to his wife in Brookline, Massachusetts. Written from Beaufort, March 9, 1862 (from *Letters from Port Royal 1862–1868*, Elizabeth Ware Pearson, ed. [New York: Arno Press, 1969])

There is also an ongoing, robust dialogue among residents about the goals of growth, both physical and economic, and preservation. At the heart of the matter is how to develop new homes and small-scale commercial areas by filling in parts of the old downtown contained in the 304-acre National Historic Landmark District. Beaufort has become a laboratory for the ideas of New Urbanism and is now a destination not only for tourists interested in history but also for planners trying to understand how to invent new places on the scaffolding of the old without causing gentrification, displacement in African American neighborhoods, and loss of open space.

The Beaufort area (and the coastal region in general) is an accessible locale—a classroom really, with sites and landscapes—to learn about Gullah Geechee culture. It is part of a federally designated heritage area (www.visitgullahgeechee.com), and many advisors who have helped develop programming are natives of Beaufort County who have deep knowledge of the community.

The nearby **Village of Port Royal** (www.oldvillageport royal.com) has an open feel, where Paris Avenue, the main thoroughfare, runs from Ribaut Road to the old port of Port Royal, now under major residential and commercial redevelopment. A left turn at its end leads to The Sands, a public beach that attracts fishermen and hunters of fossilized shark teeth. There is also a wooden viewing structure that offers excellent views of Battery Creek and Parris Island. The **Cypress Wetlands and Rookery** boardwalks are easily accessed—parking is widely available—and worth spending an hour touring, followed by visiting the town's several boutiques and restaurants (see *Where to Eat*). The website has a useful interactive map and schedule of annual events, which are delightfully funky and include free street concerts.

The area has also had its Hollywood moments: Two of native son Pat Conroy's novels have been filmed here, *The Great Santini* (1979) and *The Prince of Tides* (1991), as well as *The Big Chill* (1983) and scenes in *Forrest Gump* (1994) and *Forces of Nature* (1999). *Daughters of the Dust* (1991) and Ron and Natalie Daise's acclaimed TV series for children, *Gullah Gullah Island* (1994–1998), were set on the islands.

GETTING THERE Beaufort is 65 miles from Charleston, 45 miles from Savannah, and 30 miles from the north end of Hilton Head. The easiest route by air is via the **Savannah/Hilton Head International Airport** (912-964-0514; www.savannahairport .com), which is about an hour away and served by many major carriers and rental car agencies. **Charleston International Airport** (843-767-7000; www.iflychs.com) is about 90 minutes away.

By car: From Charleston, access Beaufort from US 17 to US 21; from Savannah (and other points north and south) via well-marked exits on I-95; from Hilton Head via US 278 to SC 170. **AMTRAK** (800-872-7245; www.amtrak.com) passes through Yemassee, about 30 miles north of Beaufort, with one northbound and one southbound train stop each day. A cab or other transportation is necessary to reach Beaufort and the islands. **Happy Taxi Cab Co.** (843-575-5000; www.happycabco.com), or **ADR Taxi Cab** (843-726-5191; www.adrtaxi.com) offer train, bus, and airport transportation, scheduled in advance. **Greyhound** (843-524-4646; www.greyhound.com) stops in Beaufort several times a day and is a short drive from downtown. Also see **What's Where in Charleston, Savannah & Coastal Islands** in the opening pages of this book.

✳ To See

ART Atelier on Bay (843-470-0266; www.atelieronbay.com), 203 West Street. Open Mon.–Sat. Home to 14 artists who are okay with you visiting their studios while they are at work and viewing or purchasing artwork. It's on the second floor of a simply renovated department store that faces Bay Street, a beloved family institution that was in business for more than 100 years. It's not overpolished, with high ceilings and sloping heart pine floors.

Beaufort Art Association Gallery (843-521-4444; www.beaufortartassociation.com), 913 Bay Street. Open Mon.–Sat. and most Sundays. The spacious storefront gallery has been a mainstay of the arts scene for 50 years. It hosts annual juried events, shows of featured artists, art walks and lectures, and original works from more than 100 members, including pottery, prints, jewelry, sculpture, photography, painting, and mixed media.

THE BEAUTIFUL BEAUFORT INN AT NIGHT GREATER BEAUFORT-PORT ROYAL CONVENTION &VISITORS BUREAU (BANKER OPTICAL MEDIA)

THE 18TH-CENTURY ARSENAL IN BEAUFORT © GINGER WAREHAM/PICKLEJUICE.COM

Charles Street Gallery (843-521-9054; www.thecharlesstreetgallery.com), 914 Charles Street. Closed Sundays. The gallery, with a garden to the side, presents an eclectic range of work that strays from the usual, with a more modern inflection to regional landscapes. An artists' community has grown here, including poets and writers. Full-service framing and regularly scheduled gallery shows.

Pinckney Simons Gallery (843-379-4774; www.ipsgallery.com), 711 Bay Street. Closed Sundays. This gallery is more polished than homegrown, represents established artists from the southeast, and offers art collecting and consulting services.

Rhett Gallery (843-524-3339; www.rhettgallery.com), 901 Bay Street. Prints and watercolors of the Lowcountry by Nancy Ricker Rhett and family, as well as antique first-edition prints and maps, Civil War and nautical materials, and hand-colored engravings.

HISTORIC AND RELIGIOUS SITES **Baptist Church of Beaufort** (843-524-3197; www.bcob.org), 601 Charles Street. This is an 1844 Greek Revival beauty. The ceiling plasterwork and ornamented cornices seem to match—in their absolute, solid mass of decoration—the abundant self-confidence of the prosperous little town of Beaufort in its heyday.

Beaufort History Museum (843-379-3079; www.beauforthistorymuseum.wildapricot.org), 713 Craven Street. Open Mon.–Sat. Housed in an arsenal built in 1799, the museum provides a comprehensive overview of the area through displays of photographs, artifacts, documents, and well-executed wall panels that trace Beaufort's history from earliest settlement to the present day. There is a rigorous training program for docents who are on-site to answer your questions. Admission $7, kids under 10 free.

Chapel of Ease, Lands End Road, St. Helena Island. The ruins of this planters' church, built in the 1740s to serve worshippers far from town, are of brick and tabby, a construction material that blends oyster shells with lime, sand, and water. The site is a wonderful place for photographs—spooky in the fog or at dawn, mellow and ageless at dusk. Just past Penn Center on the left.

John Mark Verdier House Museum (843-379-6335; www.historicbeaufort.org), 801 Bay Street. Tours are every 30 minutes, Mon.–Sat. The showcase property of the Historic Beaufort Foundation, saved from demolition in 1945, was built for a local merchant around 1805 according to the Adam-influenced decoration and floor plans of the day. It includes a formal parlor and ballroom, ornamental fireplace friezes, carved moldings, and antiques that are original both to the family and to the period of the house. Ongoing research and an exhibit area on the ground floor provide nuanced interpretations of Beaufort and the islands. A small gift shop is on-site.

Penn Center and the York W. Bailey Museum (843-838-2474; www.penncenter.com), Martin Luther King Jr. Drive, St. Helena Island. Open Mon.–Sat. Founded in 1862 by two Pennsylvania women as a school for the newly freed slaves, Penn has remained a vital institution to promote education, self-sufficiency, and cultural expression among native islanders. In the days of segregation, it was one place where Black and white people could meet together, as they did when the Rev. Martin Luther King Jr. planned his March on Washington. The York W. Bailey Museum holds a collection of cultural artifacts, African objects, and paintings, and a bookstore sells sweetgrass baskets, quilts, and books on Gullah culture and history. The entire campus is a National Historic Landmark and, most recently, a site in the National Park Service's Reconstruction Era National Historical Park. Museum admission: adults $7, children $5. Maps for a self-guided campus tour are available.

Old Sheldon Church Ruins, SC 235, 1.7 miles north of the US 17/US 21 intersection between Gardens Corners and Yemassee. Beautiful brick columns, fragile arches, and sill slabs remain from a church that was burned twice, first by the British in 1779 and then by the Union Army in 1865. It's a temple in the woods and very evocative. A fence was installed in 2019 that limits access into the ruins because of preservation concerns, but you can still see and feel this special place. A long-term plan is in the works to have docents on-site.

Parish Church of St. Helena (an Anglican Congregation), (843-522-1712; www.sthelenas1712.org), 505 Church Street. Built of brick from England in 1724, the church is adorned inside with graceful columns, upstairs galleries, and tall, multipaned

TABBY RUINS OF THE CHAPEL OF EASE, ST. HELENA ISLAND, WHERE PLANTERS WORSHIPPED IN THE 19TH CENTURY

windows with deep sills on which rest buckets of blossoming magnolias, daffodils, or narcissi in season. Its shaded, walled churchyard makes for a lovely stroll with a guide you can download from the website. Check also for the schedule of organ concerts on Fridays at noon.

Reconstruction Era National Historical Park Visitor Center (404-507-5868; www .nps.gov/reer), 706 Craven Street. Open Tues.–Sat. The modest headquarters and information hub of the newly designated park, which currently consists of several sites central to the transformative postwar period. Pick up maps, browse the exhibit, and check the schedule for free guided tours and programming.

Tabernacle Baptist Church, 907 Craven Street. A striking, white clapboard building with bell tower. In its churchyard lies the grave—and stands a fine bust—of Robert Smalls, who was born a slave, engineered a daring ship capture during the Civil War, and was later a congressman and significant figure in Beaufort's Reconstruction period.

MILITARY MUSEUMS AND SITES Beaufort National Cemetery (843-524-3925; www .cem.va.gov), 1601 Boundary Street. Created by President Lincoln in 1863 for victims of Southern battles, this 29-acre cemetery is the final resting place of some 7,500 Union soldiers from black and white regiments and more than 100 Confederates. It is still in service and is beautifully landscaped; it is listed on the National Register of Historic Places.

Fort Fremont Historical Preserve (www.fortfremont.org), Lands End, St. Helena Island. Built in 1898 to protect the coast during the Spanish-American War, the 15-acre preserve on Port Royal Sound, including fort ruins amid a classic maritime forest of oaks, palmetto, magnolia, and myrtle, is being refurbished with an interpretative center and new programming and exhibits. Follow US 21 about 7 miles from Beaufort. Turn right at the traffic light on Martin Luther King Jr. Boulevard (it becomes Lands End Road) and proceed 7.75 miles to the entrance on the right. The park was closed for construction , so check the website for news about its reopening.

Parris Island Museum (843-228-2951; www.historyofmarines.org), Marine Corps Recruit Depot, Parris Island. Open Mon.–Sat., with extended hours on graduation and family days. The museum showcases the history and development of the area on which the famous "boot camp" stands, from its earliest settlement through contemporary recruit training. Artifacts on display have been recovered from the Spanish village of Santa Elena, circa 1566; from Charlesfort, a French outpost established by Jean Ribaut in 1562; and from Fort San Marcos, circa 1576. (Excavation continues at these sites, located near the depot golf course.) Exhibits of uniforms, personal items, weapons, drawings, and documents trace the history of the Marine Corps in its worldwide engagements. You can also consult platoon books for listings of Marines and visit the gift shop. Self-guided driving tour maps are available at the Douglas Visitor Center (843-228-3650; www.mcrdpi.marines.mil), which should be your first stop. It is open on weekdays. You may also picnic in designated areas or have an inexpensive meal at a base restaurant, including the Officers' Club. This is an active military base. At the

FRISSELL HALL, PENN CENTER, ST. HELENA ISLAND, WHERE COMMUNITY SINGS AND MEETINGS CELEBRATE A HISTORY OF EDUCATION AND EMPOWERMENT FOR AFRICAN AMERICANS

entrance gate be prepared to show a photo ID, vehicle registration, and proof of vehicle insurance, and state your desire to visit the museum and visitor center. Free.

Santa Elena History Center (843-379-1550; www.santa-elena.org), 1501 Bay Street. Open Tues.–Sat. Its mission is to expand the story of North American colonization, which occurred here by the Spanish 40 years before the English settled Jamestown. Exhibits, costumed interpreters, and annual events provide insight into the first European colonial capital. Adults $10, students and kids $5.

✳ To Do

For a small town, Beaufort has a remarkable number of ways for visitors to get to know and enjoy it on land and by water; under your own power by foot, bike, or kayak; or in minivans, small skiffs, and large boats. Some businesses provide multiple modes of transportation, and many offer private tours. You can spend 55 minutes in a horse-drawn carriage or a half day on a fishing expedition. If you can tear yourself away from the seductions of the built environment, you will be rewarded by views of marshes and marine life that exist in such a pristine state in only a few places in the United States. For general information on touring and recreation opportunities, check out the **Visitor Center** (843-525-8500; www.beaufortsc.org) at 713 Craven Street, located in the historic Beaufort Arsenal. Reservations are recommended for all tours. The best event calendar and all-around source for information and suggestions about what to do is at www.eatsleepplaybeaufort.com. A list of annual events for Beaufort, Bluffton, and Edisto is at the end of the chapter.

BY CARRIAGE **Sea Island Carriage Company** (843-476-7789; www.seaislandcarriagecompany.com), 930 Bay Street, and the cleverly named **Southurn Rose Buggy Tours** (843-524-2900; www.southurnrose.com), 1002 Bay Street, depart from the downtown marina parking lot daily. Tours last about an hour. Adults $23, children $10.

BY FOOT **Beaufort Gray Line Tours** (843-473-7107; www.beaufortgrayline.com), 209 Charles Street, offers walking tours lasting around two hours with guides dressed in period costumes covering different paths in the Historic District. Adults from $20.

Janet's Walking History Tour (843-226-4412; www.janetswalkinghistory.com), 1006 Bay Street, takes visitors through the Historic District for two hours once a day. Adults $25.

BY VAN **Beaufort Tours** (843-838-2746; www.beauforttoursllc.com) introduces you to the writer Pat Conroy's Beaufort, important Reconstruction locales, settings for films, and historic buildings. Adult tickets start at $20, children $10.

Gullah-N-Geechie Mahn Tours (843-838-7516; www.gullahngeechietours.net) run Mon.–Sat. Adults $32–$42, depending on the length of the tours, which specialize in St. Helena Island sites and African American history. Reservations required.

The Spirit of Old Beaufort Heritage Tour (see **Beaufort Gray Line Tours**) also offers three-hour van tours of St. Helena that include visits to a praise house, Penn Center, and a view of a plantation house at the end of a half-mile avenue of oaks. Adults $40, children $20.

BY BOAT **Captain Dick's River Tours** (843-812-2804; www.beaufortrivertours.com). Departing from the downtown marina, the comfortable pontoon boat cruises the Beaufort River every afternoon for a 75-minute narrated trip, where you'll see dolphins and

PORT ROYAL SANDS BOARDWALK GREATER BEAUFORT PORT ROYAL CONVENTION & VISITORS BUREAU (BANKER OPTICAL MEDIA)

old houses and learn the local ecology; and for two hours on Tuesday and Saturday evenings to catch the sunset. Adults $20–$28, children $12.

Lowcountry Photo Safaris (843-524-3037; www.horanphoto.com). Join Eric Horan, a professional wildlife photographer and master naturalist, in a group of five people or fewer on a 19-foot skiff to discover and photograph the amazing array of waterfowl, shorebirds, birds of prey, and marine life that the marsh, beach, sky, and maritime forest offer. Photographers at all skill levels are welcome, and he shares tips from decades of experience. A three-hour private tour starts at $300 for one person to $475 for five; a public tour starts at $120 per person. They are designed to capture the best light, usually early morning or late afternoon, and according to wind, weather, and tides. A successful trip requires advance planning, and schedules are outlined monthly on his website, as are images from his luxurious coffee-table books.

BY KAYAK Trail guides and other information about regional paddling in the ACE Basin and nearby rivers are available through the **Lowcountry & Resort Islands Tourism Commission** (843-717-3090; www.southcarolinalowcountry.com). The **Southeast Coast Saltwater Paddling Trail** (www.secoastpaddlingtrail.com) connects 800 miles of waterway from the Chesapeake Bay to the Georgia/Florida border through sections in South Carolina. Beaufort has its own 12.6-mile round-trip, self-guided trail (www.beaufortblueways.info) that runs along the Beaufort River.

Beaufort Kayak Tours (843-525-0810; www.beaufortkayaktours.com). Trips in and around Beaufort, on the barrier islands, and in the ACE Basin are suitable for beginners to experts and include at least two hours on the water, often stopping on a sandbar for a swim. Single and tandem kayaks are available. Adults $50, children $35.

Beaufort Lands End Tours (615-243-4684; www.beaufortlandsendpaddling.net), 1152 Sea Island Parkway. As you travel on US 21 to the beach you'll see, about 8 miles from town, a fanciful cottage with outdoor sculpture and stacked kayaks for rent by the hour, day, or weekend. They will deliver kayaks for $40. Tours that last two to three hours start at the day dock in downtown Beaufort or at **Hunting Island State Park.** Adults $45; kids under 13, $30.

Higher Ground (843-379-4327; www.highergroundoutfitters.com), 95 Factory Creek Court. Tours are offered five days a week in the morning. Adults $50, kids $30. Half-day rental rates start at $40.

FISHING Fishing is thickly woven into the fabric of local life. Anthropologists note its folkways—cooking, storytelling, skills, and field ingenuity—but a Lowcountry angler is best defined by his or her passion for getting on the river; getting to the river towing a boat behind a beloved, rusted fishing car; or capturing a precious invitation to spend time at one of the area's rustic fishing camps where family traditions reign. A book written in 1856, *Carolina Sport by Land and Water* by Beaufortonian William Elliott, can be read as a nearly modern account.

Today's enthusiast can choose freshwater or saltwater sites; fish from piers, bridges, boats, banks, or the beach; or troll an artificial offshore reef. Saltwater fly-fishing is a popular specialty. The catch can range from small bream, porgy, and spot—of the family commonly known as "sailor's choice"—to flounder and big game fish like wahoo, drum, shark, and cobia. In general, the best part of the season extends from April through November. You may fish in the lagoon on Hunting Island by using light tackle with shrimp and worms for bait. Licenses are required for freshwater fishing and for saltwater fishing under certain conditions, but most visitors will not need one. For information on licenses and size and catch limits, visit the South Carolina Wildlife and Marine Resources Department website (www.dnr.sc.gov). For a comprehensive map indicating recreational fishing facilities in the Lowcountry, including marinas, boat landings, bridges and catwalks, shellfish grounds, and offshore reefs, check out the **Lowcountry & Resort Islands Tourism Commission** (843-717-3090; www.southcarolinalowcountry.com).

A sportfishing charter can take you to the Gulf Stream or to any of the dozen or so artificial reefs offshore. More than 150 years ago, the first artificial reefs used in this area were approximately 6-foot-high, log hut–like structures that were sunk to attract sheepshead. Today's reefs are far more elaborate affairs built of tires, concrete debris, and cast-off military machinery that attract dozens of species. Given that much of the sea floor off the coast is sandy, these reefs provide the hard substrate necessary to create a "live bottom" of invertebrates, small fish, coral, crabs, and sponges. They are active feeding stations for the big fish, and experienced guides know them well. Trips of this sort take a full day. Trips closer to shore, in smaller boats, can be easily enjoyed by the half day.

Rods, reels, bait, and tackle are provided; lunch or snacks are usually available, but you should check in advance; boats are equipped with safety equipment and licenses; all but the smallest have heads. Bring sunscreen, windbreakers, and a towel. Many charters will design a trip to suit your particular interest or prepare a boat for a fishing tournament. If stormy weather is forecast, call ahead to confirm that the trip is on. Also check reservation, deposit, and cancellation policies. These charter operators leave from various points around Beaufort.

Bay Street Outfitters (843-524-5250; www.baystreetoutfitters.com), 825 Bay Street. Visitors who are experienced in the art of fly-fishing, as well as those who are rank beginners, can find experienced Orvis-certified guides, instruction (Redfish School one-day seminars cost $200 per person; private fly-casting lessons are $75/hour), and a full line of gear, accessories, and specialty rods here. Guided inshore charters (fly and light tackle) for up to two people, from four to eight hours, cost $450–$650 and $50 for an extra angler.

Capt. Eddie's Fishing Charters (843-838-3782; www.fishingcapteddie1.com) launch from the Fripp Island Marina for onshore and nearshore trips lasting from four to six hours on a 21-foot boat. Cost for up to four passengers runs $425–$625. Capt. Eddie also guides two-hour dolphin watch and sightseeing cruises. If you're staying on St. Helena, Fripp, or Harbor Islands, this is the most convenient and relaxed option. He does not accept credit cards.

Cast Away Fishing Charters (843-322-1043; www.beaufortcastawaycharter

RETIRED ARMY MAJOR WALLY PHINNEY JR. WILL BE YOUR FISHING GUIDE ON *SEA WOLF VI* LOWCOUNTRY & RESORT ISLANDS TOURISM COMMISSION

.com) guides groups in 24-foot vessels seeking the trophy fish of the season, starting near Battery Creek in Port Royal. Inshore fishing rates for four-hour trips and instruction are $400–$650 for up to six anglers. The captain can arrange to have your catch prepared for your dinner at **Fishcamp on 11th Street** or at the Anchorage 1770's **Ribaut Social Club** (see *Where to Eat* and *Lodging*).

Sea Wolf VI (843-521-3372; www.seawolfcharter.com). Retired Army Major Wally Phinney Jr. is your guide from the Port Royal Marina. He offers inshore and offshore fishing using light to heavy tackle for up to six people aboard a 35-foot boat. For six people, rates are from $560–$2,100, with trips lasting from 4 to 10 hours. He has more than 60 years of experience in local waters. No smoking on board.

GOLF The Lowcountry probably has more golf courses per person than any other region in the country, and more with holes offering views of the ocean or marsh, or of deer, heron, and the occasional alligator. Weather allows for year-round play, and starting times in the summer can be as late as 5 p.m. Carts are required at peak playing times on some courses. Special prices are often posted for midday tee times in the height of summer. Courses at gated communities like Dataw, Callawassie, and Fripp are usually limited to overnight guests. Golf packages that include lodging are numerous, so ask about them. Club rentals and instruction are available at all courses.

Legends at Parris Island (843-228-2240; www.thelegendspi.com) is a public course at the Marine Corps Recruit Depot. Par 72 course redesigned by Clyde Johnston in 2000, now ranked among top 10 military courses. Tees are from 5,700 yards to 6,900 yards. Fees are $60, with a cart or walking, for nonmilitary personnel. You must have a reserved tee time to be admitted at the base's front gate.

TGC at Pleasant Point Plantation (843-986-9432; www.tgcppp.com), 8 Barnwell Drive, Lady's Island. The Russell Breeden par 72 course was overhauled in 2013 and reopened for public play. Five tees range from 4,794 to 6,602 yards. Fees are $30–$45, including a cart.

HORSEBACK RIDING **Camelot Farms** (843-838-3938; www.camelotfarmshorses .com),101 Tom & Mike Lane, St. Helena Island. Located on a 70-acre farm, Camelot offers coastline and plantation rides that last up to two hours along sandy roads and the beach overlooking St. Helena Sound and the Atlantic Ocean. Call for fees and tour schedules.

TENNIS The City of Beaufort maintains nine public courts, some of which are lit for night play, on Boundary Street across from the National Cemetery and at Battery Creek Road and Southside Boulevard. No reservations required.

✳ Green Space

Beaufort's lovely **Henry C. Chambers Waterfront Park** runs parallel to Bay Street, the main shopping and dining district downtown, and has walkways, a playground, and large "porch swings" that catch the southeastern breeze from the Beaufort River. Many restaurants offer outdoor seating that looks over the park. **Port Royal's Heritage Park,** by the entrance to the Naval Hospital and visible from Ribaut Road, has skateboard ramps, picnic seating, and is the site of the very popular **Saturday Farmers' Market,** featuring dozens of vendors of local fish, meat, produce, bread, food-to-go, and live music. It's open year-round.

BEACH ACCESS There is public access at **The Sands** in Port Royal and **Lands End** on St. Helena Island, overlooking Port Royal Sound. Both have limited free parking. **Hunting Island State Park** is a 5,000-acre preserve facing the Atlantic Ocean about 25 minutes from Beaufort on US 21. Harbor Island and Fripp Island are gated communities.

    Hunting Island State Park (843-838-2011; www.southcarolinaparks.com/hunting -island). Open daily, with extended hours during daylight saving time. Adults $5, children $3. Hunting Island is eroding, and as the water washes in, the park has taken on a haunting, wild aspect, with fallen palmettos and uprooted oaks trailing tangled roots across the beach. Hurricane Matthew in 2016 did massive damage, but even after three subsequent hurricanes it has recovered and been reconfigured. There are picnic areas and bathhouses, miles to walk at the ocean's edge, and 10 different hiking and biking trails through marsh boardwalks and maritime forest. You can kayak, paddleboard, fish off the pier, swim, camp, and visit the Nature Center. The 19th-century **Hunting Island Lighthouse** offers an expansive view of the confluence of the Ocean and St. Helena Sound (167 steps to the top) and is open daily, depending on the season. Admission $2.

BICYCLING Local bicycle enthusiasts have developed cue sheets and maps for enjoyable day trips on the emerging network of linked trails from Hunting Island State Park to the ACE Basin. The trips can be from 25 to 60 miles long and wind through scenic, rural areas and by Revolutionary War sites and movie locations.

    The Spanish Moss Trail (www.spanish mosstrail.com) is a paved Rails-to-Trails greenway that winds along marshes and creeks in Beaufort, with six designated access points for parking. It's the best new recreational opportunity in Beaufort and popular with cyclists as well as joggers and families. Ten of the proposed 16 miles are complete, making for easy round-trips along the trail. The website has a map and app.

    Lowcountry Bicycles (843-524-9585; Facebook: @locobikes), 102 Sea Island Parkway, is a good first stop for equipment, repairs, rentals, trail information, and expertise, having been dispensing it for more than 30 years. **Barefoot Bubba's Surf Shop** (843-838-9222; www .barefootbubbasurfshop.com), 2135 Sea Island Parkway, offers bike rentals near Hunting Island's park entrance.

BIRD-WATCHING As Beaufort is midway between Charleston and Savannah, see suggestions under *Nature Preserves* in those chapters. **Hunting Island State Park** is rich with shorebirds, songbirds, hawks, owls, and migrating species. Port Royal's **Cypress Wetlands and Rookery** is a nesting area for egrets, anhingas, and herons of all sizes, and its central location

THE BLUE HERON, A SHY LOWCOUNTRY ICON   LOWCOUNTRY & RESORT ISLANDS TOURISM COMMISSION

makes for an easy walk and a great stop for kids. Early morning and early evening seem to draw the birds' activity. The Carolina Bird Club (www.carolinabirdclub.org) records dates and locations of recent and notable sightings.

MARINE LIFE **The Port Royal Sound Foundation** is dedicated to education about the ecosystem and natural history of this huge river basin. Its **Maritime Center** (843-645-7774; www.portroyalsoundfoundation.org), 310 Okatie Highway, Okatie (between Beaufort and Hilton Head) offers interactive, family-friendly exhibits and programs, and docents and naturalists are on hand to answer questions. Open Tues.–Sat. Free admission.

NATURE PRESERVES Perhaps the most significant resource for those who love the outdoors and savor its hidden beauty lies off US 17, midway between Beaufort and Charleston. The **Ernest F. Hollings ACE Basin National Wildlife Refuge** (843-889-3084; www.fws.gov/refuge/ACE_basin), 8675 Willtown Road, is a consolidation of some 350,000 acres of marsh, creek, and forest to the north, east, and west of Beaufort. This crescent of landscape encompasses the forested, inland shore of the Ashepoo, Combahee, and Edisto Rivers and their small tributaries, and the vastness of St. Helena Sound. Not all the activity is on the water, either: from points on dry land, birders have identified more than 250 species of resident and migratory birds. It is open year-round from dawn to dusk. You may park and walk in; good maps are available online. Several options for visiting the ACE Basin are listed in the *To Do* sections for Charleston, Beaufort, and Edisto.

✳ Lodging

The *WPA Guide to the Palmetto State*, first published in 1941, indicates the presence of three hotels in Beaufort and a number of "tourist homes" where guests could stay. Then the preferred season was spring, although beginning in the 1920s there was an informal "winter colony" of artists, playwrights, and others who liked the laid-back town. Fall brought sportsmen from the north who hunted and fished in several vast private preserves, which by the 1940s claimed up to one-third of the acreage in Beaufort County.

Today, the visitor in the next room might be a painter, a fly-fisherman, a honeymooning couple, or a member of a wedding party. There are luxury inns and several top-notch bed-and-breakfasts to choose from—quite a selection for a small town—but ask ahead about children as guests, rules about pets, and cancellation policies. Smoking is generally permitted outside, and WiFi is common. Beach chairs and bicycles are often available to borrow. The Beaufort International Film Festival in February draws hundreds of visitors at what once was a sleepy time for tourists, so plan in advance for a stay downtown.

Anchorage 1770 (877-951-1770; www.anchorage1770.com), 1103 Bay Street. The 15-room boutique inn has the most over-the-top views of the Beaufort River and town skyline from its fourth floor (where you can have a cocktail at sunset) and has been celebrated for over 200 years as among the top few of Beaufort's impressive private mansions. Recognized by the Southern Living Hotel Collection, it defines New South luxury folded into a late 18th-century dwelling—or maybe it was its 19th-century makeover that set the expectations for a wow factor that the Anchorage fulfills. While each room capitalizes on its location (garden, third floor, waterfront, etc.) there's not a bad room among them, and the interior is sensitive to a more modern and underplayed sense of luxury. Concierge services can set you up with the best Beaufort has to offer. $$$–$$$$.

Beaufort Inn (843-379-4667; www.beaufortinn.com), 809 Port Republic Street. Trimmed in vines and rimmed with trees and flowering shrubbery, the main Victorian clapboard building with jutting bays and porches owns its busy corner. There's nothing but luxury inside: long hallways covered in plush carpet, chandeliers, and a vivid decorating style characterized by antiques, patterned wallpapers, draperies and soft curtains, and carefully hidden modern amenities. Occupying the same block are several adjoining cottages with suites, more stylishly modern apartments, and a new inn building, for a total of 48 rooms. The complex, which is located just off Bay Street, is a good choice for a family or larger group. $$–$$$$.

Beaulieu House at Cat Island (843-770-0303; www.beaulieuhouse.com), 3 Sheffield Court, a 10-minute drive from downtown toward the beach. Vibrant Caribbean pinks and greens distinguish this property, as do a full breakfast and gorgeous views. It's close enough to all the visiting options of Beaufort, but secluded and quiet, with gorgeous views. Check their room with special handicapped access. $$–$$$.

City Loft Hotel (843-379-5638; www.citylofthotel.com), 301 Carteret Street. This boutique lodging has 22 rooms on two floors, a fitness center and café, and an attentive concierge service that includes booking tours and securing privileges at a local spa and golf club. It's the hippest lodging in town, with elegant details like foam memory beds, flat-screen televisions (even in the bathrooms), walk-in showers, and sleek workstations. It's one block from the Beaufort River and within shouting distance of three excellent restaurants. City Loft is a sophisticated departure from its peers. $$–$$$.

Cuthbert House Inn (843-521-1315; www.cuthberthouseinn.com), 1203 Bay Street. The Cuthbert House has seen its

BEAUFORT'S STYLISH CITY LOFT HOTEL COURTESY CITY LOFT HOTEL

share of excitement, and its architecture tells the tale. It was moved from its original site in 1810, embellished with fine Federal-period woodcarving, served as headquarters of Union General Rufus Saxton during the federal blockade, and then enlarged with Victorian additions (sunporches and bays). Ten guest rooms include two 1-bedroom suites on the ground level and parlor suites. Its great site on Beaufort's bluff makes the full Southern breakfast, afternoon tea, evening coffee, or simply lounging a pleasure. $$$.

Rhett House Inn (843-524-9030; www.rhetthouseinn.com), 1009 Craven Street. This is Beaufort's gold standard for inns, started by a couple who left their careers in New York's fashion business and brought their perfectionism and sense of the market with them. The main house, circa 1820, is steps from the waterfront and full of sunlight and breezes. Furnished with antiques and comfortable chairs, prints, and vases of fresh flowers, the inn is flanked in the back by a garden and on the side by a courtyard fountain. Many of its 10 rooms have fireplaces or Jacuzzi tubs. The upstairs and downstairs porches are dreamy places to read or have afternoon tea and pastries. Seven rooms in a cottage complex across a quiet street have private porches and entrances, and are just as inviting.

Newcastle House is available for larger parties, with two elegant suites and a full gourmet kitchen. It is available by the month from December through February and daily at other times. Full breakfast, including homemade breads and muffins, is included, as are desserts and after-noon snacks. $$$–$$$$.

Best Western Sea Island Inn (843-522-2090; www.bestwestern.com), 1015 Bay Street. Conveniently located on Beaufort's main street, the 43-unit Best Western has a pool, exercise room, and outdoor patio tables. Continental break-fast is served in the lobby. $$.

National chain motels are well rep-resented in Beaufort and are often the choice for families of the graduating classes (many each year) of "boot camp" recruits from the Parris Island Marine Corps Recruit Depot. These are closest to the Historic District and about 15 to 20 minutes from Parris Island.

Hampton Inn (843-986-0600; www .hilton.com), 2342 Boundary Street.

Hilton Garden Inn (843-379-9800; www.hilton.com), 1500 Queen Street.

Holiday Inn & Suites (843-379-3100; www.ihg.com), 2225 Boundary Street.

Quality Inn at Town Center (843-524-2144; www.choicehotels.com), 2001 Boundary Street.

FARTHER AFIELD IN THE BEAUFORT AREA

Fripp Island Golf & Beach Resort (843-838-1558; www.frippislandresort.com), 2119 Sea Island Parkway. Fripp is a pri-vate, 3,000-acre island bordered by an ocean beach about 35 minutes by car from downtown. It's a low-key residential community with two golf courses, tennis facilities, biking trails, pools, informal restaurants, and a marina. Activity programs in the summer keep children busy. Rental properties exist in catego-ries from deluxe on down and vary in price from family homes that sleep 10 to townhouse units on the ocean, marsh, and internal sites. Weekly rates in the summer range from $1,700 to $5,000. Rentals through the resort enable you to use resort facilities. Two golf courses rim the Atlantic Ocean and Fripp Inlet. Ocean Point Course, a links-style par 72, is a George Cobb design with five sets of tees. The Ocean Creek Course, the first by Davis Love III, is a par 71 that winds through the marshes and interior wetlands. Yardage from 4,884 to 6,613. Walking is an option at both courses. Since they lie within a gated community, you must be a resort guest or renting property of a club member to play.

Harbor Island is a small private com-munity just off St. Helena Island on the way to Fripp and Hunting Island State Park. It has a pool, tennis courts, and a 3-mile beach. Find a selection of pri-vate listings and book directly through Seaside Getaways (843-868-8381; www.seasidegetaways.com) or www .visitharborislandsc.com. The latter web-site has reliable and up-to-date listings of what's open, and provides hours for local restaurants and activities. Given the current circumstances of traveling with COVID-19, these things can change quickly, but this site provides better information than most.

Hunting Island State Park (843-838-2011; www.southcarolinaparks.com/ huntingisland), 2555 Sea Island Parkway, about 30 minutes from Beaufort. There are 102 RV sites with full water and electrical hook-ups that accommodate vehicles up to 40 feet and cost about $50 per night. Rustic tent camping costs about $20 per night. Reservations are necessary (the easiest way is through the website, where you can select your spot on the park map) and require a two-night minimum stay. In the summer of 2020, the park launched a new ferry ser-vice (twice daily) for trips to nearby St. Philip's Island, where visitors can walk a pristine beach and island trails four days a week. Check the park's website for hours of service and fees. It is an incred-ible addition to the Lowcountry natural experience for individuals and families.

Palm Key (843-726-6524; www
.palmkey.com), 330 Coosaw Way,
Ridgeland. The idea at Palm Key is to
enjoy the outdoor, non-oceanfront life
of the Lowcountry—crabbing, fishing, kayaking, hiking, fossil-hunting,
bird-watching—by slowing down and
taking notice, either with a guide or on
your own. No television or telephones in
most of the 20 rental cottages, which are
attractive for families.

✻ Where to Eat

For a town of about 11,000, there are
some very good restaurants as well
as several moderately priced or more
informal ones with outdoor seating
overlooking the river. Chefs tweak the
South's favorite dishes, starting with
fresh shrimp, fish, crab, and oysters,
and have become ardent consumers of
locally grown greens and other produce
from island farms that operate year-
round. Everyone seems to be raising
chickens and selling eggs. Tomatoes are
a prominent cash crop in late spring and
early summer and are widely featured
at that time, but it's also possible to find
traditional ingredients used at the peak
of the season, like shad roe from the
Edisto River, strawberries, blueberries,
melons, Carolina dove, venison, and pork
barbecue.

If you find something you especially
like, look for the recipe in *Sea Island
Seasons,* a cookbook published by the
Beaufort County Open Land Trust (www
.openlandtrust.org), a local nonprofit
land preservation group. Within its covers you'll find out how to make such Lowcountry specialties as Frogmore Stew
(sausage, corn on the cob, potatoes, and
shrimp in broth); shrimp paste (a spread
that retains the delicate, sweet flavor of
fresh shrimp); bread-and-butter pickles;
and lemon chess pie (the secret ingredi-
ent is cornmeal).

Breakwater (843-379-0052; www
.breakwatersc.com), 203 Carteret Street.

RAW OYSTERS ARE A LOCAL FAVORITE © SELWA BAROODY/
ISTOCKPHOTO.COM

Executive chefs Gary Lang and Elizabeth
Shaw have nurtured and expanded their
restaurant from its original storefront
to a few stunning, modern rooms and a
beautiful bar that is the most interesting
night scene in town. The atmosphere is
sophisticated without being stuffy, so it
makes sense that the menu is, too. You
can create an informal meal from tapas
plates or go the distance with quail or
filet mignon. Local farmers and fishermen supply Breakwater, which has
encouraged a locavore movement. Reservations are recommended for dinner, not
so important for lunch, but it's also possible to drop by for dessert and a glass of
wine from their lengthy list. $$–$$$.

Dockside (843-379-3288; www
.docksidebeaufort.com), 71 Sea Island
Parkway. A very popular dinner choice
among locals for seafood, with patio
dining and a wonderful view of Factory
Creek and the marina. Fish off the boat,
and dressed up for gourmet diners.

Fishcamp on 11th Street (843-379-
2248; www.fishcampon11th.com), 1699
11th Street. A casual family restaurant
on Battery Creek in Port Royal, where
shrimp boats tie up and the sunsets pour
color into the sky. The menu offers fried,
steamed, and broiled seafood specialties,
as well as steak and pasta. No reserva-
tions, so expect a wait for dinner. $$.

Griffin Market (843-524-0240; www
.griffinmarket.com), 403 Carteret Street.

SHRIMP BOATS OFF PORT ROYAL ISLAND © GINGER WAREHAM/PICKLEJUICE.COM

Dinner Wed.–Sun. Seasonal offerings in the Northern Italian style with four courses, served in a quiet, modest

BEAUFORT'S BAY STREET AND ITS WATERFRONT RESTAURANTS ARE THE HEART OF THIS SMALL TOWN

setting where the food is the star. Offerings change seasonally and include artisanal pastas and risotto for the primi course, and duck breast, lamb, or scallops seasoned with figs or butternut squash puree for the secondi. Don't miss the hazelnut cake for dessert. Reservations are a must. $$$–$$$$.

Lowcountry Produce Market and Café (843-322-1900; www.lowcountryproduce .com), 302 Carteret Street. This was the former Beaufort City Hall, and the owners renovated it beautifully into a light-filled space. They serve breakfast and lunch daily, with soups, sandwiches, salads, and a selection of homemade sweets and breads. There's also a gourmet market selling wine and cheese, handmade and hand-packed goods, oils, herbs and spices, jellies, linens, local ceramics, and very pretty paper products. I've often wondered how it stays afloat because of the time and effort that must go into curating its excellent small meals and wares, but it's thriving. $.

Magnolia Bakery Café (843-524-1961; www.magnoliacafebeaufort.com), 703 Congress Street. A small, friendly restaurant with indoor and outdoor dining, specializing in homemade bread and soup, desserts, and snacks. Breakfast and lunch are served, and it's vegetarian friendly. $.

Old Bull Tavern (843-379-2855; www.oldbulltavern.com), 205 West Street. With a very lively late-dining scene, including pizza until 11 p.m. on the weekends, it's the gastro pub for Beaufort's creative class and anyone who enjoys handcrafted cocktails and menus that change daily, as do various inspirational or ironic quotes written on overhead boards. Its long, narrow layout puts the bar on the right and tables lined up in the remaining space, with a few in the back if you want a quieter experience, but the whole point is friendly congestion and an abundance of regulars and dedicated staff. You could make a meal out of the bar snacks, like wasabi deviled eggs with prosciutto or smoked mullet spread, but there's an ample menu of entrées, including a renowned burger of local grass-fed beef. $$–$$$.

Plums (843-525-1946; www.plumsrestaurant.com), 904 Bay Street. After more than 30 years, Plums is still the most reliable and popular place to eat lunch in Beaufort, inside or on its porch overlooking Waterfront Park. Hot sandwiches like grilled turkey, reubens, or po'boys are menu favorites, as are the homemade soups; there's peanut butter and jelly for the kids. A nighttime crowd spills onto the porch, nicely heated in chillier months. Live music a couple times a week. $–$$.

Saltus River Grill (843-379-3474; www.saltusrivergrill.com), 802 Bay Street. Located on the river, with a spacious outdoor deck and comfortable seating, this big, upscale restaurant takes its cues from urban restaurants housed in repurposed commercial buildings where exposed ductwork meets linen tablecloths. It's probably Beaufort's destination restaurant and doesn't disappoint. A nice feature is the chance to eat a light dinner from the full sushi and raw bar while soaking in the atmosphere of visitors having a great time. $$–$$$$.

Wren Bistro (843-524-9463; www.wrenbeaufort.com), 210 Carteret Street. There's a good price range on the menu, lots of special plates, and options from salads and sandwiches at lunch to a fuller dinner menu. It's one of the few restaurants with several vegetarian choices and one where you can drop in at 3:30 p.m. for a snack. The food is simply prepared and beautifully presented, and the surroundings, basically an L-shaped room punctuated by alcoves, are a mix of sleekly manufactured materials and fabrics or wall coverings that look as if they came off the beach. It's a sweet spot where a meal feels special but not too expensive. $–$$.

yes, Thai Indeed (843-986-1185; www.yesthaiindeed.com), 2127 Boundary

BEAUFORT-AREA OYSTERS ARE SWEET AND BRINY, AND THEIR LIQUOR CAN BE SIPPED FROM THE SHELL
© GINGER WAREHAM/PICKLEJUICE.COM

SALTUS RIVER GRILL IN BEAUFORT GREATER BEAUFORT-PORT ROYAL CONVENTION &VISITORS BUREAU (BANKER OPTICAL MEDIA)

Street. Thai food made by a Thai chef who caters to local families, people coming in after the early movie, and downtown residents who forgot to food shop. The atmosphere is welcoming, and they happily offer dietary options and a careful read of how spicy you want your curry. They sweat the small stuff to make sure it's excellent, like the homemade peanut and ginger dressings. Once a beloved hole in the wall—if I'm not mistaken, the old place was on the site of a shuttered gas station—it's now in a simple, modernist space in a shopping center complex that is itself being upgraded. $–$$.

ST. HELENA ISLAND

Whether you're on your way to Hunting Island State Park or the beach resorts— or are touring St. Helena Island, Fort Fremont, and Penn Center—you have good, non-touristy options in all price ranges and venues. The emphasis is on local sourcing and a laid-back presentation, but don't underestimate the cappuccino or liver and onions. They are located on US 21, 7 to 15 miles from Beaufort. Hours may be cut back in the winter months.

Boondock's (843-838-0821; www .boondockssc.com), 1760 Sea Island Parkway. A location close to the beach, with a laid-back vacation vibe, fried seafood, and enough choices to satisfy a burger and ribs crowd, attracts throngs in the summer months and locals year-round. $$.

Carolina Cider Company/Superior Coffee (843-838-1231; www.carolina ciderco.com), 507 Sea Island Parkway. If you want to enjoy a slice of pie and craft coffee, sit and read the free papers and magazines, or browse the shelves of spice rubs, heirloom grits and rice, and pickles and preserves, don't overlook this renovated little grocery store at the gateway to St. Helena Island that also has a little patio garden with tables and benches. $.

The Foolish Frog (843-838-9300; www .thefoolishfrog.com), 846 Sea Island Parkway. An exuberant restaurant on the marsh, with a (pet- and family-friendly) deck out back for informal musical jams and scheduled performers, it can get

SHRIMP BOATS OFF ST. HELENA ISLAND © GINGER WAREHAM/PICKLEJUICE.COM

as packed as a dive bar and now serves three meals a day. Southern staples like ribs, grilled fish, steak, and shellfish have been joined by fish tacos, so there are surprises, but probably the most popular menu items would be the fried platters. A great stop for softshell crabs in April and May. $$.

Gullah Grub (843-838-3841; gullahgrub.com), 877 Sea Island Parkway. Hours can be variable in winter, closed Sat. and Mon., but a good lunch/late lunch stop. Chef Bill Green wears many hats—horseman, trainer of hunting hounds, storyteller—and his love for and appreciation of his native Gullah heritage and culture comes through in his cooking at this tiny place. Even the not easily surprised chef and food provocateur Anthony Bourdain featured him on his television show. Bill's instructional DVDs capture the Gullah way to roast oysters and prepare standards like red rice and greens, and he also hosts cooking classes and has a mail-order business of sauces, rubs, and chowders. His wife Sara Reynolds is, among other things, an organic farmer, educator, and inspirational community leader whose Marshview Community Organic Farm and Young Farmers of the Lowcountry

program provide produce and eggs to the restaurant. $–$$.

Island BBQ Grill (843-929-9100; Facebook: @IslandFishMarket), 526 Sea Island Parkway. Open Wed.–Sat. The

CREATIVE REUSE OF EXISTING BUILDINGS TURNED AN OLD POST OFFICE INTO A NEW RESTAURANT, THE FOOLISH FROG

GATHERING AND CORN SHELLING, ST. HELENA ISLAND

When they go into the field to work, the women tie a bit of string or some vine round their skirts just below the hips, to shorten them, often raising them nearly to the knees; then they walk off with their heavy hoes on their shoulders, as free, strong, and graceful as possible. The prettiest sight is the corn-shelling on Mondays, when the week's allowance, a peck a hand, is given out at the corn-house by the driver. They all assemble with their baskets, which are shallow and without handles, made by themselves of the palmetto and holding from a half peck to a bushel. The corn is given out in the ear, and they sit about or kneel on the ground, shelling it with cleared corncobs. Here there are four enormous logs hollowed at one end, which serve as mortars, at which two can stand with their rude pestles, which they strike up and down alternately. . . . They separate the coarse and fine parts after it is ground by shaking the grits in their baskets: the finest they call corn-flour and make hoecake of, but their usual food is the grits, the large portion, boiled as hominy and eaten with clabber.

—Harriet Ware, a young abolitionist and teacher from Boston who lived and taught at Coffin Point Plantation, St. Helena Island, to her parents, May 22, 1862 (from *Letters from Port Royal 1862–1868*, Elizabeth Ware Pearson, ed. [New York: Arno Press, 1969])

barbecue is smoked in the back and, if you want, you can order and fix yourself a sandwich in the front of this tiny gem and eat it there. Or you can order ahead. The pulled pork sandwich is outstanding, but you can get racks of ribs, chicken, and fish. $.

Shrimp Shack (843-838-2962; Facebook: @ShrimpShackSC), 1925 Sea Island Parkway. Fresh seafood from the family dock—you can see the shrimp boats—accompanied by slaw, red rice, hush puppies, and beans. Their shrimp burgers (secret sauce and all that!) made

AN ISLAND PRAISE HOUSE

them famous to outsiders, but ask anyone in the know and he or she will tell you that since 1978 this has been the fast place to grab a bite at lunch. You can eat upstairs on the screened-in porch or in an adjacent gazebo. Cash and check only. $–$$.

✳ Entertainment

As Beaufort has grown, so have its cultural activities, both indigenous and imported. The annual tours of historic homes presented by the **Historic Beaufort Foundation** (843-379-3331; www .historicbeaufort.org) have gained professional thoroughness and include modern additions, like a chef's tour and a separate event focusing on new homes designed by local architects. A juried film festival in February, **Beaufort International Film Festival** (www .beaufortfilmfestival.com), culls hundreds of entries in multiple categories and draws crowds in February. The

THE BUST OF ROBERT SMALLS OUTSIDE TABERNACLE BAPTIST CHURCH LOWCOUNTRY & RESORT ISLANDS TOURISM COMMISSION

NEAR FORT FREMONT AT LANDS END LOWCOUNTRY & RESORT ISLANDS TOURISM COMMISSION

VIEW OF THE DOWNTOWN BRIDGE GREATER BEAUFORT-PORT ROYAL CONVENTION & VISITORS BUREAU (BANKER OPTICAL MEDIA)

University of South Carolina has an active exhibition and theater schedule and is the venue for an excellent chamber music series and *The Metropolitan Opera Live in HD* on many Saturdays (www.uscbcenterforthearts.com). A dozen downtown art galleries coordinate open houses on the first Friday of the month (www.downtownbeaufortsc .org). It may be enough to sit and watch the tide go out on a Friday night, but you don't have to. Comprehensive listings are at www.eatsleepplaybeaufort.com and www.yourislandnews.com. There's also a great throwback drive-in theater (843-846-4500; www.hwy21drivein.com), 55 Parker Drive, about 2 miles north of Beaufort.

✳ Selective Shopping

ANTIQUES AND HOME ACCESSORIES **Collector's Antique Mall,** 102-C Sea Island Parkway, houses dozens of vendors who sell everything from buttons to

bureaus and is located just across the Beaufort River on Lady's Island.

Lulu Burgess (843-524-5858; www .luluburgess.com), 917 Bay Street. An engaging and amusing blend of imaginative items such as jewelry, stationery, tableware, totes, and decorative accessories selected by a Beaufort native who returned home and put her good taste to work.

Macdonald Market Place (843-838-1810; www.macdonaldmarketplace .com), 853 Sea Island Parkway, St. Helena Island. Built as a general store in 1877 at the center of the island, it's now run by the fifth generation of the family and filled with a wonderful collection of local work by two dozen artisans, as well as silver and china, pillows, lamps, glassware, textiles, and furniture. There's an extensive selection of wines and specialty foods and the signature Seaside Grown Bloody Mary mix, made from the family's large commercial tomato farm.

Sweetgrass baskets made by local artists can be found on St. Helena Island on

HUNTING ISLAND LIGHTHOUSE OFFERS IMPRESSIVE VIEWS OF THE ATLANTIC AND ST. HELENA SOUND GREATER BEAUFORT-PORT ROYAL CONVENTION & VISITORS BUREAU (BANKER OPTICAL MEDIA)

AWESOME SUNSETS ARE COMMON IN SUMMER LOWCOUNTRY & RESORT ISLANDS TOURISM COMMISSION

nowhere else. Civil War albums, rare and antique volumes, as well as local writers and local history, including those by Pat Conroy.

Monkey's Uncle (843-524-6868; www .monkeysuncletoys.com), 909 Bay Street. Toys, puzzles, books, and games in a cheerful space where kids can try things out and adults can take a breather.

Nevermore Books (843-812-9460; www.nevermorebooks.com), 702 Craven Street, specializes in fiction, first editions, and art and children's books in new and gently used condition. A selection of vintage vinyl, too.

FOOD **Olive the Above** (843-379-2000; www.olivetheaboveoliveoil.com), 821 Bay Street, carries dozens of varieties of infused olive oils and balsamic vinegars, specialty foods, and kitchen accessories.

The Chocolate Tree (843-524-7980; www.thechocolatetree.us), 507 Carteret Street. A family-owned, award-winning shop selling many different kinds of chocolates, truffles, and dipped fruits made on the premises, plus candy-making accessories, gift boxes, jelly beans, cards, and gifts.

YoYo's (843-548-0300), 722 Bay Street. Add toppings such as fruit, nuts,

US 21, on the porch at the Gullah Grub restaurant, and at other roadside stands. The baskets, which incorporate palmetto fronds, pine needles, and rush with the pale grass, come in many shapes and sizes, with individual variations inspired by the utilitarian shapes used in the past. They require enormous amounts of labor and skill and are useful as well as beautiful.

BOOKS **Beaufort Bookstore** (843-525-1066), 2127 Boundary Street. A large selection and wide variety of books, from best-selling fiction and nonfiction to military and Lowcountry favorites.

McIntosh Book Shoppe (843-524-1119), 917 Bay Street. New and used books on South Carolina you'll find

SWEETGRASS BASKETS ARE A POPULAR LOCAL CRAFT © RICHARDBARROW/ISTOCKPHOTO.COM

SPORTFISHING CHARTERS CAN BE FOUND AT MANY LOCAL MARINAS GREATER BEAUFORT-PORT ROYAL CONVENTION & VISITORS BUREAU (BANKER OPTICAL MEDIA)

or candy to frozen yogurt to create your own treat, or indulge in smoothies and other chilled refreshments. Eat in or at the adjacent Waterfront Park.

CLOTHING **Barefoot Bubba's Surf Shop** (843-838-9222; www.barefoot bubbasurfshop.com), 2135 Sea Island Parkway. The store supplies everything you need to wear at the beach and all the equipment.

Bay Street Outfitters (843-524-5250; www.baystreetoutfitters.com), 825 Bay Street, carries a full line of high-end, specialized sportswear from Orvis and Barbour, as well as casual outerwear and one-of-a-kind feather bow ties made in South Carolina.

Higher Ground (843-379-4327; www .highergroundoutfitters.com), 95 Factory Creek Court, has the best selection of outerwear and accessories for sporting activities in the area, from rugged sandals to windbreakers.

SugarBelle (843-379-4141; www.shop sugarbelle.com), 905 Boundary Street. Women who like to be comfortable and

a little sassy in their look can get great guidance and abundant choices in this little shop, which was the inspiration of a successful real estate agent who followed her dreams.

LOCAL HERBS AND SPICES CREATE A DISTINCTIVE GULLAH FLAVOR IN GUMBOS, BOILS, AND FISH STEWS

IF TIME IS SHORT

Beaufort is a destination on its own and can be absorbed on a day and overnight visit, which would include guided or informal touring, dining, and shopping. Many people select it as an easy weekend trip, with planes arriving and departing from Savannah, and I recommend that. If your focus is history and architecture, a good place to start is the Historic Beaufort Foundation's John Mark Verdier House, 801 Bay Street, followed by a stroll on the wide streets of The Point neighborhood, like Prince, King, and Federal, for another hour. A number of the recommended restaurants are on your way back to Bay Street or located there, with their back porches facing the Waterfront Park and river. Fifteen minutes from town, a must-see is the historic campus and museum of Penn Center (843-838-2432; www.penncenter.com) on St. Helena Island, the nation's first school for emancipated slaves. A mile or so away are Macdonald Marketplace and numerous roadside vendors of local jellies, produce, and baskets. Continue driving south on US 21 for about 10 minutes and you come to Hunting Island State Park (843-838-2011; www.southcarolinaparks.com/huntingisland) for a walk on the beach, which is bracingly beautiful. As noted in *Where to Eat*, you can eat casually on St. Helena, too, or return back to Beaufort for another meal. All of this activity will take five to six hours. Any number of nature-related tours and activities, such as kayaking or biking, can fit into two hours if they occur in downtown Beaufort.

THE WOODS MEMORIAL BRIDGE © GINGER WAREHAM/PICKLEJUICE.COM

Edisto Island & Edisto Beach

It takes some time to get to know **Edisto,** a largely unspoiled barrier island. What remains of its "Golden Age," the period between the Revolutionary and Civil Wars, is mostly hidden, tucked away along secondary roads that wind through fields and patches of scrub oak, meandering by the North and South Edisto Rivers and their tributaries. Historic sites listed on the National Register of Historic Places include some churches but consist primarily of private plantation homes and gardens that are not open to the public except, perhaps, on an annual tour. **Edisto Beach,** where rental accommodations abound, is lively in the summer—not Hilton Head or Charleston resort lively, which is a point of pride in a modest, "we're still undiscovered" sort of way. It is quiet in the off-season. Its down-to-earth mien attracts visitors. It's a great spot for family reunions or weeklong stays that are punctuated by beachcombing, a good meal, and a kayak or boat tour. Some years ago, before social media was ubiquitous, a sickly loggerhead turtle washed up. It was nursed to health, and when the time came to release it back into the ocean, more than 300 people showed up to watch, cheer, and take pictures. They found out by word of mouth, Edisto-style. Orient yourself through the **Edisto Chamber of Commerce** (843-869-3867; www.edistochamber .com) or the **Lowcountry Resort Islands and Tourism Commission** (843-717-3090; www .southcarolinalowcountry.com). An Explore Edisto app (www.botanybayecotours.com) is available for iPhones and iPads through the Apple Store and features multiple tours enlivened with cultural and historical information.

The island lies about 45 miles south of Charleston by road, and about 75 miles north of Beaufort. From US 17, take SC 174 and follow it east for about 20 miles, threading

A RURAL, TREE-LINED ROAD IN THE LOWCOUNTRY © DENISTANGNEYJR/ISTOCKPHOTO.COM

AN OLD PIER ON EDISTO ISLAND LOWCOUNTRY & RESORT ISLANDS TOURISM COMMISSION

your way through the country and ending at the Atlantic Ocean. Original sections of the King's Highway, laid out in the early 18th century, are still in use today. The road has been designated a National Scenic Byway and notes 30 points of interest (www .edistoscenicbyway.org). Edisto is too far to travel from Charleston or Beaufort just for dinner, but it's fine for a day trip. Cab and car rental services are limited.

✳ To See

Edisto Island Museum (843-869-1954; www.edistomuseum.org), 8123 Chisolm Plantation Road at SC 174. Open Tues.–Sat. from March to October, with limited hours in other seasons. Adults $5, students $2, free to children 10 and younger. Baskets, clothing, farm tools, letters and documents, uniforms, and furniture are displayed, as well as haunting old photographs. The little gift shop sells a variety of natural history items for kids and excellent books you're not likely to find anywhere else. They include histories of Edisto Island starting in 1663; *And I'm Glad,* an oral history told by two African American islanders; and *She Came to the Island,* the Edisto diary of Mary Ames, a Northern abolitionist whose account of teaching and living among the newly freed slaves during the Civil War is among the most poignant of the genre. The museum is run by the **Edisto Island Historic Preservation Society,** which also sponsors an **October Tour of Homes** that sells out quickly. See the museum's website for tickets. At other times, book a weekday seat on a two-hour van journey at **Tours of Edisto** (843-869-1984; www.toursofedisto.com), led by an island resident whose roots go back generations.

Edisto Island Serpentarium (843-869-1171; www.edistoserpentarium.com), 1374 SC 174. More than 500 reptiles are on display in natural habitats in aquariums or in an enclosed garden with walls you can peer over. Feeding and presentations occur every hour. Days and hours of operation change monthly, and it is generally closed in winter. Admission charged.

✳ To Do

Because of its location at the confluence of the North and South Edisto Rivers, the Atlantic, and St. Helena Sound, Edisto Beach offers probably the easiest access to the ACE Basin National Wildlife Refuge (843-889-3084; www.fws.gov/refuge/ace_basin) and all sorts of fishing, boating, and water sports amid uninhabited, protected islands.

For touring the ACE Basin, ecotouring, shelling excursions, fishing charters, and kayak trips, stop by **Edisto Watersports & Tackle** (843-869-0663; www.edistowater sports.net), 3731 Docksite Road. **Captain Ron Elliott's Edisto Island Tours** (843-869-1937) provide boat trips to remote places, island rivers, and inshore fishing. You may also tour by canoe and kayak with Ron. He is a passionate naturalist and a font of Edisto lore. Rent bikes, boats, kayaks, golf carts, and beach gear at **Island Bikes & Outfitters** (843-869-4444; www.islandbikesandoutfitters.com).

✳ Green Space

In a moment of exceedingly wise land stewardship, the state of South Carolina obtained land on the northern end of Edisto and created the **Botany Bay Plantation Heritage Preserve and Wildlife Management Area** (843-869-2713; www2.dnr.sc.gov/ managedlands), a pristine, 4,687-acre tract of former cotton plantations that includes wetlands, fields, abundant wildlife habitat, and beachfront, is open for visitation daily during daylight hours. Check the website for days when it is closed for hunting dove and deer. You first obtain a day pass (no fee) at the main gate off Botany Bay Road and receive a map of the 6-mile driving loop (firm, sand roads) and the beach parking area. Volunteers are on hand to guide you. Cultural resources on Botany Bay include outbuildings from the Bleak Hall plantation. The pristine and primitive beach, littered with bleached trees deadened by rising sea level and erosion, is accessible by foot (some wheelchair accommodation) about 10 minutes from the parking lot. It is an outstanding treasure of Edisto, indeed the coastal area, and is a rare, publicly accessible site. There are no restrooms or commercial enterprises: it really is a back-to-nature walk and drive. If you're staying at Kiawah Island, or even downtown Charleston, and want to see what an island looked like before resort development, it is an easy day trip.

Edisto Beach State Park (843-869-2756; www.southcarolinaparks.com). With 1.5 miles of beach; inland walking/biking trails, including 4 miles that are ADA accessible; and boat-launching capacity to Big Bay Creek, this state park ranks just behind Hunting Island State Park in Beaufort in popularity and beauty. There are more than 100 camping and RV sites with water and electricity, and seven cabins are available by advance reservation. The beach is a wonderful place to hunt for fossils and shark teeth, better than any other public state beach. No lifeguards. Admission is $5 for adults, $3 for children.

✳ Lodging

For years Edisto Beach has been the summer getaway of South Carolina families. They take up residence in the plain, raised, two-story houses that line the boulevards for about three dozen blocks and spill across adjacent avenues. There's nothing too fancy: It's full of kids riding bikes (good bike lanes and watchful drivers here) and minivans parked in the sand. Beach access is plentiful. Near the marina, a high point of the day is watching the shrimp boats come in.

Many of these houses rent by the week, and several agencies list them. The market is organized by location: beachfront, second row (across the street from the beach, usually with an ocean view); beach walk (easy access but on a side street); condos; and homes with docks (deepwater, tidal creek, or other access, which may not be near the beach). The range of prices for a week in the summer can be from $900 to $5,000. Rental specs also include amenities like a fish-cleaning sink, a hot and cold outside shower, grills, and even a pool.

Atwood Vacations (843-869-2151; www.atwoodvacations.com).

Carolina One Vacation Rentals (843-580-0500; www.edistopropertysearch.com).

Edisto Rentals (843-869-2527; www.edistorealty.com).

✳ Where to Eat

Known to locals and return visitors as the best place to dine out, the **Old Post Office Restaurant** (843-869-2339; www.theoldpostofficerestaurant.com), 1442 SC 174, is a cozy place that serves creative Southern cuisine—this is not fried food—with local fish and shellfish entrées and a couple of veal, chicken, or rib-eye options, lightly sauced, as well as a vegetarian choice. They open at 5:30 p.m., when you can usually get a seat without a reservation, but booking ahead is advisable. Seasonal hours are usually Tues.–Sat., with a limited off-season schedule. $$–$$$.

The Seacow Eatery (843-869-3222; www.theseacoweatery.com), 145 Jungle Road, offers a varied breakfast menu, from standard bacon and eggs to shrimp and eggs. At lunch you can order the veggie melt, deli sandwiches, or a shrimp po'boy. Their dinner menu features your choice of fried or grilled seafood, steaks, and chicken, and there is a kids' menu. Informal is the byword, and you can eat on a back porch. Open daily. $–$$.

The Waterfront (843-869-1400; www.waterfrontrestaurantedisto.com), 136

SHRIMP BOATS ARE A COMMON LOCAL SITE
© GINGER WAREHAM/PICKLEJUICE.COM

Jungle Road. You can't get more local than this: local seafood caught by the chef/owner's family and local vegetables from his wife's family farm. No longer on the water with the view, but no one minds. The menu aims to please with a build-your-own approach to sides, customized salads, and all-you-can-eat options. $–$$.

Whaley's (843-869-2161; www.whaleyseb.com), 2801 Myrtle Street, is an old filling station that has been turned into a beachy café, serving crab cakes, fresh seafood, steaks, wings, pork chop sandwiches, and the "Big Ugly" burger. Open for lunch and dinner but limited off-season hours. Discovery and accolades by the national press have not turned its head or changed its down-home/dive bar vibe. $–$$.

✴ Selective Shopping

Local and regional artwork and crafts are represented informally at **With These Hands** (843-869-3509; www.withthesehandsgallery.com), 547 SC 174, which specializes in American crafts. **The Edistonian Gift Shop & Gallery** (843-869-4466), 406 SC 174, is where you're likely to find a vase, bag, or home accessory with a nautical theme. The **Edisto Island Bookstore** (843-869-1885; edistobookstore.com), also at 547 SC 174, sells new and used books, great maps, and titles pertaining to Edisto life and culture. It provides a reminder of the integral role books and reading play in a small community, although there are lots of fun beach reads for sale, too.

Bluffton

Historic Bluffton Village, now branded Old Town Bluffton, was one of the Lowcountry's last cul-de-sacs. There were a couple of "Historic" this-and-that signs nailed up, but what you thought it ought to be and whether or not it ever got scrubbed-up was of no concern. It had all the charm of a barefoot kid. That's changed. About a decade ago, the town annexed a bazillion acres in the southern part of Beaufort County (Hilton Head is a different address, over the bridges), so when you hear about how special "Bluffton" is to visit, people are probably talking about Old Town—which is special and has grown delightfully in Bluffton's signature quirky way—rather than the new residential neighborhoods and gated communities. An hour or two spent walking around the 1-square-mile Historic District, with its 19th-century frame houses that were the core of its cotton planters' summer community; gazing off the May River bluff; browsing art galleries; and dining and shopping makes for a day or half day. Visitor information can be found at www.oldtownbluffton.com.

From Beaufort (about 40 minutes), follow SC 170 and continue as if you were going to Hilton Head, across the Broad River Bridge. About 8 miles ahead, exit right at the sign to Hilton Head and loop around. You are now on US 278 (William Hilton Parkway), the main Hilton Head access. After a couple of miles, you will see SC 46 marked as a right turn. Take it into Bluffton. From Hilton Head (about 30 minutes), follow US 278 across the Graves Bridge, turn left on SC 46, and follow it to Boundary Street. It is about a half-hour drive from Savannah and the closest airport.

✴ To See

In 1863 Bluffton was nearly burned to the ground by Union troops. Eight antebellum buildings remain; another 16 or so houses were built after the Civil War. Taken together, they give a view of classic Low-country village life. They are not mansions, as in Beaufort, but are nonetheless suffused with a sense of form appropriate to the landscape and to their function as seasonal dwellings.

The Heyward House Museum (843-757-6293; www.heywardhouse.org), 70 Boundary Street, serves as a welcome center and is open Mon.–Sat. It's a classic 1840s Carolina farmhouse with a summer kitchen and a cabin for the enslaved workers. Walking tours of the village originate here and reservations are necessary, but not for house tours. There is a nominal charge. Pick up a self-guided walking tour or biking map. It's worth it to browse the small gift shop and pick up books produced by the Bluffton Historical Preservation Society, which runs the site, to learn the town's history. Check website for current opening information.

BLUFFTON'S MID-19TH-CENTURY CHURCH OF THE CROSS, ONE THE FEW BUILDINGS IN THE VILLAGE TO SURVIVE THE CIVIL WAR COURTESY OF THE HILTON HEAD ISLAND VISITOR & CONVENTION BUREAU

ART GALLERIES Bluffton has emerged as a center for working artists, and galleries primarily located on Calhoun Street are open daily and feature rotating shows of fine art and photography, crafts, and work in many media that capture the light, land, and sea of this corner of the world. **The Red Piano Art Gallery** (843-842-4433; www.redpianoartgallery.com), 40 Calhoun Street, is the granddaddy of the art scene and has the broadest and best inventory of work by four dozen painters and sculptors. Founded in 1994, the **Society of Bluffton Artists Gallery** (843-757-6586; www.sobagallery.com), 6 Church Street, is a nonprofit run by artists and presents new shows monthly. The working studio of potter **Jacob Preston** (843-757-3084; jacobprestonpottery.com), 10 Church Street, between Boundary and

THE BLUFFTON FARMERS' MARKET SC LOWCOUNTRY TOURISM COMMISSION

Calhoun Streets, is a light-filled showcase of his work, which has graced area homes for 40 years. **Ben Ham Gallery** (843-815-6200; www.benhamimages.com), 210 Bluffton Road, is one of two locations (the other is in Charleston) that display stunning black and white photographs captured by a large-format camera and influenced by the grace and respect for nature demonstrated by Ansel Adams.

✳ To Do

If Bluffton is more than a stopover, you can get on the May River and its tributaries to fish, watch birds and dolphins, collect shells and stories, and learn about the ecology of this unique habitat. You can even ride a Jet Ski or take a sunset cruise. Trips can be as short as 90 minutes or as long as a day, and costs begin at around $30 per person. **May River Excursions** (843-304-2878; www.mayriverexcursions.com), 81 Calhoun Street, is a little more oriented toward sightseeing and fishing, and **Spartina Marine Education Charters** (843-338-2716; www.spartinacharters.com) toward ecotouring and education.

✳ Lodging

Refer to lodgings in Savannah, Beaufort, and Hilton Head, which have easy access to Bluffton; all of the major hotel and motel chains have lodgings in greater Bluffton. **Old Town Bluffton Inn** (843-707-4045; www.blufftoninnsc.com), 1321 May River Road, opened in spring 2019. Some of its 14 rooms have balconies that overlook downtown Bluffton or the May River in the distance, and they are all luxury standard. $$$.

The most sensational addition in the highest-end-possible category in lodging from Charleston to Savannah has been **Palmetto Bluff** (866-706-6565; www.palmettobluff.com), a Montage resort and residential community located on 20,000 acres and one of the nation's top wedding venues. You can stay in cottages (each with a kitchen), at the inn, or rent a resplendent home and visit seven places to eat without leaving the compound. There's a par 72 golf course for guests, as well as tennis, swimming, boating, fishing, sporting clays, and miles of hiking and biking trails. Coming in later to the Lowcountry resort and residential game, and not on the ocean and not at all touristy, Palmetto Bluff has built conservation and education into its identity, and it shows.

✳ Where to Eat

The Pearl Kitchen & Bar (843-757-5511; www.thepearlbluffton.com), 55 Calhoun Street. Open for lunch Thurs.–Sat. and dinner daily. The Pearl serves very fresh and local seafood and large salads, with vegetables and greens drawn from local farmers. You'd have to go to a much bigger town to get the creative cocktails they come up with. The menu is like a French bistro's in that it doesn't oversell and the food is just exceedingly well executed. $–$$$.

The Cottage Café, Bakery & Tea Room (843-757-0508; www.thecottagebluffton.com), 38 Calhoun Street, serves breakfast and lunch daily and dinner on the weekends. It's funky and homegrown, and you can eat on a little porch of the old house. While it's not a classic Lowcountry fish place, it offers food with similar abundance, and you get lots of veggies and greens, too. Sunday brunch starts early and is a real winner. $–$$.

✳ Selective Shopping

Bluffton Farmers' Market operates Thursday afternoons on Calhoun Street and gathers a wonderful mix of artists, craftspeople, chefs, farmers, gardeners, and musicians who represent the inclusive and creative spirit of the town.

Eggs 'N' Tricities (843-757-3446; Facebook:@eggsntricities), 5 Lawton Street. Local and best known for dressing women in cashmere, patterned shirts, and cute jackets, it also has a riotous selection of housewares, tableware, candles, and accessories.

Spartina 449 (843-815-9000; www.spartina449.com), 32 Calhoun Street. What started as a crisp linen and leather handbag and accessories business on Daufuskie Island has exploded in popularity, clearly tapping into a vision for what independent, stylish women want in a palette inspired by vivid Lowcountry colors and attention to workmanship in bags, jewelry, dresses, scarves, and gifts.

The Storybook Shoppe (843-757-2600; www.thestorybookshoppe.com), 41 Calhoun Street. A large selection of children's books, classic and new.

✳ Special Events

SPRING *February:* **Beaufort International Film Festival** (843-522-3196; www .beaufortfilmfestival.com). A juried festival that highlights feature films, documentaries, shorts, and animated work made by professionals and students.

May: **Beaufort Gullah Festival** (www .originalgullahfestival.org). Held Memorial Day weekend, this event features a big outdoor market with a quirky variety of vendors, dance performances, concerts of spiritual and gospel music, and demonstrations of boatbuilding, net-weaving, and other skills related to the West African heritage of the Sea Islands.

SUMMER *July:* **Beaufort Water Festival** (843-524-0600; www.bftwaterfestival .com). A 10-day festival starting in mid-July that features special events each day and entertainment at night: croquet, fishing, golf tournaments, a juried art show, kids' day, parade, and several outdoor dances with live music. The air shows and acrobatic waterskiing demonstrations are especially fun to watch. It's a reunion for locals who have moved away and maintains a small-town feel.

FALL *October:* **Historic Beaufort Foundation Fall Festival of Houses & Gardens** (843-379-3331; www.historicbeaufort .org). A weekend of candlelight and daytime tours of homes and gardens in and around Beaufort. The final day often features tours of outlying plantations, such as the rarely seen Auldbrass, designed by Frank Lloyd Wright and meticulously restored inside and out.

Historic Bluffton Arts & Seafood Festival (843-757-2583; www.blufftonarts andseafoodfestival.com). A weeklong fair in mid-October showcasing a hundred local and regional artists, historical exhibits and tours, music, events on the river, and food vendors galore.

Edisto Historic Preservation Society Tour of Homes (843-869-1954; www .edistomuseum.org). Daylong tour of homes that are not usually open to the public and not often visible from public roads. Tickets go on sale in August and often sell out.

November: **Music to Your Mouth** (www.palmettobluff.com). Held annually at Palmetto Bluff, this ingenious, expensive, and popular multiday event mixes Southern music, chef's demonstrations, and special meals and tastings. There are classes and demonstrations, oyster and pig roasts, storytelling and art.

Penn Center Heritage Days (843-838-2432; www.penncenter.com), St. Helena. Held the second weekend in November on the historic Penn Center campus, Heritage Days celebrates Sea Island culture in its many forms. It features islanders in a children's theater production on Penn's history; local church choirs and a community sing; lectures; an art exhibit; and an old-fashioned fish fry with musical entertainment. Saturday highlights start with a parade full of bands and floats that shuts down the central highway on the island and continue with performances that include Gullah games and storytelling, dance, music, and demonstrations of traditional crafts and cooking.

WINTER *December:* **A Night on the Town** (843-525-6644; www.downtown beaufort.com). Join in an informal street party thrown by the downtown Beaufort merchants, usually on the first Friday of the month. There are decorations everywhere, jazz musicians, carolers, and even Santa. The following night, **Light Up the Night Christmas Boat Parade** includes hundreds of crafts in all shapes and sizes motoring down the Beaufort River, a joyful scene easily enjoyed from the seawall at Waterfront Park.

OPPOSITE: HILTON HEAD IS A BOATER'S PARADISE

HILTON HEAD

HILTON HEAD

nlike the rest of the Lowcountry, Hilton Head is a place of condensed and organized pleasures. The island is 12 miles long and 5 miles wide; fronts the Intracoastal Waterway, the Atlantic, and Port Royal Sound; and is laced by creeks. The commercial districts are discreetly screened from view, and even the busiest thoroughfare, US 278 (William Hilton Parkway), lacks neon signs. Summer is the busiest time, when the year-round population of about 38,000 sees a turnover of 10,000 visitors a week; more than 2.5 million visitors come every year.

Until 1955, when the first bridge linked Hilton Head to the mainland, the island's history resembled that of its Sea Island neighbors. Slaves worked on 16 or so plantations until the Civil War, when it became a federal base defending the entrance to the Broad River and the railways and Confederate strongholds further inland. Unlike other islands, Hilton Head's native islanders remained rural and self-sufficient well into the mid-1960s. The African American families farmed and fished; the visitors who came were gentleman hunters, millionaires from the North. Packet steamers, sailboats, motorboats, and barges supplied transportation, and more often than not their market destination was Savannah, for Hilton Head is the southernmost area of Beaufort County.

Years of scholarly research have yielded new information about **Mitchelville,** considered the first self-governing African American community in the country, established as a result of the federal occupation and liberation of the plantations.

Resort development led to the modern "plantation" layout that orders the island's geography. In the summer of 2020, several gated communities using the word "plantation" as part of their corporate identity and signage took steps to remove the word. The gated communities remain, and you may get short-term rentals there, based on their rules: same entity, slightly different name. To native islanders and, finally to some others, the marketing concept of "plantation" had become objectionable. Within and around them are the dozens of golf courses, tennis courts, and marinas that define island recreation. Stores and restaurants are usually gathered in mall clusters and shopping pods, like **Harbour Town,** the **Village at Wexford, Coligny Plaza,** or **Main Street.** Locally, and on local maps, you'll see the island divided into the South, Mid, and North areas. Many smaller residential areas lie scattered across the island, some of them "gated" communities, others not.

As the island's topography has changed (much of it sculpted into golf courses), so has its population. Census figures categorize residents by race (90 percent white) and by age (some 30 percent over 60 years old). Spillover development into greater Bluffton (as opposed to Old Town Bluffton) has blurred the "Hilton Head" brand, meaning a restaurant may actually be off-island. The listings in this chapter are almost always located on Hilton Head Island.

If you mostly want to play golf or tennis or stay near the beach, look for options in the *Lodging* section for "stay-and-play" packages. If you're traveling with friends or family, you may want to rent a house or villa unit. If you decide upon a resort, you may not need a car—most resort amenities are within walking and biking distance, and you will usually be provided with airport transportation from Savannah. For touring without a car, rent a bike and explore the island's bike trails.

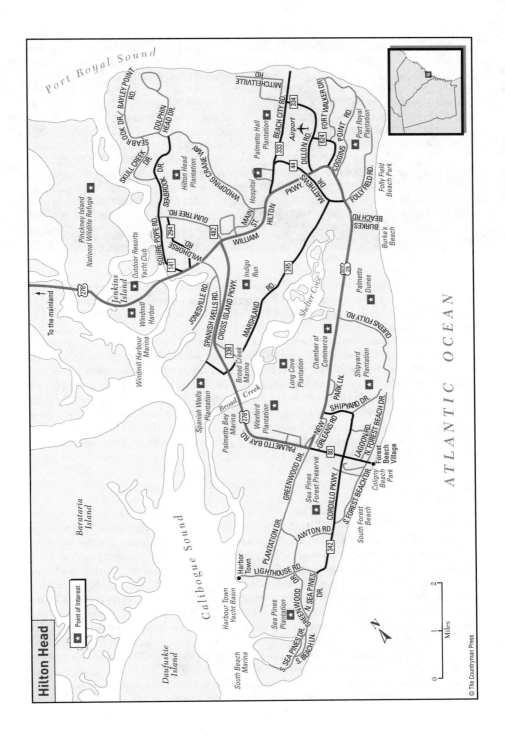

COVID-19

Due to the COVID-19 pandemic, travel in the Lowcountry, as everywhere else, requires more planning for every activity to ensure appropriate social distancing. This means that you should call or check a venue's website to confirm, among other things, if reservations are required where walk-in activity was once the norm. It also means that providers of services from hotels to restaurants or boat rides to carriage tours are likely to be running their businesses differently from in the past, with fewer visitors engaged at any one time. If you are a family group, be sure to mention that, because it may make a difference in the business owner's risk calculations. Ask if there is outdoor seating available at restaurants—many venues have changed their layouts to include more outside dining while they reduce the numbers of tables inside. Meals to go, food service delivery, and curbside pick-up options have expanded dramatically in the spring and summer of 2020; check to see if those options are still available. Annual events, including professional golf and tennis tournaments and house and garden tours, have shifted their dates and ticketing procedures. You'll have a more rewarding travel experience if you arrive prepared and flexible.

The high season starts in March, when families come on spring vacation, and lasts through October. Some 2.5 million guests visit annually. When the island is crowded, expect traffic congestion on the bridges, especially on the weekends, and on all island roads.

Savannah/Hilton Head International Airport (912-964-0514; www.savannah airport.com) and the county-owned **Hilton Head Island Airport** (www.hiltonhead airport.com) are gateways. Flights to Hilton Head are increasing in range of service and frequency due to recent facility upgrades. Rental cars are available and there's a taxi stand. Expect to pay between $17 and $36, depending on your destination. Resorts don't generally provide pickup service at the Hilton Head Island Airport as they do at Savannah. By car, take Exit 8 from I-95 to US 278, the link to Hilton Head. It's about 25 minutes by car from the exit to the north end of the island and Bluffton locations, but count on an hour to get to the island's south end.

✳ To See

HISTORIC SITES AND MUSEUMS Sites are often off the beaten path, and a guide or a bit of research will enhance their context. Two places to start are the websites of the **Coastal Discovery Museum** (843-689-6767; www.coastaldiscovery.org) and the **Heritage Library Foundation** (843-686-6560; www.heritagelib.org), a research library with old photographs and maps where you can explore your roots. Guided by native islanders with an abundance of expertise and warmth, **Gullah Heritage Trail Tours** (843-681-7066; gullaheritage.com) include visits to praise houses, cemeteries, and the original location of **Mitchelville,** the first freed African American township in the country. Tours leave daily from the Coastal Discovery Museum. Adults $32, children $15. It's a must-do on Hilton Head if you want to understand Gullah culture and its place in and contributions to American history.

Baynard Ruins within Sea Pines Plantation. The remains of a plantation house and outbuildings first constructed circa 1800 can be seen on a short, self-guided walk at the site. The ruins are made of tabby, a popular, homemade Lowcountry building material that resulted from burning oyster shells (to make lime), which were then mixed with whole shells, sand, and water. This is one of few sites where you can still see it. $8 gate fee to access Sea Pines.

Coastal Discovery Museum (843-689-6767; www.coastaldiscovery.org), 70 Honey Horn Drive, is located at the north end of the island. Archaeological digs have yielded a collection of artifacts related to the island's history and culture, and these are on display along with models, dioramas, interactive displays, and explanatory panels and videos. You can hear and see oral history interviews capturing decades of small farming, fishing, oystering, and the timbering industry. The gift shop offers an excellent selection of books on the Lowcountry as well as maps, field guides, and activity kits for kids. Open daily, the museum offers many tours of the marsh, beach, and other natural areas and historic sites, including the steam cannon, Mitchelville, and Fort Walker. Fees vary; reservations -suggested.

Fish Haul Plantation off Beach City Road near Mitchelville. Only the chimneys of slave dwellings remain at what

HARBOUR TOWN AT DUSK COURTESY OF THE HILTON HEAD ISLAND VISITOR & CONVENTION BUREAU AND THE HARBOUR TOWN LIGHTHOUSE AT SEA PINES RESORT

TABBY RUINS ON DAUFUSKIE ISLAND LOWCOUNTRY & RESORT ISLANDS TOURISM COMMISSION

BE SURE TO ORDER OYSTERS © GINGER WAREHAM/PICKLEJUICE.COM

was once a thriving Sea Island cotton plantation. Federal troops camped here from the time of Union occupation in November 1861.

Fort Howell off Beach City Road at Dillon Road. A large earthwork built by Union troops in 1864 to strengthen the defense of Mitchelville.

Historic Mitchelville Freedom Park (843-255-7301; www.exploremitchelville.org), 229 Beach City Road. Mitchelville was the first self-governing town of free Africans in the country, where formerly enslaved people built their own homes, churches, schools, and stores. A growing series of tours, cultural programming, exhibits, and annual events, like the extremely popular Juneteenth celebration, highlight its history in the Civil War and Reconstruction periods. The site itself is evocative, but currently no buildings remain, so signing up for a walking tour is worthwhile.

Indian Shell Ring, Sea Pines Forest Preserve. Native Americans occupied Hilton Head and other sea islands some 4,000 years ago and left their mark in huge rings and shell middens. It is thought that this site represents the refuse of oyster shells piled behind each of many huts that stood in a small circle.

Zion Chapel of Ease, William Hilton Parkway at Mathews Drive. A small chapel built circa 1786 for the convenience of worshippers who lived too far from the Episcopal Church at Beaufort once occupied this site. The circa-1846 Baynard Mausoleum within its cemetery is the largest antebellum structure extant on the island.

✲ To Do

The towns of Bluffton and Beaufort are easy day trips; see entries in those chapters for touring, exploring, and dining. Savannah is about an hour away, and you could tour the

Historic District, wander around and have at least one meal, and be back in time for sunset on Hilton Head. A trip to Charleston requires more time and planning, including approximately four hours by car, round-trip.

Several large and fully equipped marinas serve as the visitor's jumping-off point for water-based tours, fishing, water sports, and boat rentals. They also provide transient berths, launching ramps, fuel, shower facilities, ship's stores, and repair shops. Rates for berthing vary, from $1–$2.50 per foot, or by the week/month. Charter fishing boats, small powerboats, sailboats, and yachts as long as 150 feet are berthed side by side, offering a striking example of the many ways residents and visitors choose to enjoy the water.

Broad Creek Marina (843-681-3625; www.broadcreekmarinahh.com), 18 Simmons Road. Located mid-island with many excellent seafood restaurants nearby.

Harbour Town Yacht Basin (843-363-8335; www.seapines.com/marina). The gem of Sea Pines waterfront, with a high-end shopping district.

Palmetto Bay Marina (843-785-5000; www.palmettobaymarinahhi.com), 86 Helmsman Way.

Shelter Cove Harbour & Marina (866-661-3822; www.sheltercovehiltonhead.com). Located in a village-like area of shops and restaurants.

Skull Creek Marina (843-681-8436; www.theskullcreekmarina.com), Hilton Head Plantation.

South Beach Marina (843-671-6498; www.sbinn.com). Located in Sea Pines on the south end, originally envisioned as a New England–style village harbor.

Windmill Harbour (843-681-9235; www.windmillharbourmarina.org). Set on the northwest coast of Hilton Head Island on the Intracoastal Waterway. Enter via a lock system. About 250 slips accommodating boats up to 70 feet. Very few transient slips available; reservations a must.

TOURS ON THE WATER **Adventure Cruises** (843-785-4558; www.hiltonheadisland .com), Shelter Cove Harbour. Dolphin-watch nature cruises lasting nearly two hours, as well as sunset cruises. Adults $20, children $10.

Dolphin Nature Tour (843-681-2522; www.hiltonheadtours.com), Broad Creek Marina. Narrated environmental tours (90 minutes) aboard the 16-passenger SS *Pelican*, a restored Navy Motor Whaler with canopy, or the *Island Queen*, which holds up to 40 passengers. Adults $20, children $10.Wheelchair accessible. Advance purchase recommended.

Flying Circus and *Pau Hana* (843-686-2582; www.hiltonheadislandsailing.com), Palmetto Bay Marina. *Flying Circus* is a fast catamaran offering two-hour daylight and sunset cruises for a maximum of six passengers. *Pau Hana*, a larger catamaran, can carry 49 passengers. Tickets for two-hour tours, which usually depart three times a day are $45 for adults, $25 for children.

Island Explorer (843-785-2100; www.dolphintourshiltonhead.com) offers dolphin watching and eco-tours that last from one to three hours on a 12-person motorized skiff. Rates start at $25.

Lowcountry Nature Tours (843-683-0187; www.lowcountrynaturetours.com) depart from Shelter Cove Marina. Limiting its load to six passengers, it's a nice option for multigenerational parties, and tours can be customized.

An excursion to **Daufuskie Island** (www.daufuskieisland.com), the setting for Pat Conroy's book *The Water Is Wide,* makes for a nice day trip, or even a half day, starting with a ferry ride and golf cart tours that can be arranged in advance to see historic cemeteries, churches, and communities. They offer the best way to see the rural island. A small section has luxury homes, but it remains in proud isolation—with a couple of art studios and informal places to eat, and expansive beaches and marshes.

Daufuskie Island Ferry (843-940-7704; www.daufuskieislandferry.com) leaves from Buckingham Landing at the foot of the bridge on the Bluffton side four times daily, and there's an evening trip in the summer. Parking is free. Fares are $17.50 each way. You can take bikes and dogs.

Outside Daufuskie (800-686-6996; www.outsidedaufuskie.com) offers private charters and customized trips.

Vagabond Cruise (843-363-9026; www.vagabondcruise.com), Harbour Town Marina, Sea Pines. Vessels take you to Savannah's River Street and pick you up four hours later on Tuesdays and Thursdays. A good way to avoid the driving/parking hassle and get a sense of why Savannah was and is such a significant port. Adults $60, kids $25.

BOATING **Commander Zodiac** (843-671-3344; www.commanderzodiac.com), South Beach Marina. Visit the dolphins in engine-powered rubber rafts and rent small sailboats. There's an extensive camp and junior sailing program for kids.

H2O Sports Center (843-671-4386; www.h2osports.com), Harbour Town Marina, Sea Pines. Provides rentals for, and instruction in, parasailing, wave running on Jet Skis, kneeboarding, paddleboarding, and kayaking.

Palmetto Bay Water Sports (843-785-5000; www.pbmarinahhi.com), Palmetto Bay Marina. If you want more than paddle, kayak, or wind power, you can rent a variety of watercraft by the hour to go on your own or join a group tour in Broad Creek.

HILTON HEAD IS A MAJOR RECREATIONAL PORT FOR LOCAL AND VISITING BOATERS

CANOEING, KAYAKING, AND PADDLE-BOARDING Amid the opportunities to play golf and tennis or be a spectator in a beautifully manicured and maintained resort landscape, a visitor can forget that Hilton Head has its own world-class, low-tech, low-impact recreational options. They are found in the creeks and on the perimeter that makes Hilton Head an island, after all.

Today you can explore miles of waterways in a canoe or kayak, on your own or with a guided tour, by the half day, the day, at sunset, by moonlight, or on an overnight expedition. No experience is necessary, all safety equipment and basic instruction is provided, and kids are welcome. You may end up paddling out to a sandbar, fishing, taking a birding tour, or winding through the maze of coastal marshlands, pristine rivers, and nature preserves.

Here are public landings to launch from. Note that while you can park for free, the spaces fill quickly.

Broad Creek Boat Ramp (Helmsman Way, under the Charles Fraser Bridge).

C. C. Haigh Jr. Boat Landing (off US 278 at Pinckney Island).

Marshland Road Boat Ramp (Marshland Road).

HAVE AN ACTIVE DAY ON THE WATER © GINGER WAREHAM/ PICKLEJUICE.COM

Some outfitters offer extended-day programs for teens. For paddlers who feel comfortable going out on their own, day-rate rental charges for kayaks start at $60 for a single, $70 for a double; kayaks may be rented for as long as six days. Two-hour guided tours of local waters like Broad Creek, where you are likely to see lots of birds and fish in action, start at $40 per person, $30 for kids 12 and younger. Longer tours run about $125 per person, depending on the arrangements. Customized trips and overnight camping/biking expeditions are available by request. Reservations are suggested for tours.

Outside Hilton Head (843-686-6996; www.outsidehiltonhead.com), 50 Shelter Cove Lane. This longtime island business and outfitter offers clinics, teen camps, weekend retreats, and lessons, as well as tours on every imaginable thing that floats. Trips vary in length and season but always include two-hour and daylong excursions. It's the best-run and most comprehensive tour/rental/instructional operation on Hilton Head.

FAMILY FUN Beachcombing, bike-riding, flying a kite, sunset children's concerts, putt-putt golf after dinner, and weekly summer fireworks displays are part of the Hilton Head experience. **Outside Hilton Head** (843-686-6996; www.outsidehiltonhead .com) offers kayak camps for kids as young as 7, as well as teen activities. Free concerts generally occur nightly under the Liberty Oak in Harbour Town and in Shelter Cove Park. Various musicians, puppeteers, and clowns also turn up at Coligny Plaza (off

Pope Avenue) Monday through Friday nights to entertain families. At South Beach Marina you can enjoy music while the sun sets over the docks.

Playgrounds are located at Harbour Town in Sea Pines ($8 gate fee for nonguests), Shelter Cove, and Crossings Park. Check *The Island Packet* (www.islandpacket.com) to find special family-oriented events.

Adventure Cove Family Fun Center (843-842-9990; www.adventurecove.com),18 Folly Field Road. Miniature golf and arcade.

Legendary Golf (843-686-3399; www.legendarygolfhhi.com), 900 William Hilton Parkway.

Pirate's Island Adventure Golf (843-686-4001; www.piratesislandgolf.com), 8 Marina Side Drive.

Zipline Hilton Head (843-682-6000; www.ziplinehiltonhead.com), Broad Creek Marina. Eight interconnected ziplines, up to 75 feet high, course above the marsh and sound. A "ride" or tour lasts two hours. They also offer group aerial adventures in a park with six different ability courses (no ziplines) that are easier for younger kids to explore.

FISHING The options are too numerous to list, but the diversity indicates the number of customized possibilities: size of the boat, length of the day, level of challenge, location, number of anglers, type of catch, and, of course, the probability of success. (All but the last can be provided.) Fly-fishing is also available. Boats are fully equipped with tackle, etc., and depart from several marinas for inshore waters, flats, artificial reefs, and the Gulf Stream. Catches include tarpon, marlin, and sailfish; amberjack, shark, king mackerel, and bluefish closer to shore; and flounder, red drum, sea trout, and sheepshead in the coastal flats. Prices for four to six passengers for a half day of fishing start at about $475. A Gulf Stream expedition (about 14 hours) starts at about $2,300 for six passengers. A good overview is at www.hiltonheadisland.org, or check the marina websites listed above.

Blue Water Bait & Tackle (843-671-3060; www.bluewaterhhi.com), South Beach Marina. Trophy fishing, taxidermy services, and a full gear shop. The fleet has boats from 17 to 32 feet long for fishing offshore and inshore.

Capt. Hook (843-785-1700; www.captainhookhiltonhead.com), Shelter Cove. A good family and budget choice for four- to six-hour inshore and offshore trips on a 70-foot boat with enclosed cabin and restrooms. Food on board.

Tallboy Fishing Charters (843-575-2550; www.tallboyfishingcharters.com). Capt. Richard Pollitzer was raised on the water in Beaufort (as were several generations of family before him). He knows the fishing and islands landscape as well as anyone and has been chartering for 25 years. On his 31-foot *Ocean Master* (with head and plenty of covered and open space for fishing) he offers inshore, nearshore, and offshore trips that start at three hours and cost $450 for up to six people. He will customize a trip according to your needs.

FITNESS Major resorts such as the Westin and Hilton have in-house spas, but the industry in general, including yoga studios, is growing. Here are a few establishments that have been around for a while.

Island Yoga (803-420-2829; www.hhislandyoga.com), 1012 William Hilton Parkway, has classes, including yoga on the beach, that cater to practitioners at all levels.

Jiva Yoga (843-247-4549; www.jivayogacenter.com), 1032 William Hilton Parkway. This studio offers stand-up paddleboarding yoga as well as multiple classes daily.

Le Spa (843-363-6000; www.lespahiltonhead.com), 71 Lighthouse Road, Sea Pines. A wide selection of massages is available: long and short, shiatsu, hot rock, deep tissue, reflexology, or any combination.

The Sanctuary (843-290-1062; www.sanctuary-spa.com), 32 Palmetto Bay Road. A full-service spa for men and women, it specializes in European techniques, with facial peels, waxing, and unique beauty treatments.

Seeds of Calm Spa (843-686-5525; www.seedsofcalmspa.com), 18 Executive Park Road. You can detoxify your body with a wrap, rejuvenate with an herbal rub, undergo deep massage therapy, or have an acupuncture session.

GOLF Golf culture has shaped life here and determined modern Hilton Head's identity. Today there are some 30 courses in the Hilton Head area (on and just off the island) that are a mix of public, semiprivate, and resort play. The list below is a sampling. Golf is expensive, and Hilton Head is no different—anywhere from $95 to $250 for prime time, with the average about $125, including cart and fees. Early morning or later afternoon play costs less, as do resort packages or packages sold by bundling brokers. Public course play starts at about $50. (Walking is permitted on several courses—check ahead for caddie help.) During the low season—winter months—prices can drop by 40 percent. Good sources for information are www.hiltonheadisland.org, www.hiltonheadgolf.com, and the resorts' individual websites if you're staying at one.

Reservations to secure tee times are essential—some courses accept reservations from nonresort guests up to 90 days in advance, others just 30 to 60 days in advance. (It gets crowded—800,000 rounds of golf are played annually at Hilton Head.) Unless noted, all courses are 18 holes. Appropriate dress calls for shirts with collars for men and no blue jeans, gym shorts, or jogging shorts. If you're looking to improve your game, inquire about clinics, private instruction, and programs from half a day to three days at **The Golf Learning Center at Sea Pines Resort** (843-785-4540; www.golfacademy.net) or the **Palmetto Dunes Golf Academy** (888-909-9566; www.palmetto dunes.com).

Hilton Head Plantation

Country Club of Hilton Head (843-681-2582; www.clubcorp.com). Par 72; 5,373-yard ladies course to 6,919-yard champion course. Designed by Rees Jones.

Oyster Reef Golf Club (843-681-1750; www.oysterreefgolfclub.com). Par 72; 6,071-yard forward course to 7,018-yard champion course. Designed by Rees Jones.

Indigo Run

Golden Bear Golf Club at Indigo Run (843-689-2200; www.clubcorp.com). Par 72; 4,965-yard forward course to 7,014-yard champion course. Designed by Jack Nicklaus.

HILTON HEAD'S DOZENS OF GOLF COURSES DRAW YEAR-ROUND VISITORS AND PGA TOURNAMENTS COURTESY OF THE HILTON HEAD ISLAND VISITOR & CONVENTION BUREAU

Palmetto Dunes Resort

Arthur Hills Course (888-909-9566; www.palmettodunes.com). Par 72; 4,999-yard forward course to 6,651-yard champion course. Designed by Arthur Hills.

George Fazio Course (888-909-9566; www.palmettodunes.com). Par 70; 5,273-yard ladies course to 6,873-yard champion course. Designed by George Fazio. Named one of Fodor's *Golf Digest*'s 100 top American courses.

Robert Trent Jones (888-909-9566; www.palmettodunes.com). Par 72; 2,625-yard junior to 7,005-yard champion course. Designed by Robert Trent Jones/Roger Rulewich. Junior tees allow young golfers to play a classic course.

Palmetto Hall Plantation

Arthur Hills Course (843-342-2582; www.palmettohallcc.com). Par 72; 4,956-yard forward course to 6,918-yard champion course. Designed by Arthur Hills.

Robert Cupp Course (843-342-2582; www.palmettohallgolf.com). Par 72; 5,220-yard forward course to 7,079-yard tour course. Designed by Robert Cupp.

Port Royal Golf & Racquet Club

Barony Course (843-681-1750; www.portroyalgolfclub.com). Par 72; 5,183-yard forward course to 6,543-yard champion course. Designed by George Cobb.

Robber's Row Course (843-681-1750; www.portroyalgolfclub.com). Par 72; 4,902-yard forward course to 6,675-yard champion course. A Pete Dye renovation of a George Cobb course near what was Fort Walker, a Civil War camp.

Sea Pines Plantation

Atlantic Dunes (843-842-8484; www.seapines.com). Par 72; 7,065 yards. Davis Love III designed a complete reconstruction of the island's first course while maintaining the feel of the dune landscape and ocean views and adding masses of indigenous plants along its edge.

Harbour Town Golf Links (843-842-8484; www.seapines.com). Par 71; 5,208-yard green course to 7,107-yard "Heritage" course. Designed by Pete Dye. The RBC Heritage is played on this course—rated among the top 75 in the world and among the top 50 in the United States—every April.

Heron Point (843-842-8484; www.seapines.com). Par 72; 5,261-yard ladies course to 7,103-yard champion course. Designed by Pete Dye.

Shipyard Plantation

Shipyard Golf Club (843-681-1750; www.hiltonheadgolf.net/shipyard-golf-club). Par 36 for 9 holes and 72 for 18 holes on four tees set up across three linked courses: Brigantine, Galleon, and Clipper, a 5,391-yard forward course to 6,848-yard champion course. Designed by George Cobb/Willard Byrd. A favorite of the senior PGA Tour.

Off-Island/Public

Crescent Pointe Golf Club (843-706-2600; www.crescentpointegolf.com), US 278, Bluffton. Par 71; four tees from 5,219 yards to 6,772 yards. Designed by Arnold Palmer for "Arnie's Army."

Eagle's Pointe Golf Club (843-757-5900; www.eaglespointegolf.com), US 278, 7 miles west of Hilton Head. Par 71; 5,112 yards to 6,780 yards. Designed by Davis Love III, a five-time Heritage Classic winner.

Hilton Head National (843-842-5900; www.hiltonheadnational.com), US 278, Bluffton. Par 72; 4,649-yard forward course to 6,779-yard champion course. Designed by Gary Player/Bobby Weed. Advance reservations up to one year.

Island West Golf Club (843-823-6222; www.islandwestgolf.net), US 278, Bluffton. Par 72; 4,948-yard ladies course to 6,803-yard champion course. Designed by Fuzzy Zoeller/Clyde Johnston.

Old South Golf Links (843-785-5353; www.oldsouthgolf.com), US 278, Bluffton. Par 71/72; 4,776-yard red tee ladies course to 5,772-yard green tee champion course. Designed by Clyde Johnston.

HORSEBACK RIDING **Lawton Stables** (843-671-2586; www.lawtonstables.com), Sea Pines. One-hour walking trail rides for adults and kids cost $65–$75, including trips through the 600-acre Sea Pines Forest Preserve. Reservations required.

TENNIS There are more than 300 tennis courts spread through 19 clubs on Hilton Head, with several clubs open for public play. Pickleball is getting big here, too. Call ahead for reservations—the staff may be able to set you up with a game. Pros offer lessons, daily stroke clinics, and intensive camps year-round; fully stocked shops provide stringing services and sales of equipment, clothing, and accessories. Reserved court rental fees range from $20–$25 per hour, but some clubs offer reduced walk-on rates for midday play (noon–4 p.m.) and off-season use. Free exhibitions take place at 5:30 p.m. Monday through Thursday and Sunday afternoons at different clubs on a rotating basis.

Hilton Head Island Beach & Tennis Resort (800-475-2631; www.hhibeachandtennis .com), 40 Folly Field Road. Ten courts, pro shop, and instruction.

Palmetto Dunes Tennis Center (888-909-9566; www.palmettodunes.com), Palmetto Dunes Oceanfront Resort. Twenty-three clay, two hard courts. Hard courts and eight clay courts are lit for night play.

Port Royal Racquet Club (843-686-8803), Port Royal Resort. Ten clay, four hard courts.

Sea Pines Racquet Club (843-363-4495; www.seapinestennisresort.com), Sea Pines Plantation. Champion Stan Smith, a longtime resident, has made this the island's classiest tennis arena, with 21 clay courts and top-notch teaching.

Van Der Meer Tennis Center (843-785-8388; www.vandermeertennis.com), Deallyon Road. Seventeen hard courts, including four covered and lit. The center is internationally known for its rigorous teaching programs and camps for kids and pros, as well as serious players. The island's top youngsters often train here.

Van Der Meer Tennis/Shipyard Racquet Club (843-686-8804), Shipyard Plantation. Twenty courts: 13 clay, 7 hard.

✳ Green Space

BEACHES Twelve miles of gently sloping beaches define the island's ocean edge. They can be as wide as 600 feet at low tide, providing a hard surface for fat-tire bicycles. Although gated communities limit access to residents and guests, the beach is public to the high-water mark, good for long walks. The town maintains several entry points where there is parking (metered and nonmetered) and where you can swim;

some are muddier and marshier but serene to visit. Maps and descriptions are at www
.hiltonhead.com.

The public and most popular beaches with facilities, designated swimming areas,
and seasonal lifeguards are: **Alder Lane** (S. Forest Beach Drive); **Coligny Beach Park**
(1 N. Forest Beach Road), **Folly Field Beach Park** (55 Starfish Drive), **Driessen Beach
Park** (64 Bradley Beach Road), and **Islanders Beach Park** (94 Folly Field Road). As of
2019, they were accessible to wheelchairs via boardwalks and beach matting. Coligny
has free WiFi.

Other gems include **Fish Haul Creek/Mitchelville Beach Park** (124 Mitchelville
Road) and **Burkes Beach** (60 Burkes Beach Road) limited parking but near **Chaplin
Community Park,** where you can leave your car, visit the dog park, or play tennis and
basketball.

On some nights (May through October) you can watch the amazing loggerhead turtle, an endangered species, crawl ashore and lay its eggs in nests it digs on the beach,
or see hundreds of loggerhead hatchlings make their way back to the ocean. Volunteer
groups monitor the beach and sometimes move the eggs to higher ground or protected
sites, away from tides and hungry raccoons. The turtles are slow moving and docile
but chary: do not disturb them with light or touch the nests. Just seeing these huge
creatures is magical. Check the Coastal Discovery Museum's beach and turtle watch
tours (www.coastaldiscovery.org).

There are lots of beach rules. They are widely posted. Here are a few: Dogs are
not permitted on the beach from 10 a.m.–5 p.m. from the beginning of Memorial Day
weekend through Labor Day. They have to be leashed in those hours from April 1–
September 30. Motor vehicles, alcohol, glass containers, nudity, and general boor-
ishness are not allowed. Fishing, boating, surfing, ballplaying, and similar activities

THERE ARE MORE THAN 12 MILES OF OCEANFRONT BEACH IN HILTON HEAD, WITH MANY POINTS OF PUBLIC ACCESS AND
MULTIPLE PLACES TO RENT BIKES OR BEACH CHAIRS COURTESY OF THE HILTON HEAD ISLAND VISITOR & CONVENTION
BUREAU

are prohibited in designated swimming areas. You can't dig deep holes and leave them unfilled when you leave for a person or animal to stumble in. You have to take away the equipment you came with, like tents and umbrellas. All pretty common sense, but it's amazing what people in swimsuits and tanning lotion forget about.

BICYCLING Bikes are easy to come by, and you can expect island-wide pickup and delivery. If you're traveling with youngsters, you'll be able to get baby carriers, helmets, bikes with training wheels, hook-on "trailers," and jogging strollers. Paths are marked—there are now more than 40 miles of them—and they extend from the tip of North Forest Beach to the end of South Forest Beach, along Pope Avenue, and up William Hilton Parkway to Squire Pope Road. Take detours to the beach and marsh. Bike paths also thread through the private plantations. At low tide, ride on the beach. Rental charges for bicycles start at $15 per day and $20–$30 per week for a simple cruiser model.

PALM TREES ARE EVERYWHERE ON HILTON HEAD

Bike Doctor (843-681-7531; www.bikedoctorhhi.com), 80 Beach City Road. They can also repair your bike. There is a second location at 21 New Orleans Road, Suite B (843-681-7532).

Hilton Head Bicycle Company (843-686-6888; www.hiltonheadbicycle.com), 112 Arrow Road.

Island Cruisers (843-785-4321; www.islandcruisersbikerentals.com), 13 Executive Park Road.

Pedals (843-842-5522; www.pedalsbicycles.com), 71 Pope Avenue.

BIRD-WATCHING Hilton Head still has some quiet places for birds to nest and feed. According to the island's Audubon Society chapter, some 200 species of birds regularly visit, and in the past 10 years more than 350 species have been sighted. Among the most distinctive "frequent flyers" are the snowy egret, great blue heron, white ibis, and osprey. Catch a glimpse of them for yourself during daylight hours at the following sites, where paths and boardwalks can accommodate hikers, bikers, and joggers.

Audubon Newhall Preserve, Palmetto Bay Road, 0.75 mile from Sea Pines Circle. A 50-acre sanctuary, open daily from dawn to dusk, that preserves the Lowcountry environment for plants and animals. Trees and plants are labeled for self-guided walks on woodland trails, and lists of bird sightings are posted on a bulletin board at the entrance. Interpretive walks are offered in the spring and fall. To arrange a group tour, contact the local Audubon organization through their website (www.hiltonheadaudubon.org).

Pinckney Island National Wildlife Refuge (843-784-2468; www.fws.gov/refuge/pinckney_island), 0.5 mile west of Hilton Head Island on US 278. Open daily dawn to dusk. This pristine, 4,035-acre landscape features the best birdwatching during the spring and fall and an easy 4-mile bike trail to White Point, site of an early Native American settlement.

Sea Pines Forest Preserve, Sea Pines Plantation. This 400-acre site with a shell ring and old rice field offers a self-guided walking tour, which takes one to two hours. $8 fee to enter Sea Pines.

Whooping Crane Pond Conservancy (www.hhilandtrust.org). Visitors can email for a day pass to enter Hilton Head Plantation, where this 137-actre tract is located. It features a boardwalk and self-guided nature trail.

✳ Lodging

When I stopped counting, there were more than 3,000 hotel and motel rooms and 6,000 rental units on Hilton Head, including cottages, houses, and villas scattered across the island, from sites on or near the beach to those around golf courses, marinas, lagoons, in residential subdivisions or low-rise housing complexes, even on the main highway. Another 1,000 units are dedicated to "time-share" arrangements and may be available for rent, too. Your accommodations may be elegant or simple; offer as much or as little privacy as you wish; come with or without kitchens; and lie within walking distance, or not, from the beach and recreational amenities.

Rates vary from as little as $70 per night (off-season) for an economy motel room to $8,500 per week for an ocean-front home with a swimming pool. The range reflects differences in size and location—oceanfront is premium; resort privileges add to the price—and also the time of year. Rates are highest during the vacation seasons, March through April and June through mid-August. The shoulder seasons of late April and May, then September and October bring ideal golfing conditions, so prices stay high, though not at the seasonal peak. In the winter months, rates can be half what they are in the high season.

Like many resort areas, Hilton Head adds an accommodations tax to lodging bills, and some establishments place a surcharge on credit card payments. Ask for an estimate of your total bill when you are booking and inquire about special rate packages or coupons offered for restaurants. Many hotels have discounts for golf and tennis; some have family plans, including activities for kids. In larger hotels, children often stay for free. WiFi is widely available; however, cell phone service can be spotty though it is improving all the time.

The easiest way to make reservations in a hotel or motel is by phone or website. To inquire about home and villa rentals, call a property management company or the resorts themselves. Central reservation agencies can give you a sense of the big picture, and they may be especially helpful in designing a package tailored to your specific interests. Good places to start are www.hiltonheadisland.org or www.explorehiltonhead.com.

Prices quoted are for high-season accommodations and do not include taxes, surcharges, or any special recreation/entertainment discounts. Note that the rates for luxury accommodations are at least in the "very expensive" category; they can easily run higher. Villa and home rentals generally run from Saturday to Saturday during peak season. **Evergreen Pet Lodge** (843-681-8354; www.evergreenpetlodgehhi.com) and **Southpaw Pet Resort** (843-342-7200; www.sphhi.com) offer boarding options and care for your pet.

HOTELS AND LARGER INNS **The Inn & Club at Harbour Town** (843-785-3333; www.seapines.com), 32 Greenwood Drive, Sea Pines Plantation. The most luxurious and private resort on the island, it's located in the Harbour Town complex, a Mediterranean-style marina village whose lighthouse is the most-recognized symbol of Hilton Head. The inn is situated just off the water in a quieter location by the golf courses. It's more thoughtfully designed than the functional fun-and-sun architecture of the big beachfront hotels, and its focus on service and serenity seem to suggest another way to enjoy the resort experience: to be in it, but not of it. $$$$.

Marriott Hilton Head Resort & Spa (843-686-8400 www.marriott.com), 1 Hotel Circle, Palmetto Dunes. It's the largest hotel on the island, with 512 rooms, indoor pool, Olympic-sized outdoor pool, and children's pool. Health club, tennis courts, three golf courses, sailboat and bicycle rentals, and lots of beachfront. Four restaurants, including casual poolside dining. A children's program (for an additional fee) is available weekends year-round, daily during the summer. $$$–$$$$.

Omni Oceanfront Resort & Spa (843-842-8000; www.omnihotels.com), 23 Ocean Lane, Palmetto Dunes. A luxury 323-room hotel that claims the largest rooms on the island—550 square feet each—with private balconies and kitchenettes. At the oceanfront setting there's an adults-only pool and a family pool, whirlpools, a fitness center, 25 tennis courts, and three golf courses. There is biking, canoeing, and kayaking on the 11-mile lagoon system. In the summer months, activities for kids ages 4 to 16 can be arranged. Restaurants and nightclubs are within the complex. $$$–$$$$.

Sonesta Hotel (843-842-2400; www .sonesta.com/HiltonHeadIsland), 130 Shipyard Drive, Shipyard Plantation. A 340-room oceanfront hotel with full concierge service, two restaurants, and a popular lounge for evening entertainment. Two pools on-site, golf courses within a mile and accessed by complimentary shuttle, nearby tennis courts

and a day spa, and sailing and water sports by arrangement. $$$.

Westin Hilton Head Island Resort and Spa (843-681-4000; www.marriott .com), 2 Grasslawn Avenue, Port Royal Plantation. Considered the most luxurious of the island's oceanfront resort hotels, with more than 400 rooms and 32 suites. The Westin is praised for its spa, the elegant decorations, and rooms with balconies. Guests may play golf on three courses and tennis on hard and clay courts. Heated, covered pool and two outdoor pools. There are six restaurants, from elegant to casual, including a poolside café and several bars. $$$$.

SMALLER INNS **The Beachhouse: A Holiday Inn Resort** (855-474-2882; www .thebeachhousehhi.com), 1 S. Forest Beach Drive. A popular public-access beach is at your doorstep, plus a poolside restaurant and volleyball courts on the beach, where there is most always a pickup game available. The Tiki Hut bar is a great place for people watching. Kids, who stay free, will enjoy nearby Coligny Plaza, with its touristy gift and T-shirt shops, informal restaurants, and movie theater. It tends to attract bargain-minded international guests and young people and can be noisy, but it has an upbeat, friendly vibe. $$.

Palmera Inn and Suites (843-686-5700; www.palmerainnandsuites.com), 12 Park Lane. An all-suite hotel with rooms that are larger than average and feature a small kitchen. There is a pool and recreation area including grills and benches, and trails for bicycling, jogging, and walking are close by. A good option for families or groups of friends. $$$.

South Beach Marina Inn (843-671-6498; www.sbinn.com), 232 S. Sea Pines Drive, Sea Pines Plantation. This small, casual option in the Sea Pines resort sits above waterfront shops and restaurants in a New England–style marina village. The rooms are condominium suites, with living and dining areas and kitchenettes overlooking the courtyard or marina.

With tennis, water sports, restaurants, and the beach close by, you could pretend you're on Cape Cod . . . with much warmer water. $$–$$$.

BUDGET CHOICES Each of these national chain motels of approximately 100 rooms has a swimming pool and is close to inexpensive restaurants or shopping areas. They tend to be several blocks from a beach access point.

Hampton Inn (843-681-7900; www .hamptoninn.com), 1 Dillon Road.

Quality Inn (877-424-6423; www .choicehotels.com), 200 Museum Street.

Red Roof Inn (843-686-6808; www .redroof.com), 5 Regency Parkway.

RECREATIONAL VEHICLE PARKS/ CAMPING **Hilton Head Island Motorcoach Resort** (843-593-9755; www .hhimotorcoachresort.com), 133 Arrow Road. Full hook-ups, 401 sites, six tennis courts, pool, artificial lake, shuffleboard, horseshoes, basketball, playground, dog park, WiFi, laundry, and bathrooms with tubs and saunas.

Hilton Head Harbor RV Resort & Marina (843-681-3256; www.hilton headharbor.com), 43 Jenkins Island Road. Full hook-ups on 200 sites, bathhouses, two pools, three tennis courts, laundry, WiFi, exercise room, sauna, and whirlpool.

RENTALS Most vacation rental properties are concentrated on the south end of the island in Sea Pines, Shipyard, South Forest Beach, and Palmetto Dunes. Several villa rental complexes are located mid-island on or near Folly Field Beach. The northern half of the island is geared mainly toward permanent residents; the island's other private communities do not generally permit short-term rentals.

Villas and homes usually rent by the week. The least expensive summer rates are about $1,000 per week, which can buy you a small unit outside a plantation more than a half mile from the beach. In the summer, $9,000 per week can secure a top-of-the-line oceanfront home. From November to February, rates drop substantially.

Agencies manage properties in a variety of sizes, shapes, and locations. A desirable vacation rental would offer swimming in a shared villa pool or a private home, free or discounted tennis, discounts on golf, and would be within walking distance of the beach. Before you sign a rental agreement, make sure you understand policies regarding deposits, refunds in the event of cancellation, times of arrival and departure, and charges for cleaning services. If you have special needs such as handicapped-accessible rooms, or will be renting cots, cribs, bicycles, or beach chairs, alert the agent from the start. The agencies listed below are just some of many.

Beach Properties of Hilton Head (800-671-5155; www.beach-property .com). Most if not all rental homes have pools, and villas have access to one.

Island Getaway Rentals (843-842-4664; www.islandgetaway.com). The company has a smart way of sorting properties, not just on the beach, and has many winter/off-season rentals.

Resort Rentals of Hilton Head Island (843-686-6008; www.hhivacations.com). More than 200 properties in Sea Pines, South Forest Beach, North Forest Beach, Shipyard, and Palmetto Dunes, including in villa complexes with access to a community pool.

Vacation Homes of Hilton Head (843-715-2208; www.vacationhomesofhilton head.com).

✳ Where to Eat

Listed are just some of the 300 places to eat or relax and listen to music that have a track record of good food and ambience and do not just cater to tourists. There are selections in every price category. Where you go may depend on whether you're traveling with children (if you're at a resort, ask the concierge about babysitting services or specifically family-friendly restaurants); on a guy's golf weekend or with the ladies for spa treatments; celebrating in a quiet way; or seeking a later-night bar scene. Prices represent per-person expenses estimated without tax, tip, or bar beverages. In general, dining out is more expensive on Hilton Head than in similar restaurants elsewhere, although there are savings to be found in eating before the crowd (5 p.m. specials) or if the restaurant is running a promotion of some kind, which is why you should check their websites and menus. Taxi service for night owls 24/7 is Yellow Transportation (843-686-6666; www .yellowtransportationhhi.com).

Charlie's L'Etoile Verte (843-785-9277; www.charliesgreenstar.com), 8 New Orleans Road. Open weekdays for lunch and Mon.–Sat. for dinner. For more than 30 years, Charlie's, run by a local family, has been welcoming locals and return visitors with consistently delicious and creative French-inflected cuisine. The menu changes daily based on the freshest seafood, and it also features such favorites as rack of lamb and filet mignon. Charlie's is known for its extensive wine list and cozy atmosphere and is often considered the island's best fine dining restaurant. $$$–$$$$.

Crave by Daniel's (843-341-9379; www.cravebydanielshhi.com), 2 N. Forest Beach Drive. Small dinner tapas plates feature the cuisines of Asia, India, and the Americas. It pushes back the chairs at night and becomes a dance club and local favorite bar scene. $$–$$$.

Hudson's Seafood House on the Docks (843-681-2772; www .hudsonsonthedocks.com), 1 Hudson Road, on the north end of the island. Open daily for lunch and dinner. A large, informal family restaurant, one of the first on the island, in a rustic indoor/outdoor setting overlooking the Intracoastal Waterway and the shrimp trawlers and fishing boats docked at Skull Creek. Known for its sunsets, crowds,

and commitment to the community by its family owners. Classic entrées include fried local seafood platters, but there are blackened and boiled options. No reservations—go early on a summer night or risk waiting two hours to be served. $$–$$$.

Lucky Rooster (843-681-3474; www .luckyroosterhhi.com), 841 William Hilton Parkway. Open for dinner Mon.–Sat. Southern soul food is mashed up with a French-ish bistro menu and craft cocktails. You can get small and large plates, and most of the ingredients are locally sourced. Vegetarians will have options. $$–$$$.

Michael Anthony's (843-785-6272; www.michael-anthonys.com), 37 New Orleans Road. Open for dinner nightly except Sun. Family owned and run, the kitchen elaborates on northern Italian classics like homemade gnocchi, ossobuco, and veal tenderloin. Seasonal additions include game in the fall and specialty mushrooms and truffles when available. An elegant room is divided lengthwise by a curving, granite bar illuminated by pinpoint lights, and the dining area is accented by walls the color of terra-cotta and pale wood furnishings. The work of the pastry chef attracts diners for nightcaps, wine by the glass (for which they are noted), and dessert in the bar. $$$–$$$$.

One Hot Mama's (843-682-6262; www .onehotmamas.com), 7A-1 Greenwood Drive. Bar atmosphere (and there's a great bar menu), and the specialties are barbecue, baby back ribs, and wings with a dozen sauces. A plus is the late-night menu in small portions. $$.

Palmetto Bay Sunrise Café (843-686-3232; www.palmettobaysunrisecafe .com), 86 Helmsman Way, by the Palmetto Bay Marina. Breakfast and lunch daily starting at 6 a.m. Better known to locals, professional fishing guides and boaters, it's casual and family friendly. $.

Red Fish (843-686-3388; www .redfishofhiltonhead.com), 8 Archer Road. Open Mon.–Sat. for lunch and dinner. Red Fish is popular because of its creative menu of spiced seafood (like the Cajun shrimp and lobster burger) and steak, although you can order entrées simply grilled with oil and lemon. They source from their own farm. A stunning dining room feels like an art gallery, but relaxed. It's captured the Hilton Head style of sophistication. The attention to its wines and the on-site wine market with more than 1,000 bottles from which you may choose have garnered national recognition. Reservations for dinner recommended. $$$–$$$$.

Skull Creek Boathouse (843-681-3663; www.skullcreekboathouse.com), 397 Squire Pope Road. Open daily for lunch and dinner. Casual. No reservations, but there are lots of places to sit or walk around if you have to wait, a robust outdoor bar, and a play area for kids. The menu moves from a traditional Southern seafood restaurant to include sushi and sashimi, rice bowls, and choose-your-own Asian or South American flavorings. The number of choices boggles the mind. $$$.

Vine (843-686-3900), 1 N. Forest Beach Drive. Open daily for dinner. A tiny, casual bistro that takes its farm-to-table philosophy seriously but without any pretension. Excellently curated wine list. It's not at all typical Hilton Head—it's much more intimate and hip. Anonymously located right off the busiest beach access at Coligny. No children under 14 allowed. $$–$$$.

Wise Guys (843-842-8866; www.wiseguyshhi.com), 1513 Main Street. Dinner nightly until midnight, later on weekends. Known for its mixed seafood grill entrées and a hefty cowboy ribeye with brandied peppercorn sauce, as well as other serious chops and cuts. But they bow to gluten-free tastes and pork, veal, and lamb, too. The look is cool, urban, and sleek. $$–$$$.

✳ Entertainment

The beat goes on and on at Hilton Head, especially in summer, when crowds jam the dance floor or couples find quieter music in lounges or late-night eateries.

Big Bamboo (843-686-3443; www.bigbamboocafe.com), 1 N. Forest Beach Drive. Two floors of a burger restaurant and live music and dancing in a pretend World War II–era South Pacific retro setting.

Charbar Co. (843-785-2427), 33 Office Park Road. Casual place for late-night specialty burgers, with live music every night and outdoor bar and patio dining.

Coligny Theatre (843-686-3500; colignytheatre.com), Coligny Plaza. Independent and art house films are screened every day. A real treasure.

Jazz Corner (843-842-8620; www.thejazzcorner.com), Village at Wexford. National and regional jazz artists perform nightly in an intimate 99-seat venue. Check the schedule to find your favorites: big band, swing, rhythm and blues, and classic jazz. There are usually two sets a night. In addition to being a

THOUGH IT'S KNOWN FOR ITS BEACHES, GOLF COURSES, AND BOATING, HILTON HEAD HAS A VIBRANT NIGHTLIFE AS WELL

grown-up place to hear great music, it has a wonderful menu. This is dinner and a show that can compare to the big city. Reservations recommended.

Rooftop Bar at Poseidon (843-341-3838; www.poseidonhhi.com), 38 Shelter Cove Ln. House DJ, live music, and dancing Wed.–Sat.

✱ Selective Shopping

Harbour Town, in Sea Pines Plantation, the Hilton Head classic venue with its Instagrammable striped lighthouse, features upscale shops around the marina basin. **Shelter Cove Towne Centre** is mid-island, where new, shiny condos, fancy restaurants, and an expansive park add a touch of glamour. **Main Street Village** (just inside the entrance to Hilton Head Plantation—no gate fee) feels like a few downtown blocks in a prosperous suburb, with its specialty boutiques, pubs and restaurants, and "real" stores that sell ordinary things like beer and diapers. **Village at Wexford** (1000 William Hilton Parkway) has the most interesting collection of clothing stores, restaurants, and "artsy" locales, like a gallery, a jazz club, and craft and cooking shops. **Coligny Plaza** is oriented toward kids and tourists, a good place to find toys and togs for the beach and Hilton Head souvenirs. There are also suggestions outside of the main hubs that are unique.

Just off the island on US 278 are Target and other big "box stores." At Tanger Outlet 1 and 2, there are bargains in every category: housewares, toys, shoes, eyeglasses, children's clothing, linens, high fashion, and sportswear. Dozens of brand-name manufacturers include Adidas, Ann Taylor, Columbia, Coach, Brooks Brothers, J. Crew, Donna Karan, Lucky Brand Jeans, Nike—the list goes on forever.

ARTS **Art Café** (843-785-5525; www .artcafehhi.com), 5 Lagoon Road. A hands-on pottery studio where you select

CHAPELS OF EASE LIKE THIS ONE WERE BUILT FOR THOSE WHO COULD NOT REACH THE MAIN CHURCH LOWCOUNTRY & RESORT ISLANDS TOURISM COMMISSION

an unadorned object (mug, plate, bowl, something else), choose the glazes and tools, and decorate it until it's unique. They finish it in the kiln within two or three days. A good family project.

High Tide Beads (843-686-4367; www .hightidebeads.com), 32 Palmetto Bay Road. Beads from all over the world are sold here as well as supplies for making necklaces, earrings, and bracelets. Bring a piece in need of repair or redesign to owner Steve Mardell, who makes glass beads and designs jewelry, and he will do or create a new adornment with you.

Needlepoint Junction (843-842-8488; www.needlepointjunctionhhi.com), Village at Wexford. A boutique for all needle crafters, with stitchery supplies like thread, yarn, canvas, and kits.

BOOKS **Barnes & Noble** (843-342-6690), 20 Hatton Place. A well-curated and large brick-and-mortar store that has an excellent section on Lowcountry history, culture, and fiction.

CLOTHING AND SPORTSWEAR

Knickers (843-671-2291; www.knickers menswear.com), 149 Lighthouse Road, Harbour Town. Classic outfits in linen, cotton, tweeds, and madras for a designed preppy resort look. An institution.

Outside Hilton Head (843-686-6996; www.outsidehiltonhead.com), 50 Shelter Cove Lane. Top-of-the-line durable sports clothing and gear (Patagonia, The North Face, Teva), as well as heavy-duty stuff, like electric bikes and kayaks.

Palmetto Running Company (843-815-1718; www.palmettorunningcompany .com), 28 Shelter Cove Lane. The center of action for Lowcountry runners provides clothing, gear, and customized orthotics and has great suggestions for local trails.

Player's World of Sports (843-842-5100; www.playersworld.com), 38 Shelter Cove Lane. Hilton Head's largest sporting goods store specializes in tennis equipment and accessories but also carries other athletic gear and accessories for the beach and pool.

Spartina 449 (843-342-7722; www .spartina449.com), 28 Shelter Cove Lane. Inspired by the colors and soft light of the Lowcountry but tricked out with gold, linen, and leather accents, Spartina's lines of handbags, accessories, home goods, fashion, and jewelry are defining a new look for the Hilton Head and Lowcountry resort brand.

S. M. Bradford–Lilly Pulitzer Shop (843-686-6161; www.forlp.com), Village at Wexford. The bright florals for women and children that are the designer's trademark, with accessories and home goods, too.

GALLERIES **Art League of Hilton Head Gallery** (843-681-5060; www .artleaguehhi.org/gallery), 14 Shelter Cove Lane, has shows by local artists and national visual artists nearly every month and features more than 500 members. They offer off-site exhibits in various locations on the island.

The Iron Fish (843-842-9448; www .ironfishart.com), 168 Benjies Point Road, Daufuskie Island. Chase Allen is a self-taught artist who creates metal sculptures of fish and other marine life in his open-air studio and forge on Daufuskie, where he landed about 20 years ago. National collectors and designers have since discovered him. A trip to his website might be easier than the ferry ride to Daufuskie, but there you can see his unique pieces that cross between folk art and fine art in context.

Smith Galleries (843-842-2280; www .smithgalleries.com), Village at Wexford. More than 300 American artisans are represented in media such as glass, wood, metal, clay, and textiles.

HOME GOODS **J. Banks Design Studio & Retail Showroom** (843-682-1745; www .jbanksdesign.com), 35 N. Main Street. High-end home accents and tableware, not just meant for resort or beach life.

Le Cookery (843-785-7171; lecookeryusa.com), Village at Wexford. Gorgeous tableware, place settings, glass, and kitchen tools, including Smithey cast-iron cookware designed and manufactured in Charleston.

REAL ESTATE If you came to the Lowcountry and couldn't bear to leave without owning a piece, take your place in line. Practically every new resident who has settled here was once in your position. The population in Beaufort County alone has increased 40 percent in the past 10 years. The fastest-growing segment of the market is in traditional, single-family homes and in new "walking communities," which try to reproduce the feel of a small town. Gated communities—glorified subdivisions which may or may not be resorts—are

of them may also be your golf instructor or bartender. For starters, pick up the free, widely available real-estate magazines, published weekly, to get a general idea of the market. Resorts usually rely on exclusive sales teams. Walk-ins are welcome, but if you can't find what you're looking for, ask for referrals in other towns.

✳ Special Events

SPRING *February:* **Native Islander Gullah Celebration** (843-255-7303; www.gullahcelebration.com). A monthlong look at island culture and its African roots through concerts, lectures, performances by gospel choirs, storytelling, art exhibits, and tours.

April: **RBC Heritage Presented by Boeing** (www.rbcheritage.com), Sea Pines Plantation. Falling about a week after the Masters at Augusta, this premier golf tournament brings thousands of spectators and the top PGA players to the Harbour Town Golf Links. It's by far the biggest event on Hilton Head and showcases the island nationally. Many ticket and related event packages are available online. If you're planning a vacation around it, make all the reservations you can for lodging and dining in advance.

FALL *November:* **Concours d'Elegance** (843-785-7469; www.hhiconcours.com). Held at locations on Hilton Head Island and in Savannah, this weekend event brings together more than 150 classic cars and motorcycles and vintage aircraft before judges and onlookers, with motor races and aerial exhibitions.

FOLK ART IN ALL KINDS OF MEDIA TAKES ITS INSPIRATION FROM THE REGION'S PLANTS, ANIMALS, AND GULLAH HERITAGE

rapidly eating up the Bluffton countryside. If you want to be on the water, be certain about rules regarding dock permits and building in flood zones, which, after four hurricanes in a row, are under reconsideration. Rapidly rising annual insurance rates in these areas should be factored into any purchase.

There are hundreds of real estate agents, many independent, some affiliated with national brokerage firms. One

BIBLIOGRAPHY

Lowcountry life is well documented, and bookstores have growing "local history" sections. Many out-of-print volumes are back in circulation; originals may still be found in secondhand bookstores and online. Here is a list of some classics, the books you're likely to find in residents' libraries. Don't overlook self-published histories, for they contain gems of regional lore. And, since the best part of a trip is often reliving it at home, check your local bookstore upon returning. The boxed quotes scattered throughout this book are taken from those included in the list below. The list is by no means complete; think of it as a mere guide to the shelves.

Art & Architecture

Cole, Cynthia, ed. *Historic Resources of the Lowcountry.* Yemassee, SC: Lowcountry Council of Governments, 1979, 2nd. ed. 1990. 202 pp., illus., photos, index, $29.95. The definitive four-county survey of historic houses and sites, with fine historical and architectural explanation.

Dugan, Ellen, ed. *Picturing the South: 1860 to the Present.* Atlanta, GA: Chronicle Books, the High Museum of Art, 1996. 213 pp., index, $29.95. Based on a 1996 exhibit at the High Museum in Atlanta, the selection of photographs (from the Library of Congress collections, private donors, historical societies, and museums) is honed to perfection, and the accompanying essays by several Southern writers of the first rank are excellent. The book is moving without being sentimental.

Green, Jonathan. *Gullah Images: The Art of Jonathan Green.* Columbia, SC: University of South Carolina Press, 1996. 214 pp., $49.95. More than 180 gorgeous color reproductions of paintings by Jonathan Green tell the story of Sea Island life and its rituals and pleasures as he experienced them growing up in Beaufort County. Foreword by Pat Conroy.

Lane, Mills. *Architecture of the Old South: South Carolina.* Savannah, GA: Beehive Press, 1984. 258 pp., photos, $75. Exquisite, large-format, black-and-white photos.

———. *Architecture of the Old South: Georgia.* Savannah, GA: Beehive Press, 1986. 252 pp., photos, $75.

Ravenel, Beatrice St. Julian. *Architects of Charleston.* Columbia, SC: University of South Carolina Press, 1992. 338 pp., photos, index, bibliog., $19.95. First published in 1945, a detailed examination of the lives and works of the city's builders, engineers, and architects.

Rosengarten, Dale. *Row Upon Row: Sea Grass Baskets of the South Carolina Lowcountry.* Columbia, SC: McKissick Museum, 1986. 64 pp., photos, $10. A thorough and lovingly documented catalog of a vibrant Sea Island art. It is the authoritative text on the shapes, weaving style, and uses of island baskets.

Severens, Kenneth. *Charleston Antebellum Architecture and Civic Destiny.* Knoxville, TN: University of Tennessee Press, 1988. 330 pp., photos, index, $49.95. A specialized topic explained in clear prose for the interested amateur or professional architect.

Severens, Martha R. *Charles Fraser of Charleston*. Charles L. Wyrick Jr., ed. Charleston, SC: Carolina Art Association, 1983. 176 pp., illus., $14.95. The subject was a miniaturist of the 19th century whose portraits of local gentry, in the collection of the Gibbes Museum of Art, are exquisite and incisive.

————. *The Charleston Renaissance*. Charleston, SC: Robert M. Hicklin Jr., Inc., 1999. 232 pp., illus., $65. A scholarly, beautifully illustrated chronicle of the artists in early 20th-century Charleston who were inspired by the city's heritage and story and expressed themselves in a variety of media.

Talbott, Page. *Classical Savannah: Fine and Decorative Arts 1800–1840*. Savannah, GA: Telfair Museum, 1995. 320 pp., illus., $24.95. An overview of a period during which Savannah was deeply influenced by English Regency and Continental architecture and interior style.

Vlach, John Michael. *Back of the Big House: The Architecture of Plantation Slavery*. Chapel Hill, NC: University of North Carolina Press, 1993. 236 pp., illus., photos, index, $18.95. A serious, well-written, and fundamental study of the relationship of plantation "spaces"—the outbuildings, the quarters, the "Big House," the allées or avenues, fields, docks, and waterways—to the enslaved and free people who lived there, and to each other. Numerous plantation plans are cited.

Autobiography, Biography, Diaries & Letters

Bartram, William. *Travels through North & South Carolina, Georgia, East & West Florida*. New York: Viking Penguin, 1988. 452 pp., $7.95. The account of an 18th-century trip through the Lowcountry by the famous botanist.

Chesnut, Mary Boykin. *A Diary from Dixie*. Cambridge, MA: Harvard University Press, 1980. 608 pp., $12.95. A classic account with good detail on Charleston society.

Daise, Ronald. *Reminiscences of a Sea Island Heritage*. Columbia, SC: Sandlapper, 1986. 103 pp., photos, $18.95. Archival black-and-white photos accompanied by text and stories of Sea Island Gullah culture. Ronald and his wife, Natalie, were the creators and stars of the TV series for children, *Gullah Gullah Island,* and they continue to perform nationally and as community activists and curators.

Egerton, Douglas. *He Shall Go Out Free: The Lives of Denmark Vesey*. Madison, WI: Madison House, 1999. 272 pp., illus., $34.95. A complete, well-researched, and well-argued account of the failed slave uprising in Charleston in 1822.

Elliott, William, and Theodore Rosengarten. *William Elliott's Carolina Sports by Land and Water, Including Incidents of Devil-Fishing, Wild-Cat, Deer, and Bear-Hunting, Etc.* Columbia, SC: University of South Carolina Press, 1994. 296 pp., illus., $14.95. A reprint of Elliott's 1850s original, it is still funny, easy to read, and as full of suspense as ever.

Forten, Charlotte L. *The Journal of a Free Negro in the Slave Era*. New York: W. W. Norton, 1981. 286 pp., index, $8.95. The vivid impressions of a Northern teacher who came to the Sea Islands to educate the newly freed slaves.

Georgia Writers' Project, ed. *Drums and Shadows*. Athens, GA: University of Georgia Press, 1986. 352 pp., $11.95. The collection of oral histories first published under the Federal WPA program in 1940. It allows you to hear the voices of the coast.

Higginson, Thomas Wentworth. *Army Life in a Black Regiment*. New York: W. W. Norton, 1984. 279 pp., appendix, index, $6.95. Higginson, a Boston Brahmin, was the white commander of the 1st South Carolina Volunteers, headquartered in Beaufort during the Civil War. This honest, self-effacing narrative of camp life, leadership among the formerly enslaved volunteers, observations of nature, and military skirmishes is invaluable.

Kemble, Frances Anne. *Journal of Residence on a Georgia Plantation in 1838–1839*. Athens, GA: University of Georgia Press, 1984. 488 pp., $11.95. Although the setting is the coastal Georgia plantation of the author's husband, Pierce Butler, her insights into plantation life and the culture of enslaved women make this perhaps the best account of that time.

McTeer, J. E. *High Sheriff of the Lowcountry*. Beaufort, SC: JEM Co., 1995. 101 pp., $19.70. Newly reprinted, it contains the colorful recollections of the author's days as a Lowcountry lawman and his encounters with voodoo and witch doctors, rumrunners, and local scoundrels.

Olmsted, F. L. *A Journey in the Seaboard Slave States*. Westport, CT: Negro Universities Press, 1969. Illus., index, $35. A reprint of the 1856 edition in which the author acutely observes the coastal region and standards of living there.

Pearson, Elizabeth Ware, ed. *Letters from Port Royal, 1862–1868*. New York: Arno Press, 1969. $14. In 1862, dozens of Northern abolitionists flocked to the federally occupied area around Beaufort to educate the newly freed slaves and manage the abandoned cotton plantations. This collection of letters by the Boston contingent is as forceful and moving a commentary on race relations and liberal expectations and failures as exists.

Pennington, Patience. *A Woman Rice Planter*. Cambridge, MA: Belknap Press of Harvard University Press, 1961. The author was a Lowcountry native who managed her father's rice plantations after the Civil War and wrote about the experience for New York newspapers. The illustrations are by Alice Ravenel Huger Smith, a lyrical interpreter of the rural Lowcountry.

Pinckney, Roger. *The Beaufort Chronicles*. Beaufort, SC: Pluff Mud. 110 pp., $9.95. A collection of remembrances and essays on small-town life and its simple pleasures.

Towne, Laura. *Letters and Diary Written from the Sea Islands of South Carolina, 1862–1884*. New York: American Biography Series, 1991. 310 pp., $79. Another wonderful journal of a teacher; she established Penn School, the first school for freed slaves in the United States.

Verner, Elizabeth O. *Mellowed by Time*. Charleston, SC: Tradd Street Press, 1978. $15. Sketches and memories of old Charleston by a distinguished artist who favored etchings and pastel and pencil drawings.

Cultural Studies

Bluffton Historical Preservation Society. *No. II: A Longer Short History of Bluffton, South Carolina and its Environs*. Bluffton, SC: Bluffton Historical Preservation Society, 1988. 49 pp., photos, $9.95. An excellent local history with photographs of classic Lowcountry cottages.

Carawan, Guy, and Candy Carawan, eds. *Ain't You Got a Right to the Tree of Life? The People of Johns Island, South Carolina—Their Faces, Their Words, and Their Songs*. Athens, GA: University of Georgia Press, 1989. 256 pp., photos, $29.95.

Garrity, Janet. *Goin' Down the River: Fish Camps of the Sea Islands*. Hilton Head Island, SC: Lydia Inglett Publishing, 2012. 128 pp., photos, $39.95. A beautiful presentation of the fish camps that dot the hummocks and creeks, with stories of multigenerational families who built and use them still, and their collective history as special places from the time of Native American settlements. Original and archival photos.

Johnson, Guion G. *A Social History of the Sea Islands*. Westport, CT: Greenwood Press, 1969. 185 pp., index, bibliog., $38.50. A reprint of the 1930 edition of a series in which scholars from the University of North Carolina examined the lives, speech, culture, and folkways of Sea Island natives. Others in the series include *Folk Culture on St. Helena Island* by Guy B. Johnson and *Black Yeomanry* by T. J. Woofter, which, if you can find it, has stirring documentary photographs.

Jones-Jackson, Patricia. *When Roots Die: Endangered Traditions on the Sea Islands*. Athens, GA: University of Georgia Press, 1987. 189 pp., photos, bibliog., $19.95.

Lee, Matt, and Ted Lee. *The Lee Bros. Southern Cookbook*. New York: W. W. Norton, 2006. 589 pp., $35. The brothers relocated with their family to Charleston as pre-teens, and by messing around in the creeks and the kitchen, found, as they put it, that in the Lowcountry food is life. They became entrepreneurs of boiled peanuts in Manhattan because they missed their favorite snacks, and it wasn't long before their amusing prose, goofy self-deprecation, and honest devotion to Lowcountry foodways garnered praise and fans. Another volume is *The Lee Bros. Charleston Kitchen*. New York: Clarkson, Potter, 2013. 240 pp., $35. It's an homage to Charleston cooking of the past and present, with old recipes they've researched and updated, archival photographs, stories of local farmers and fishermen, and even walking and driving tours to orient you to the homes where cooking has been essential to the city's culture for more than two centuries.

Parrish, Lydia. *Slave Songs of the Georgia Sea Islands*. Athens, GA: University of Georgia Press, 1992. 252 pp., photos, musical notation, $19.95. A reprint of the 1942 original by the wife of artist Maxfield Parrish, documenting the islanders' songs from the praise house to the play yard.

Taylor, John Martin. *Hoppin' John's Lowcountry Cooking*. New York: Bantam, 1990. 345 pp., illus., $24.

———. *The New Southern Cook: 200 Recipes*. New York: Bantam, 1995. 287 pp., illus., $27.95. A superb follow-up to Taylor's first book, this one ranges a bit further but maintains the author's discriminating judgments and lack of pretension.

Vernon, Amelia Wallace. *African Americans at Mars Bluff, South Carolina*. Columbia, SC: University of South Carolina Press, 1995. 200 pp., illus., photos, index, bibliog., $16.95. A wonderful documentary account of an African American community north of Charleston.

Welty, Eudora. *The Eye of the Story: Selected Essays and Reviews*. New York: Vintage International, 1990. 355 pp., $14.

Westmacott, Richard. *African American Gardens and Yards in the Rural South*. Knoxville, TN: University of Tennessee Press, 1992. 175 pp., illus., photos, index, bibliog., $24.95. One of the most thoughtful and inspired books ever written on African American rural life (some in the Lowcountry), it focuses on several families and the way they create color, style, whimsy, and usefulness in their immediate landscape. It is part scholarship, part oral history, and the tone is just right.

Wolfe, Michael C. *The Abundant Life Prevails: Religious Traditions of St. Helena Island*. Waco, TX: Baylor University Press, 2000. 181 pp., bibliog., extensive chapter notes, $39.95. A tremendously thoughtful book that examines the religious traditions of St. Helena Islanders, in particular the role of Penn School and the missionary tradition.

Fiction

Berendt, John. *Midnight in the Garden of Good and Evil*. New York: Random House, 1994. 388 pp., $22. A wild romp in Savannah—and it's all true.

Conroy, Pat. *The Water Is Wide.* New York: Bantam, 1972. 320 pp., $4.95. This was the book based on Conroy's experiences as a Beaufort County schoolteacher on isolated Daufuskie Island. His other books include *The Great Santini, The Prince of Tides,* and *Beach Music,* and have Beaufort as their setting (even in the movie versions).

Griswold, Francis. *Sea Island Lady.* Beaufort, SC: Beaufort Book Co., 1984. 964 pp., $19.95. A reprint of the 1939 original—a big, fat Southern novel set in Beaufort.

Heyward, du Bose. *Porgy.* Charleston, SC: Tradd Street Press, 1985. 130 pp., illus., $20. A reprinting of the great tale set in and around Charleston.

A SOUTHERN MAGNOLIA SC LOWCOUNTRY TOURISM COMMISSION

Humphreys, Josephine. *Rich in Love.* New York: Viking Penguin, 1987. 262 pp., $8.95. Set in Mount Pleasant, near Charleston, this novel (basis of the 1993 movie) captures the world view of a precocious 17-year-old girl. The author's other novels, *Dreams of Sleep* (1984) and *The Fireman's Fair* (1991), are also set in the Charleston area.

Naylor, Gloria R. *Mama Day.* New York: Random House, 1989. 312 pp., $9.95. A magical story set in a mythical place that nearly mirrors the Georgia/South Carolina Sea Islands.

Peterkin, Julia. *Scarlet Sister Mary.* Marietta, GA: Cherokee Press, 1991. 352 pp., $18.95. A reprint of the 1928 edition.

Powell, Padgett. *Edisto.* New York: Farrar, Strauss & Giroux, 1984. 192 pp., $11.95. A boy's coming of age on a Sea Island.

———. *Edisto Revisited.* New York: Henry Holt, 1996. 145 pp., $20.

Sayers, Valerie. *Due East.* New York: Doubleday, 1987. 264 pp., $15.95. The first novel in a group that chronicles life in a town like Beaufort, where the author grew up. Others include *How I Got Him Back* (1989) and *Who Do You Love* (1991).

Worthington, Curtis, ed. *Literary Charleston: A Lowcountry Reader.* Charleston, SC: Wyrick & Co., 1996. 360 pp., $24.95.

History

Bridenbaugh, Carl. *Myths and Realities: Societies of the Colonial South.* New York: Atheneum, 1963. 208 pp., index, bibliog., from $4 used.

Dollard, John. *Caste and Class in a Southern Town.* Madison, WI: University of Wisconsin Press, 1989. 466 pp., index, $14.50. A reissue of the 1937 work which, while not specifically about the Lowcountry, has everything to say about race relations in small towns throughout the region.

Jacoway, Elizabeth. *Yankee Missionaries in the South: The Penn School Experiment.* Baton Rouge, LA: LSU Press, 1980. 301 pp., index, bibliog., from $5 used.

Jones, Katharine M. *Port Royal Under Six Flags.* Indianapolis, IN: Bobbs-Merrill, 1960. 368 pp., illus., bibliog., from $15 used. A good general introduction to the area, with long passages quoting original documents.

Rogers, George. *Charleston in the Age of the Pinckneys.* Columbia, SC: University of South Carolina Press, 1984. 198 pp., index, $9.95. If there is one book you should read about Charleston's heyday, this is it.

Rose, Willie Lee. *Rehearsal for Reconstruction: The Port Royal Experiment.* New York: Oxford University Press, 1976. 450 pp., index, bibliog., $13.95. A beautifully written and meticulously researched account of the Northern abolitionists who went to the Sea Islands of Beaufort at the time of the Civil War. If you have a serious interest in the subject, the bibliography of this book is where you should start. Many writers and historians stand on Rose's shoulders.

Rosen, Robert. *A Short History of Charleston.* San Francisco: Lexikos, 1982. 160 pp., illus., photos, bibliog., $8.95. A popular introduction to Charleston by a native son.

Rosengarten, Theodore. *Tombee: Portrait of a Cotton Planter.* New York: McGraw, 1988. 752 pp., index, $15. This prize-winning book reproduces the diaries of an antebellum St. Helena Islander, Thomas B. Chaplin, and creates a context of explanation for them. This is the story—not the myth—of life on a cotton plantation, its boredom, isolation, suspicions, and random cruelty handled in vivid prose by the region's best historian.

Rowland, Lawrence, Alexander Moore, and George Rogers. *The History of Beaufort County, South Carolina: 1514–1861.* Columbia, SC: University of South Carolina Press, 1996. 480 pp., index, bibliog., maps, $39.95. The first volume (succeeded by two volumes that chronicle Reconstruction and changes brought in the 20th century) of the authoritative yet readable history of the area, which brings the Native American story into new focus and weeds out the antebellum myths about Beaufort and plantation culture.

Stampp, Kenneth. *The Peculiar Institution: Slavery in the Antebellum South.* New York: Vintage, 1989. Index, $10. A classic study first published in 1956.

Wise, Stephen R. *Lifeline of the Confederacy: Blockade Running during the Civil War.* Columbia, SC: University of South Carolina Press, 1988. 403 pp., illus., index, $16.95.

———. *Gate of Hell: Campaign for Charleston Harbor, 1863.* Columbia, SC: University of South Carolina Press, 1994. 218 pp., illus., index, $29.95.

Wood, Peter. *Black Majority: Negroes in Colonial South Carolina from 1670 through the Stono Rebellion.* New York: W. W. Norton, 1975. 384 pp., index, $9.95.

Photographic Studies

Blagden, Tom. *The Lowcountry.* Greensboro, NC: Legacy Publications, 1988. 104 pp., photos, $49.95. Views of the coastal world by an immensely talented photographer. His words of introduction and praise for the region's natural beauty resonate with visitors and locals alike.

———. *South Carolina's Wetland Wilderness: The ACE Basin.* Englewood, CO: Westcliffe Publishers, Inc., 1992. 110 pp., $29.95. A sumptuous study of the land and estuarine ecosystem in and around the Ashepoo, Combahee, and Edisto Rivers; much of the area is protected by federal, state, local, and private organizations.

Dabbs, Edith, ed. *Face of an Island.* New York: Wyrick & Co., 1971. New edition. It's very difficult to find; expect to pay in the hundreds of dollars. An album of early 20th-century photographs taken on St. Helena Island by Leigh Richmond Miner and reproduced from the glass plates. A treasure.

Ellis, Ray. *South by Southeast.* Birmingham, AL: Oxmoor House, 1983. 122 pp., $50. Watercolors of the coastal region by a noted painter and former Hilton Head resident.

Isley, Jane, Agnes Baldwin, and William P. Baldwin. *Plantations of the Low Country*. Greensboro, NC: Legacy Publishing, 1987. 151 pp., $19.95. Color photographs and histories of historic homes.

Schultz, Constance, ed. *A South Carolina Album, 1936–1948*. Columbia, SC: University of South Carolina Press, 1992. 143 pp. A collection of photographs taken under the auspices of the Farm Security Administration and later under the direction of its chief, Roy Stryker.

Recreation & Travel

Baldwin, William P. III. *Lowcountry Daytrips: Plantations, Gardens, and a Natural History of the Charleston Region*. Greensboro, NC: Legacy Publications, 1993. 283 pp., illus., photos, index, bibliog., maps, $18.95. Written by a Lowcountry native, it is a model of organization (with maps and mileages clearly spelled out), good design, practicality, and a writing style that lends itself to reading aloud.

Ballantine, Todd. *Tideland Treasures*. Columbia, SC: University of South Carolina Press, 1991. 218 pp., $15.95. A general primer on local ecology and nature that is a classic and can be enjoyed by adults and kids.

Federal Writers' Project Staff. *South Carolina: The WPA Guide to the Palmetto State*. Walter B. Edgar, ed. Columbia, SC: University of South Carolina Press, 1988. 514 pp., photos, index, $16.95. A reprint of the superb guide.

Georgia Conservancy. *A Guide to the Georgia Coast*. Savannah, GA: The Georgia Conservancy, 1989. 199 pp., illus., index, $6.

INDEX

Page numbers in *italics* refer to illustrations.

A

ACE Basin: bicycling, 117; boating, 46, 114; Ernest F. Hollings ACE Basin National Wildlife Refuge, 50, 118, 135; turtles, 13
Adam style, 39, 109
Adams, Henry, 24
Adventure Cove Family Fun Center, 150
Adventure Cruises, 147
Adventure Sightseeing, 45
Affordabike, 46
Aiken-Rhett House, 36, 56
American Missionary Association, 77
Ames, Mary, 134
Andrew Low House, 78–79
Angel Oak Park, *59*
Anglin Smith Fine Art, 36
Animal Forest, 43
Anne (ship), 76, 80
Annual NOGS Tour, 80
Architectural Tours of Savannah, 83
Army Life in a Black Regiment, 18, 24
Arsenal, Beaufort, 108, *108*, 112
Art Café, 161
Art League of Hilton Head Gallery, 162
Arthur Hills Course, 152
Ashepoo, 50, 118, 170
Ashley River, *34*, 37, 55, *57*
Ashley River plantations, 25, 33, 56
Atelier on Bay, 107
Atlantic Dunes, 152
Audubon Newhall Preserve, 155
Audubon Swamp Garden, 39
Avery Research Center for African American History and Culture, 42
Avid Angling Fishing Charters, 47

B

Bacon Park, 85
Bacon Park Golf Course, 84
bamboo, 85–86
Baptist Church of Beaufort, 108
Barbadian design, 34

Barefoot Bubba's Surf Shop, 117, 131
Barony Course, 152
Barrier Island EcoTours, 50–51
Bartram, William, 14, 16, 17
Battery, *45*, 46, 56, 60
Battle of Secessionville, 40
Baynard Ruins, 144
Bay Street Outfitters, 115, 131
Beach Institute African American Cultural Center, 77
Beachwalker Park, 28, 49
Bear Island, 49
Beaufort, 102–32
Beaufort Art Association Gallery, 107
Beaufort County Library, 27
Beaufort District Collection, 27
Beaufort Gray Line Tours, 112
Beaufort Gullah Festival, 140
Beaufort History Museum, 108
Beaufort International Film Festival, 118, 127, 140
Beaufort Kayak Tours, 114
Beaufort Lands End Tours, 114
Beaufort National Cemetery, 110
Beaufort Tours, 112
Beaufort Water Festival, 140
Ben Ham Gallery, 138
Berendt, John, 72
Bicycle Shoppe, The, 46
Big Bamboo, 160
Big Bay Creek, 135
Big Chill, The, 106
bird-watching, 49, 85, 117, 155
Bleak Hall plantation, 135
Blue Water Bait & Tackle, 150
Bluffton, 12, 137–40
Bohicket Marina, 47
boll weevil, 102, 105
Bonaventure Cemetery, *13*, 79
Botany Bay Plantation, 135
Bourdain, Anthony, 125
Breeden, Russell, 116
Broad Creek Marina, 147, 150

Broughton Street, 75, 96
Brown, Alphonso, 45
Brown, Morris, 38
Bull, William, 76
Bull River Marina, 83–84
Bulldog Tours, 44
Bulls Island, 50

C

canoeing. *See* boating
Cape Island, 50
Cape Romain National Wildlife Refuge, 50
Capers Island, 50
Captain Dick's River Tours, 112
Captain Mike's Dolphin Tours, 83
Captain Ron Elliott's Edisto Island Tours, 135
Capt. Eddie's Fishing Charters, 115
Capt. Hook, 150
Carolina Bird Club, 118
Carolina Sport by Land and Water (Elliot), 114
Carriage House, 79
Cast Away Fishing Charters, 115
Caw Caw Interpretive Center, 50
Chapel of Ease, 108, *109*, 146, *161*
Charbar Co., 160
Charles Street Gallery, 108
Charleston, 30–70
Charleston Aquarium, 41
Charleston Gallery Association, 36
Charleston Renaissance school of artists, 36
Charleston RiverDogs, 64
Charles Towne Landing, 34, 42
Charles II, 34
Chesnut, Mary Boykin, 19
Church of the Cross (Bluffton), *138*
Citadel Museum, The, 40
Clamagore, 41
Classic Carriage Tours, 45
Coastal Discovery Museum, 144, *145*, 154
Coastal Expeditions, 46, 50
Coastal Georgia Botanical Gardens, 85
Coastal River Charters, fishing, 84
Coligny Plaza, 142, 149, 157, 160, 161
Coligny Theatre, 160
Colleton, John, 34
Colleton State Park, 46
Combahee, 50, 118, 170
Commander Zodiac, 148
Concours d'Elegance, 163
Connect Savannah, 77, 95
Conroy, Pat, 20, 28, 106, 112, 147
Cooper River Bridge Run, 69
cotton, 18, 22, 35, 72, 83, 102, 105
Country Club of Hilton Head, 151

COVID-19, 32
Creek, 76
Crescent Pointe Golf Club, 152
Cypress Wetlands and Rookery, 106, 117

D

Daffin Park, 85
Daufuskie Island, *100*, *145*, 147, 148, 162
Davis, Ulysses, 77, 89
Declaration of Independence, 38, 54, 76
Denmark Vesey rebellion, 18, 38
Dock Street Theatre, 64, *64*
Dolphin Magic Tours, 83
Dolphin Nature Tour, 147
dolphins, 13, 89, 112, 115, 138, 148
Douglas Visitor Center, 111
Drayton Hall, 18, 26, 33, 37, *38*, 56

E

Eagle's Point Golf Club, 153
East Bay Street, 56, *61*
East Coast Paddleboarding, 84
Edisto Island & Edisto Beach, 13, 102, 133–37, *134*, 140
Edisto River, 46, 50, 118
Edmonston-Alston House, 37, 54
Eggs 'N' Tricities, 139
Elliott, William, 114
Ellis, Ray, 77
Emancipation Proclamation, 80
Ernest F. Hollings ACE Basin National Wildlife Refuge, 50, 118
Evans, Walker, 105
Eye of the Story: Selected Essays and Reviews, The (Welty), 105

F

farmers' markets: Beaufort, 116; Bluffton, *138*, 139; Charleston, 68; Savannah, 85, 97
Farm Security Administration photos, 20, 105
Festival of Houses & Gardens, 32, 69
First African Baptist Church (Savannah), *78*
Fish Haul Plantation, 145
fishing, 46, 84, 114–15, 131, 150
fitness, 150
Flora (steamboat), 24
Flying Circus and *Pau Hana*, 147
Folly Beach County Park, *28*, 49
food and wine festival, 33
Foolish Frog, 124, *125*
Footprints of Savannah, 83
Forsyth Park, 85, 89, *90*, 97
Fort Fremont Historical Preserve, 111
Fort Howell, 146
Fort Jackson, 80

Fort Lamar Heritage Preserve, 40
Fort McAllister Historic Park, 80
Fort Moultrie, 35, 40, *41,* 50
Fort Pulaski, 19, 80, 83, 89
Fort San Marcos, 111
Fort Sumter, 19, *30, 30,* 41, 46, 48, *104*
Francis Beidler Forest in Four Holes Swamp,
    50
Francis Marion National Forest, 46
Free African Society, 38
Freedom Trail Tour, 83
French Protestant (Huguenot) Church, 38
French Quarter, 32, 33, *37,* 52, 55
Fripp Island, 115–17, 120
frogs, 14

G
Garden Club of Savannah, The, 80
Garris Landing, 50
Gaye Sanders Fisher Fine Art Gallery, 36
George Fazio Course, 152
Georgia State Railroad Museum, 81
Ghost Talk Ghost Walk, 83
"Gideon's Band," 19–20
Gibbes Museum of Art, 36
Girl Scouts, 78, 79, 83
Givhans Ferry State Park, 46
Golden Bear Golf Club at Indigo Run, 151
Golf Learning Center, 151
golf, 27; Beaufort, 116, 120; Charleston,
    47–48, 58; Hilton Head, 151–53; Savan-
    nah, 84, 88
Green-Meldrim House, 79
Gullah Geechee, 18; Beach Institute African
    American Cultural Center, 77; Beaufort,
    106, 109, 112, 125, 140; Charleston, 35,
    45, 69; Gullah Grub, 125; *Gullah Gul-
    lah Island,* 106; Gullah Heritage Trail
    Tours, 144; Gullah Tours, 45; Gullah-N-
    Geechie Mahn Tours, 112; Hilton Head,
    140, 144, 163; Mount Pleasant Sweet-
    grass Festival, The, 69; Native Islander
    Gullah Celebration, 163; Penn Center
    Heritage Days, 140; Savannah, 77; York
    W. Bailey Museum, 109

H
Harbour Town, 142, *145,* 149–50, 161
Harbour Town Golf Links, 152, 163
Harbour Town Yacht Basin, 147
Harris Neck National Wildlife Refuge,
    85
Headshaker Charters, 47
Helena Fox Fine Art, 36
Henry C. Chambers Waterfront Park, 116
Heritage Library Foundation, 27, 144
Heritage Park, Port Royal, 116

heron, 20, 46, 117, *117,* 155
Heron Point, 152
Heyward House Museum, The, 138
Heyward-Washington House, 38
Hidden Gardens of Savannah, 98
Higginson, Thomas Wentworth, 18, 24
Higher Ground, 114, 131
High Tide Beads, 161
Hilton Head, 12, 142–63
Hilton Head Island Beach & Tennis Resort,
    153
Hilton Head National, 153
Historic Beaufort Foundation, 109, 127, 132
Historic Beaufort Foundation Fall Festival of
    Houses & Gardens, 140
Historic Bluffton Arts & Seafood Festival,
    140
Historic Charleston Foundation, 27, 36, 39,
    67, 69
Historic Mitchelville Freedom Park, 146
Historic Savannah Foundation, 20, 27, 79
H. L. Hunley Exhibit, 41
Horan, Eric, 114
horseback riding, 55, 116, 153
H2O Sports Center, 148
Huguenot, 13, *32,* 38
Hunting Island Lighthouse, 117, *129*
Hunting Island State Park, 114, 117, 120,
    129
hurricanes, 23, 105, 117
Hutty, Alfred, 36

I
Indian Shell Ring, 146
indigo, 35, 102
I'on Swamp, 49
Iron Fish, The, 162
Isaiah Davenport House, 20, 79
Island Bikes & Outfitters, 135
Island Explorer, 147
Island West Golf Club, 153
Isle of Hope, 80, 83
Isle of Palms County Park, beaches, 49

J
Janet's Walking History Tour, 112
Jay, William, 72, 77, 79, 89
Jazz Corner, 160
Jepson Center, 79, 81
joggling board, 67
John Carroll Doyle Art Gallery, 36
John Mark Verdier House Museum, 109,
    132
Johns Island, 59, *59,* 68
John Tucker Fine Arts, 77
Johnston, Clyde, 48, 116
Jones, Noble, 80

Joseph Manigault House, 39
Juliette Gordon Low Birthplace, 79

K
Kahal Kadosh Beth Elohim, 37
kayaking. *See* boating
Kiawah Island: beaches, 49; Botany Bay, 135;
    golf, 27, 48, 58; resorts, 12, 56
Kiawah River, 46
Kiawah tribe, 34, 43
King, Martin Luther, Jr., 80, 109
King-Tisdell Cottage, 79
Kobo Gallery, 77

L
Laffey, 41
Lake Mayer Park, 85
Lands End, 117, *127*
Laurel Grove Cemetery, 79
Lawton Stables, 153
Lee, Robert E., 80
Legendary Golf, 150
Legends at Parris Island, 116
Letters from Port Royal 1862–1868 (Pearson),
    106, 126
Liberty Oak in Harbour Town, 149
Light Up the Night Christmas Boat Parade,
    140
lighthouse, 81, 117, *129*, *145*, 157, 161
live oaks, 16, 91, 104
Low, Juliette Gordon, 78, 79
Lowcountry Bicycles, 117
Lowcountry Nature Tours, 147
Lowcountry Photo Safaris, 114

M
Macdonald Marketplace, 132
Magnolia Plantation, 26, *28*, 33, 39
Main Street Village, 161
Manigault, Gabriel, 39
Marion Square, 51–52, *52*, 68
Marshview Community Organic Farm,
    125
May River, 12, 137–39
McKevlin's Surf Shop, 49
Memorial Park in Mount Pleasant, 47
Mercer Williams House, 79
Metropolitan Opera Live in HD, 128
Middleton Place, 18, *25*, 39, 56, *57*
Middleton Place Foundation, 36
Midnight in the Garden of Good and Evil
    (Berendt), 72, 79, 82, 92
"Mighty Eighth," 81
Mills House, 52, *53*
Miss Judy Charters, fishing, 84
Mitchelville, 142, 144, 145, 146
mock-bird, 17

Moja Arts Festival, 69
Mother Emanuel, 38
Mother Emanuel African Methodist Episco-
    pal Church, 38
Mount Pleasant, 47, 49, 69
Mount Pleasant Sweetgrass Festival, 69
Museum Mile on Meeting Street, 36
Musgrove, John, 76
Musgrove, Mary, 76
Music Farm, 64
Music to Your Mouth, 140

N
Nathaniel Russell House, 39, *39*
National Museum of the Mighty Eighth Air
    Force, 81
Native Islander Gullah Celebration, 163
Nature Adventures Outfitters, 46
nature preserves and refuges, 50, 85, 118,
    149
Needlepoint Junction, 161
Neema Fine Art Gallery, 36
New Urbanism, 106
Night on the Town, A, 140
North Island Surf & Kayak, 84

O
Oatland Island Wildlife Center, 85
Ocean Master, 150
Ocean Surf Shop, 49
October Tour of Homes, 134
Oglethorpe, James, 76
Old Charleston Walking Tours, 44
Old Savannah Tours, 82
Old Sheldon Church Ruins, 109, *110*
Old Slave Mart Museum, 43, 56
Old South Carriage Co., 45
Old South Golf Links, 153
Old Town Trolley Tours, 82
Outside Daufuskie, 148
Outside Hilton Head, 149, 162
Owens-Thomas House & Slave Quarters, 79,
    81, 89
Oyster Reef Golf Club, 151

P
paddleboarding. *See* boating
Palmetto Bay Marina, 147
Palmetto Bay Water Sports, 148
Palmetto Bluff, 12, 139, 140
Palmetto Carriage Works, 45
Palmetto Dunes Golf Academy, 151
Palmetto Dunes Tennis Center, 153
Parish Church of St. Helena, 109
Parris Island, 13, 106, 111, 116
Parris Island Museum, 111
Pat Conroy Literary Center, 28

Pat Conroy Literary Festival, 28
Patriots Point Naval and Maritime Museum, 41
Pearson, Elizabeth Ware, 106, 126
Pei Ling Chan Garden for the Arts, 78
Penn Center, 11, 105, 109, *111*, 112, 132, 140
Philbrick, Edward S., 106
Phinney, Wally, Jr., *115*, 116
Piccolo Spoleto, 63, 69
Pinckney Island National Wildlife Refuge, 86, 155
Pinckney Simons Gallery, 108
Pineapple Fountain, 70
Pirate's Island Adventure Golf, 150
pluff mud, 17
Point, The, 102, 132
Port Royal Experiment, 105
Port Royal Island, 19, 117, *122*.
Port Royal Plantation, 157
Port Royal Racquet Club, 153
Port Royal Sound, 13, 19, 105, 111, 118
Port Royal Village, 106, *113*, 116, 117, 121
praise house, 18, 112, *126*, 144
Preston, Jacob, 138
Prince of Tides, The (Conroy), 20, 106

R
Raccoon Key Island, 50
Rainbow Row, *56*
Ralph Mark Gilbert Civil Rights Museum, 81
Randolph Hall, *43*
Ray Ellis Gallery, 77
RBC Heritage Presented by Boeing, 163
Reconstruction Era National Historical Park, 20, 109, 110
Red Piano Art Gallery, The, 138
Rhett Gallery, 108
Ribaut, Jean, 13, 111
rice, 18, 23, 35, 37, 49, 50, 86, 102
River Street, 75, 83, 94, 96, 99, 148
Robber's Row Course, 152
Robert Cupp Course, 152
Robert Trent Jones, 48, 152
Rodman Cannons, *30*
Rooftop Bar at Poseidon, 161
Russell, William Howard, 19

S
Safdie, Moshe, 74
salt marsh, 16–17, *44*
Saltus River Grill, 123, *124*
Sand Gnats, 72
Sand Hills, 16
Sandlapper Water Tours, 45
Sands, The, 106, 117
Santa Elena, 111–12

Savannah, 72–100
Savannah Bike Tours, 83
Savannah Canoe and Kayak, 83
Savannah College of Art and Design, 72, 77
Savannah Ghosts & Folklore Tour and Haunted Pub Crawl Tour, 83
Savannah Grayline, 83
Savannah Heritage Tours, 83
Savannah Jazz Festival, 98
Savannah Music Festival, 96, 98
Savannah National Wildlife Refuge, 85, 86
Savannah-Ogeechee Canal, 86
Savannah Scottish Games and Highland Gathering, 98
Savannah Stopover, 98
Savannah Tour of Homes and Gardens, 80, 98
Savannah Walks, 83
SCAD Savannah Film Festival, 78, 96, 100
Seabrook Island, 47, 48, 58
Sea Kayak Georgia, 83
Sea Pines Forest Preserve, 146, 153, 156
Sea Pines Plantation, 144, 152–53, 156, 157, 161, 163
Sea Pines Racquet Club, 153
Sea Wolf VI, *115*, 116
Second African Baptist Church, 80
shark teeth, 106, 135
"Shell Road," 24
Shelter Cove Harbour & Marina, 147
Shelter Cove Park, 149
Shelter Cove Towne Centre, 161
Sherman, W. T., 24, 72, 75, 79, 80
Ships of the Sea Maritime Museum, 81
Shipyard Golf Club, 152
shopSCAD, 78
Skidaway Island, 83, 85, 91
Skull Creek Marina, 147
slavery, 18, 42, 75–76, 83
Smalls, Robert, 17, 110, *127*
Smith, Alice Ravenel Huger, 36
Smith Galleries, 162
Society of Bluffton Artists Gallery, 138
South Beach Marina, 147, 148, 150
South Carolina Aquarium, 43
South Carolina Historical Society in Charleston, 27, 50
Southeast Coast Saltwater Paddling Trail, 114
Southeastern Wildlife Exposition, 70
Spanish moss, 16–17
Spanish Moss Trail, The, 117
Spanish Village, Santa Elena, 111
Spartina 449, 139, 162
Spartina Marine Education Charters, 139
Spirit Line Harbor Tour, 46
Spirit of Old Beaufort Heritage Tour, 112

Spoleto Festival, 32, 56, 62, 63, 69
St. Helena Island, 24, 105, *109*, 124, 132;
    beach access, 117; Chapel of Ease, 108;
    corn-shelling, 126; Fort Fremont His-
    torical Preserve, 111; Gullah-N-Geechie
    Mahn Tours, 112; Harbor Island, 120;
    Henry Adams, 24; horseback riding,
    116; Macdonald Market Place, 128;
    Penn Center and the York W. Bailey
    Museum, 109, *111*; shrimp boats, *125*;
    Sweetgrass baskets, 128
St. Helena Sound, 13, 116–18
St. Michael's Church, 39
St. Patrick's Day Parade, 72, 98, *100*
St. Philip's Church, 40
Stell Park, 84
Storybook Shoppe, The, 139
Sullivan's Island, 35, 40, 49–50
Sundial Nature and Fishing Tours, 84
sweetgrass baskets, 36, 66, 69, 109, 128,
    130

T
Tabby Ruins, 80, 109, *145*
Tabernacle Baptist Church, 110, *127*
Tallboy Fishing Charters, 150
Taylor, Anna Heyward, 36
Telfair Academy, 79, 81
Telfair Museum, 74
Temple Mickve Israel, 80
TGC at Pleasant Point Plantation, 116
tide, popping, 17
Tomochichi, 76
Torah scrolls, 80
Travels of William Bartram, 14, 16, 17
Trustees, 75–76
Trustees' Garden, 76, 86
turtles, loggerhead, 13, 43, 50, 133, 154
Tybee Island, 81, 83–85, 87, 89, 90–91, 94

U
University of South Carolina, 128
USS *Housatonic*, 41
USS *Yorktown*, 41–42, *42*

V
Vagabond Cruise, 148
Van Der Meer Tennis Center, 153
Van Der Meer Tennis/Shipyard Racquet
    Club, 153
Vesey, Denmark, 18, 38
Victoria Bluff Heritage Preserve, 87
Victorian District, 75
Village at Wexford, 142, 160–62
Volvo Car Open, 49, 69

W
Ware, Harriet, 126
Washington, George, 38, 51, 53
Washington Square, 60, *60*
Wassaw Island, 84, 85
Water Is Wide, The (Conroy), 147
Waterfront Park, 56, 60, *70*, 104, 116, 132, 140
Welty, Eudora, 105
Whitaker Street, 75, 92, 96–98
White Point Garden, *16*, *55*
Whooping Crane Pond Conservancy, 156
Wild Dunes, 48, 58
William Scarbrough House, 81
Williams, Jim, 79
Wilmington Island Club, 84
Wilmington Island Community Park, 85
Windmill Harbour, 147
Wolcott, Marion Post, 105
Woods Memorial Bridge, *132*
Wormsloe State Historic Site, 80
WPA Guide to the Palmetto State, 33, 118
Wright Square, 75, 83, 96

Y
Yamacraw, 76
Yemassee Indians, 102
yoga, 150
York W. Bailey Museum, 109
Young Farmers of the Lowcountry, 125

Z
Zion Chapel of Ease, 146
Zipline Hilton Head, 150